Sounding Bodies

Sounding Bodies

Identity, Injustice, and the Voice

Ann J. Cahill and Christine Hamel

methuen | drama

LONDON • NEW YORK • OXFORD • NEW DELHI • SYDNEY

METHUEN DRAMA
Bloomsbury Publishing Plc
50 Bedford Square, London, WC1B 3DP, UK
1385 Broadway, New York, NY 10018, USA
29 Earlsfort Terrace, Dublin 2, Ireland

BLOOMSBURY, METHUEN DRAMA and the Methuen Drama logo are trademarks of
Bloomsbury Publishing Plc

First published in Great Britain 2022

Cover design by Charlotte Daniels
Cover image © Henrik Sorensen / Getty Images

A catalogue record for this book is available from the British Library.

A catalog record for this book is available from the Library of Congress.

ISBN: HB: 978-1-3501-6959-3
ePDF: 978-1-3501-6961-6
eBook: 978-1-3501-6960-9

Typeset by Newgen KnowledgeWorks Pvt. Ltd., Chennai, India

To find out more about our authors and books visit www.bloomsbury.com
and sign up for our newsletters.

For Shelley
with all kinds of love

Contents

Acknowledgments

The Coauthors:

Cowriting a book requires the assistance and support of many persons and organizations, and we are both particularly grateful for the sabbaticals that we received from our home institutions (especially because they overlapped for a semester!). We also appreciate the assistance provided by our colleagues in our universities' libraries, who ensured that we had access to a wide-ranging set of scholarly sources. Travel funding from Elon University's Faculty Research and Development Committee, as well as the Provost's office, supported multiple (pre-pandemic) in-person meetings that moved the project forward in crucial ways; without these multiple forms of institutional support, this work would not have been possible.

Portions of this book found earlier expressions in two journal articles: *Voice and Speech Review* published the coauthored "Toward Intervocality: Linklater, the Body, and Contemporary Feminist Theory" in 2019 (13[2]: 130–51), and *PhiloSOPHIA: A Journal of Continental Feminism* published Cahill's "Vocal Politics" in 2020 (10[1]: 71–93). Anonymous reviewers from both journals provided insightful and productive feedback that helped us to improve the articles significantly, and we thank them for their efforts. We also thank Kat J. McAlpine and Art Jahnke for their coverage of our work in Boston University's research publication *The BRINK*. We presented aspects of this work at a variety of conferences, including at the meetings of the Association for Feminist Ethics and Social Theory, the American Philosophical Association, the Society for Analytic Feminism, the Voice and Speech Trainers Association/Association for Theatre in Higher Education, and BU's "Day of Collective Engagement: Racism and Antiracism, Our Realities and Our Roles," and we are appreciative of the generative discussion afforded at those gatherings.

Two anonymous readers provided welcome advice on how to revise the manuscript prior to publication; their insights helped us to sharpen and clarify our analysis, and we are grateful for the time and energy they dedicated to their close and critical reading of our work. Charlotte Moon, Jack Williams, and Alexa Rasmussen checked and rechecked the citations and references, and whipped our formatting into shape. Any mistakes that remain are solely our responsibility!

Christine Hamel:

I am very fortunate to have an artistic home at Boston University School of Theatre where I am endlessly inspired by my colleagues who have always beautifully centered students' journeys as they themselves also shift, change, and grow as artists. I particularly want to thank Adam Kassim, Kirsten Greenidge, Michael Kaye, Judy Braha, Elaine Vaan Hogue, Yo-EL Cassell, McCaela Donovan, Betsy Polatin, Judith Chaffee, Sid Friedman, and the late Jon Lipsky for their friendship and wisdom. I also thank Jim Petosa and Susan Mickey for their bold and wholehearted leadership.

A special thanks to my teachers and colleagues in voice: to Nina Pleasants for her kind mentorship, to Penny Bitzas for her clarity and support, to Paula Langton for her rigor and deep care of the work. I also owe a huge debt to the late Kristin Linklater who helped me to grow immeasurably as a teacher, and whose work has opened up pathways for growth, purpose, and change for so many.

I profoundly value ongoing friendships and conversations about teaching, theatre, and life with colleagues in the field, especially Megan Sandberg-Zakian, Antonio Ocampo-Guzman, Anne Gottlieb, Erika Bailey, Jessica Webb, Craig Mathers, and Naomi Bailis. I am indebted to all of my students, and I hold dearly the conversations about identity, representation, and injustice I've been lucky to have with Micah Rosegrant, John Tomlinson, Bishop Edwards, and so many others, without whose insights many concerns shared in this book surely would have remained unarticulated.

I really don't know how to begin to express my humility and gratitude to Ann for taking my half-formed thoughts about the ethics of voice seriously, and for inviting (and trusting) me to work so very far outside my disciplinary comfort zone. Her ability and willingness to rescue me from doubt at nearly every turn is something I wish I had learned to bottle for safekeeping, and I will sorely miss the nourishment of all of the time we were able to spend in each other's company these past few years. I have long been inspired by Annie's dizzying insightfulness, integrity, and generosity of spirit, and it was a true privilege and pleasure to dare greatly together on this project.

The last twelve months have been particularly long, and I am grateful for all of the ways I have felt support and care moving in and out of crises of various sorts. I thank my good fortune for Leah, Miquel, Beth, and Colin for providing much needed good cheer, good food, and grown-up company; Meg and Sam, who continue to inspire from afar but are sorely missed; and my dear parents for the many traditions created and maintained that have helped to keep us all close during these difficult times.

Ann J. Cahill:

I am grateful, as always, to be part of a university that recognizes the ways in which research and teaching are interconnected, and finds creative and effective ways to support both. In addition to a full-year sabbatical and travel funds for in-person meetings, Elon's FR&D Committee provided two summer fellowships that laid the groundwork for this book. The project could not have been completed without that support.

I hit the professional jackpot when I landed in a philosophy department with colleagues who are generous of spirit, eager to celebrate each other and work together to find ways to make the discipline of philosophy more alive, more just, and more meaningful to our students. I am particularly grateful for the friendship of Nim Batchelor, Anthony Weston, John Sullivan, Stephen Bloch-Schulman, Ryan Johnson, and Lauren Guilmette; beyond the philosophy department (and now, for some of them, beyond Elon), Brooke Barnett, Toddie Peters, Kirstin Ringelberg, and Leigh-Anne Royster keep me sane, honest, and fired up about learning new things. It is my great good fortune to be able to lean on such ludicrously wise and witty folk in good times and bad.

I also rely on and revel in friendships with philosophers developed in conference meetings, workshops, joint projects, and invited talks, many of whom graciously listened and asked probing, insightful questions as the ideas in this book took shape. I am particularly indebted to Sarah LaChance Adams, Linda Martín Alcoff, Susan Brison, Mercy Corredor, Louise du Toit, Nicola Gavey, Kim Q. Hall, Jennifer Hansen, Cressida Heyes, Ada Jaarsma, Melissa Jacquart, Ruthanne Crapo Kim, Claire Lockard, Russell Marcus, Sarah Clark Miller, Kate Norlock, Gaile Pohlhaus Jr., Rebecca Scott, Dianna Taylor, Helga Varden, Caleb Ward, and George Yancy.

At a presentation of our work, one philosopher asked in a somewhat bewildered tone, "But how does cowriting work? I imagine it would be positively painful!" She imagined incorrectly. I could never have written this book without Chris, whose expertise, good cheer, and honesty simply never failed. Over and over again, I thanked my lucky stars to be able to work through ideas, struggle over phrasing, and worry over whether we were saying anything at all with such a brilliant friend. This project has brimmed with both delight and challenge, and I am indebted to her for taking it up with me.

This project spanned a tumultuous five years, both politically and personally. I was humbled and inspired by the many activists with the courage to stand against the forces of xenophobia, anti-Black racism, climate change denialism, sexism, white supremacy, homophobia, ableism, and cisnormativity, in favor of more democratic, more just, and more inclusive ways of being-with. Close to home, the ladies of FIND (Friends of Immigrant Neighbors facing Detention) showed me how to undertake meaningful, local actions to challenge the US detention and deportation system, and the board and staff at FaithAction International House modeled for me time and again what it meant to keep doing the work with integrity and grace. All across the country, health care workers, frontline responders, essential workers, and hundreds of thousands of people who lost their lives (or who continue to live with long-lasting, often devastating health conditions) bore the brunt of the individual and collective failures to respond to the Covid-19 pandemic in effective, ethical, and responsible ways. I am sorry that we let them all down. I hope we at least have the decency, at some point, to acknowledge our failures.

As the pandemic raged, and antidemocratic forces turned to violence to achieve their ends, and institutions that had seemed solid and sure teetered, Mary, Maggie, Sarah, and Abby, and their utterly delightful progeny and partners, made sure that I laughed and ranted in good company on the regular. May I never live to face a challenge without my sisters beside me.

The Coauthors (Again):

A global pandemic brings many things into stark focus; among them, for both of us, is how fortunate we are to cohabitate with loving, funny, fascinating family members. Cowriting this book over five years meant that, prior to the pandemic shut-downs, we were able to spend more time with each other's family than we would have otherwise, and we loved every minute. And so, together, we blow kisses to them all: Shelley, Neil, Anne Joy, Seannie, and Foster. Y'all are the best.

About the Authors

Ann J. Cahill is Professor of Philosophy at Elon University. She is the author of *Overcoming Objectification: A Carnal Ethics* (2010) and *Rethinking Rape* (2001). Her research interests lie in the intersection between feminist theory and philosophy of the body, and she has published on topics such as miscarriage, beautification, and sexual assault.

Christine Hamel currently serves as head of the BFA Acting Program at Boston University School of Theatre where she is Assistant Professor of Voice and Acting. She is a professional actor, voice/dialect coach, and director whose credits include work on Broadway, off-Broadway, and regional theatre. A Designated Linklater Voice Teacher certified in the Michael Chekhov acting technique, she founded *Femina Shakes*, a BU initiative committed to feminist retellings of Shakespeare exploring a wide range of gender identities unconstrained by the limitations of conventional gender narratives.

Introduction

As embodied beings immersed in a sonorous world, vocal humans generate sound replete with social and political meanings that exceed linguistic signification. Yet there are few explorations, in any discipline, of those meanings, how they are shaped, and how they in turn shape subjects, shared worlds, and injustices of all sorts. In *Sounding Bodies*, we argue that the meanings that voices carry, and the ways in which voices are carried (both by those who generate them and by those who receive them) are inextricably, and complexly, interwoven with dynamic social structures marked by injustices and oppression. Unpacking those meanings requires a new conceptualization of voice—one that refuses the (perhaps related) assumptions that language, as opposed to sound, is the properly privileged conveyor of meaning and that bodily phenomena are to be understood as reducible to biological and apolitical forces. It also requires a keen awareness of the sonorous possibilities of human vocalizations, possibilities borne of complex physiological events, all of which always and only occur within specific social contexts.

Our aim as coauthors in initiating this scholarly conversation embracing two distinct fields (feminist philosophy and theatre studies) is to focus attention on the politics of voice and to increase attunement to various forms of vocal injustice. We invite our readers, who may include theorists and voice practitioners alike, to dally with, consider, and take time to examine the voice—an under-theorized subject—as an embodied site worthy of ethical attention. In the wake of the social, political, and racial reckoning of our time, there is a call for voice pedagogues to question every aspect of teaching and coaching practices; we aim in this text not simply to provide (or rush to the edification of) "best practices" (though some possibilities will be provided) but, first, to develop a set of theoretical principles and frameworks out of which new practices may be born. Our desire to collaborate, as practitioner and theorist, centers philosophy itself as a practical tool—one that can navigate a thorough conceptualization of voice and help us take responsibility for the event of embodied human sound as it either sustains justice or enacts harm.

As we will establish, the lived, embodied, often quotidian phenomenon of voice is ineluctably marked by material and social/political realities, including systemic inequalities related to gender identity and presentation, race, class, ability, and others. Our analysis unpacks how the sonorous capacities of voiced human beings are deployed, taken up, experienced, and constructed by complex social and political relations. Such a project necessarily requires a multidisciplinary approach, particularly given significant lacunae in each of our respective fields.

The field of philosophy, represented by Cahill, brings to the analysis highly developed theories of embodiment, the self, and systemic oppression, and our analysis is particularly influenced by the extensive scholarship that feminist theorists have produced demonstrating that bodily phenomena long considered to be natural or pre-political are in fact deeply shaped by social and political forces.[1] However, while feminist philosophers of the body have grappled with a wide scope of modes of embodiment (see Iris Marion Young's classic description of feminine bodily comportment [2005]; Patricia Hill Collins's analysis of Black female sexuality [2004]; or Cressida Heyes's exploration of bodily transformations, including weight loss and cosmetic surgery [2007]), the phenomenon of voice has been largely neglected. When philosophers have turned their attention to voice, their analyses have been largely apolitical (Ihde 2007 and Appelbaum 1990), highly focused on questions of language rather than sound (Kristeva 1984 and Roudiez 1984), and/or centered on musical phenomena (James 2010). Even historical analyses of the profound links between the political oppression of women and the control of women's voices (Carson 1995 and Beard 2017) provide neither a detailed theory of voice itself nor a fine-grained description of how those controlling forces and listening practices are experienced. The few philosophical works that do address the ethical and political meanings of voice (e.g., Cavarero 2005), as we will argue in the first two chapters, do not take into sufficient account theories of systemic injustice, identity, and intersubjectivity that we hold to be central to our analysis. What is needed from the discipline of philosophy, and what we hope to contribute here, is a more carefully developed critical phenomenology of voice.

Crucial to such a phenomenology is a nuanced understanding of not only the physiology of the voice (the specific muscles, bodily cavities, tissues, and mechanisms involved in its production as human-generated sound), but also its grounding in a complex interplay of vocal, psychological, and emotional bodily events. This is where Hamel's expertise as a voice and speech trainer comes in, as she has worked extensively with the expressive, embodied voices of actors, with a particular pedagogical emphasis on psychophysical approaches to both voice and acting. Yet this discipline has not consistently engaged with the cutting-edge theories of embodiment and systemic injustice that feminist theory has developed, and there are gaps to be addressed in voice trainers' fluency with the underlying philosophical assumptions embedded in the practical matters of voice work. The arena of speech training (as distinct from voice training) has received the preponderance of critical analysis (including Knight 1997, Brown 2000, Colaianni 2011, Ginther 2015, Oram 2019, 2020a, Coronel et al. 2020) centering primarily on the racist, classist, imperialist demands of "standard" accents. Such analyses emphasize "authenticity" as a marker of culturally embodied language and frame "liberation" as resisting erasure by shedding prescribed, highly constructed standards of "good," "neutral," or "clear" speech so that culturally (ethnic-, class-, ability-, etc.) specific speech markers may be retained, valued, and centered. However, liberatory models of voice training consistently align "authenticity" with the absence of—or freedom from—cultural or social markers (and therefore "limits") in the voice, thus tethering it to the pre-cultural, pre-social, and pre-political realms of the universal and/ or natural. This model of vocal freedom does not adequately acknowledge that the voice is, in fact, deeply social (as well as constructed) from the outset, rendering it vulnerable to enacting various injustices in the name of liberation. A more thorough investigation into the mechanics of oppression within voice methodologies is therefore needed, not only because there is a deep interest within the field to engage with voice as an anti-oppression tool—in performance as well as beyond—but because voice as a site of embodiment warrants ethical attention.

One challenge/problem that occurs across many disciplines, particularly in the work of scholars who seek to understand and challenge oppressive systems, is that references to voice are often only metaphorical (Dunn and Jones 1994a: 1). Carol Gilligan (1982) referred to women's "different voice" to articulate gendered patterns in moral thinking; "finding" one's "voice" is constituted as both an end and a means in the struggle to dismantle oppressive systems (e.g., Bacharach 2018); and exhortations for the inclusion of marginalized persons and groups call for "more voices at the table." Such metaphors point to the identification of the voice with both the self and the self's (often distinctly epistemological, but also ethical) worth. However, they also deflect ethical attention from the embodied voice, the sonorous phenomenon of human-generated sound involving muscles, air, mucous membrane, and bone. What is both missing and mystified in the persistent use of vocal metaphors within academic and activist discussions of inequality is the possibility of the ethical, social, and political relevance of the embodied voice as sound—not (only) as a vehicle for thought, language, and expression of interiority, but as a sonorous, embodied phenomenon replete with meaning on its own terms.

Unpacking the many salient aspects of the ethical and political meanings of voice as human-generated sound has required us to engage substantially with cognate fields such as sound studies, musicology, and voice studies. In doing so, we hope to initiate an ongoing, multidisciplinary scholarly conversation on the politics of voice, and foster a heightened attunement to vocal injustice. The material, embodied voice matters: to one's sense of self, to systems of oppression, to the meanings of personal interactions and public discourse, and to the ways that all three co-constitute each other.

The Object of Analysis: Parameters, Caveats, Pitfalls

We center our explorations of voice as employed in a range of informal and formal vocal interactions, with a particular interest in everyday human experience, thus distinguishing our focus from scholarship grounded in musicology, which focuses primarily on the singing and/or performing voice. In addition, we will largely confine our considerations to the sonorous experience of human voice and its phonemic content, touching only occasionally on matters related to linguistic or semantic content. Our focus on the sounding of voice thus distinguishes our work from that of feminist linguistics such as Deborah Tannen (2007), who analyze gendered patterns of word choice and rhetoric. Yet in focusing on sound rather than on linguistic content, we do not mean to imply that the meaning of human vocalization can be separated entirely from speech; sounded voices are constructed in linguistic contexts, and those contexts leave sonorous marks. We suggest that there is no voice unmarked by speech, though it is not necessarily the case that vocal sound's destination is always, necessarily, language.

Some philosophers of voice, such as Karmen MacKendrick (2016), move so quickly from the spoken voice to the authorial written voice, word choice, and linguistic meaning, as to risk conflating the two. Mladen Dolar's Lacanian analysis of voice (2006) avoids that conflation, yet retains the centrality of questions of language and signification. His analyses of the politics and the ethics of voice do not address, as ours do, the ways in which voice is implicated in and utilized by oppressive social structures, but rather how the figure of voice has been deployed in philosophical theories of politics and ethics. Thus, while Dolar illuminates the role that voice plays in the psychoanalytic drama of the emergence of signification and the construction of the embodied, linguistic subject, he says little about how the sonorous phenomenon of voice reveals patterns of structural injustice regarding race, gender, class, ability, and so on. Our discussion also parts ways with the philosophical critique of phonocentrism, often understood as instigated by Derrida's *Of Grammatology* (1976; although at least one scholar [Siisiäinen 2012] has argued that Foucault anticipated Derrida's point by several years) on similar grounds. Derrida argues that philosophers, linguists, and anthropologists, ranging from Jean-Jacques Rousseau to Edmund Husserl to Levi-Strauss, have associated the spoken voice with unmediated authenticity, thus endowing it with a privileged relationship to both truth and reality, in contrast with which the written word is considered to be mediated, partial, and tainted with the specter of absence that voice manages to escape. Derrida's criticism of phonocentrism is aimed less at the sonorous aspects of voice itself, and more at the ways in which voice was conscripted into a metaphysics of presence that undergirds (in Derrida's view, profoundly mistaken) theories of language, being, and the linguistic human being.

We agree with Derrida that a theory of the voice that assumes it to be a neutral medium by which interior thoughts are expressed, or that aligns it with self-contained subjectivity and presence, is deeply flawed. Indeed, the very association between voice and authenticity that Derrida diagnoses would serve as a barrier to our lines of inquiry, as our approach to the embodied phenomenon of voice holds that human voices are neither self-contained or self-defined; to the contrary, they are fundamentally relational and always marked by the other. Moreover, the conversation about phonocentrism seems inextricably implicated in questions about the nature of language and the linguistic being, while we seek to bracket (not entirely, but substantially) questions about language in order to place the sonorous, sounded voice—and its implication in inequality—at the center of our inquiry.

If our analysis largely parts ways with the phonocentrism controversy, it cannot fail to engage with the challenge of audism, the "normalizing discourse [that] privileges hearing bodies, spoken communication, and hearing culture over Deaf bodies, signed communication, and Deaf culture" (Levitt 2013: 77). There is a clear connection, of course, between phonocentrism and audism—if the spoken voice is the incarnation of the authentic subject, then beings who do not receive or generate the spoken voice in normative ways can all too easily be dismissed as less than human, and should they engage in non-spoken languages, such as American Sign Language, the very linguistic value of their modes of communication can register as dubious (Bauman 2008, Bauman and Murray 2014). How can a philosophical analysis of voice as a phenomenon of human-generated sound refrain from perpetuating the audist assumptions of the centrality of voiced speech to human identity and existence, the cognitive superiority of voiced language to signed language, and the insistent pathologizing of forms of human embodiment with nonnormative capacities for sound generation and reception?

Our attempt to bracket the linguistic aspects of voice is an asset in this regard. By homing in, by and large, not on the linguistic content of vocalizations, but rather on their sonorous qualities, we sidestep the questions of language and being that make the stakes of comparing the merits and possibilities of spoken and signed language so very high (a comparison that is morally questionable from the outset). Moreover, our more nuanced, physiologically complex, and intersubjective approach to voice as a phenomenon of human-generated sound serves as a fruitful basis from which to undermine the hearing world's flawed assumption that D/deaf individuals live in a world absent of all experience of sound.

There are at least two aspects of this audist mistake that are relevant here. First, sound is received by bodies in multiple ways, a fairly obvious fact frequently missed by a cultural imaginary about sound that assigns an unearned monopoly to the ear. That D/deaf individuals experience a range of sonorous phenomena narrower than or otherwise different from the range experienced by many hearing people does not exile the former from the world of sound entirely. Deaf artist Christine Sun Kim describes how her transition from a painter to a sound artist hinged upon her encountering the dominance of auditory art in Berlin in 2008:

> Now sound has come into my art territory. Is it going to further distance me from art? I realized, that doesn't have to be the case at all. I actually know sound. I know it so well—that it doesn't have to be something just experienced through the ears. It could be felt tactually, or experienced as a visual, or even as an idea. So I decided to reclaim ownership of sound and to put it into my art practice. And everything that I had been taught regarding sound, I decided to do away with and unlearn. I started creating a new body of work. (2015: 4:35)

Ableist assumptions and norms, including impoverished understandings of the experiences of D/deaf individuals; a failure to recognize the unnecessary, but persistent, structural barriers to full participation of D/deaf individuals in many central aspects of social life; and a general inability to understand deafness as a particular mode of embodiment that offers assets as well as limitations (Bauman and Murray 2014) are frequently grounded in impoverished understandings of lived experience of sound. Correcting for the monopoly of the ear in philosophical understandings of sound, as our analysis does, can thus provide important tools for countering anti-deaf ableism, while scholarship from the field of Deaf Studies can similarly ground more comprehensive theories of sonorous phenomena (see, for example, Summer Loeffler's analysis of Deaf music [2014]).

Second, and perhaps even more importantly, the construction of D/deaf experience as simply the totality of hearing subjectivity minus a certain capacity (one assumed to be so inherently valuable that its absence constitutes only a deficiency) is not only a descriptive mistake, but, as Ernst Thoutenhoofd articulates, a crucial foundation for the oppression of D/deaf people: "But deaf people never are merely 'like myself but without being able to hear sound'" (2000: 275). Even when the lived experience of deaf individuals is self-described as one that is marked by the absence of sound, as in Teresa Blankmeyer Burke's description (2017), to understand that absence as merely deprivation (rather than as a particular way of experiencing and moving through the world) would render the capacitating effects of such an embodied modality—effects that Burke describes in compelling and illuminating detail—unperceivable.

In seeking to explore the ethical, political, and social meanings of the sonorous elements of human interaction, then, we are not excluding D/deaf experiences, but rather understanding them as one of many sites at which different forms of human embodiment (with different relationships to sound and voice) are hierarchized. It is true, of course, that in keeping our focus on sound and voice, we will fail to sufficiently explore important aspects of D/deaf experience that exceed the sonorous realm (e.g., the visuality of signed language, and the question of the role that iconicity plays in it; see Rée [1999] and Thoutenhoofd [2000] for opposing views on that matter). But our point, particularly in this introduction, is to emphasize that we reject the ableist intuition that assumes that focusing on sound and voice inevitably excludes D/deaf experiences.

The question of ableist exclusion becomes perhaps even more acute when posed in relationship to our understanding of voice as deeply implicated in various forms of identity, including gender, race, class, and ability. In making this claim we are not arguing that having a voice (in the nonmetaphorical sense) is central or necessary to being human, however one understands that term. Vocal capacity is a widely, but not universally, shared trait among human beings, and while it frequently plays a central role in human interactions, it is certainly not a requirement for either language use or communicative interactions with other human (and other-than-human) beings. As mentioned above, much of the philosophical conversation regarding the phonocentrism of Western metaphysics has at its core a set of concerns about the construction of the distinctly linguistic subject, the subject formed by psychoanalytic and linguistic dynamics themselves structured by processes of individuation and (paradoxical) alterity. Although our analysis does include a consideration of the sonorous aspects of the womb, our interest in prenatal experiences of vocalizations is generated not by questions of how the human being per se comes to be, or what its essential qualities are, but rather by questions of how this particular human capacity emerges.

In addition, to say that the voice is implicated in identity is not to say that vocalized and/or sonorous aspects of identity are more salient, or more revealing, or necessary to senses of self than other aspects of identity (such a presumption would commit us to the flawed "audiovisual litany," which is described by Jonathan Sterne [2003] as a comparison between hearing and seeing that posits a focus on hearing as a corrective to a Western focus on the visual, which is associated with logos, rationality, and order). Nor are we turning to voice or sound as modalities that can ground new and liberatory political frameworks to counter the downfalls of modernity and postmodernity; Robin James (2019) has argued persuasively that instantiations of the sonic episteme that make such promises, either implicitly or explicitly, in fact reinscribe the very systems of domination and subordination that they ostensibly transcend. Our argument here is far less metaphysically burdened: as feminist scholars, we are interested in voice because it is an undertheorized embodied phenomenon, not because it is particularly well-suited to countering phallocentric networks of meaning and power. We argue that the phenomenon of voice as human-generated sound (like many other phenomena, such as mobility, appearance, etc.) is related to identity in important ways, and that it is precisely those relations to identity that are both required and constructed by systemic forms of inequality.

Although this project does not aim at developing a comprehensive account of identity writ large (and thus does not engage with the many aspects of identity that are not sounded or voiced, such as some forms of disability, marital status, political persuasion, and so on), it is undergirded by a general understanding of identity as a sense of self that is under constant construction, profoundly influenced and shaped by relations of all sorts, from overarching political structures to personal relationships. We take seriously, and do not view as contradictory, lived experiences that include both strong and weak senses of identity (i.e., experiences where one's identity seems to be clearly defined and persisting over stretches of time, and those where one's identity is ambiguous, uncertain, fragmented, or inaccessible). Although we will rely on the term "identity" for ease and consistency, its meaning should be taken as roughly equivalent with phrases such as "(inter)subjective becoming" or "self-in-process." In a related vein, we will make frequent references to "structural" or "systemic injustice," or "oppressive systems," using these terms as shorthand for complex interlocking networks of institutions, norms, habits, epistemologies, policies, and practices that result in unjust social hierarchies along axes of gender, race, ability, economic class, national origin, and other identity factors. While these networks are regrettably resilient, they are also dynamic, constantly shifting in intensity, orientation, and expression; they are not necessary features of social life but are contingent forms of sociality that can and should be transformed into more just ways of being-with.

Finally, we persistently train our attention on the phenomenon of voice as human-generated sound, seeking to identify ways in which the soundedness of voice is ethically, socially, politically, and existentially meaningful. We are aware, of course, that voice is not the only sound generated by human beings and that much could be said about the ethical, political, and social meanings of nonvocal human sounds (clapping, foot stomping, snapping, etc.). Moreover, we recognize that Aristotle's limitation of voice to human animals is certainly mistaken, and that much could be written about the meanings of other-than-human vocalizations. Both categories, however, are beyond the scope of this particular work.

Chapter Summaries

In the foundational concepts of the first chapter, we offer an understanding of voice as simultaneously material and political; relying heavily on contemporary feminist theories of the body, we argue that the embodied nature of the voice is inseparable from its social meanings, and cannot be understood in isolation from them, or conceptualized as standing in opposition to the forces of social order. While we distill important insights from Don Ihde and David Appelbaum, we note that their ostensibly apolitical approaches to vocal phenomena leave critical elements unexplored. We also reject persistent descriptions of the recorded or transmitted voice as "disembodied," noting that such descriptions privilege visuality and efface the materiality of vocalization. We provide an extended explanation of intervocality, a term referring to the fact that the material phenomenon of human vocality always emanates from, takes place in the context of, and is sonorously marked by human relations. Understanding voiced human beings as intervocal reveals the constitutive role of receiving sound in the construction of any vocal event, thus demonstrating that a specific vocal event cannot be reduced beyond the level of the relational. We conclude the chapter with an extended discussion of vocal identity, using Linda Martín Alcoff's work on visible identity to establish the existential meaningfulness of voice to both a sense of individual identity and of group belonging.

We turn in the second chapter to the matter of vocal injustice, beginning with a brief description of the multiple forms of vocal injustice that mark contemporary US politics. Relying on scholarship produced by media studies, rhetoric, psychology, and other fields, we present empirical evidence regarding various identity markers (including gender and race) and what we're terming "vocal social goods" (e.g., volume, airtime, and freedom from vocal critique and correction), while also noting important gaps in that data. We then explore three approaches to vocal justice emanating from distinct disciplines: Adriana Cavarero's philosophical critique of the devocalization of logos, Kristin Linklater's vocal pedagogy of liberation, and Nina Eidsheim's analysis of sound and racial injustice, grounded in musicology and sound studies. We argue that all three approaches fail to sufficiently recognize the complex dynamics of intervocality. If vocal injustice is not to be ameliorated by relying on individuality (Cavarero), freeing the voice from the effects of socialization (Linklater), or conceptualizing racial vocal identities as solely produced by oppressive listening practices (Eidsheim), we are left to ask: how might we approach the problem of vocal injustice?

Our third chapter argues that attending to vocal justice requires attending to the social, political, and material conditions in which voices emerge, are received, and are shaped, a complex phenomenon which we term "envoicing." We develop in this chapter a notion of respiratory responsibility that highlights the phenomenon of breath as an essential building block of voice, and air as a relational and political material carrying with it (in a literal sense) the effects of social practices, policies, and norms. We also analyze how different vocal possibilities and traits are profoundly shaped by the specific individual bodies who receive vocal emanations, extending the work of musicologists and sound studies thinkers who have emphasized the environmentally intersubjective nature of sound. An ethical approach to envoicing must value a multiplicity of vocal patterns and possibilities; push back against the ways in which vocal capacities are marshalled to reify and perpetuate various forms of systemic injustice; situate human voices as irreducibly emerging from a complex set of social and political relations; and conceptualize the material, embodied phenomenon that is human-generated sound as replete with both existential and political meaning. We argue that *vocal generosity* (a notion grounded in Rosalyn Diprose's concept of corporeal generosity [2002]), understood as a particular way of both comprehending and taking up the demands of respiratory responsibility, can provide a starting point for the development of such an approach.

Our next several chapters provide opportunities to deploy our notions of intervocality, respiratory responsibility, and vocal generosity in distinct social and political sites. The fourth chapter takes up questions of envoicing and gender identity. We argue against a biologically essentialist approach to the gendered voice, positing instead that such gendering occurs at the intersection of materiality and social and political norms and practices. We delve into the gendered ways in which people speak to babies, toddlers, and children to argue that the contemporary sonorous, vocal environments in which voices develop are marked indelibly by gender politics. Relying on the work of Judith Butler, we argue that the gendered voice is the result of vocal events and situations, and emphasize that the gendered voice is marked sonorously by a complex set of intersecting practices, norms, and materialities related to a wide variety of identity factors, including race, class, ability, and culture. Building on the insights of Anne Carson, Mary Beard, and Robin James, we hold that central to the social construction of nonnormative voices (including those racialized as non-white, and gendered as feminine, gender nonconforming, or insufficiently masculine) is their positioning as more appropriate targets of vocal policing than their normatively masculine, white counterparts. That is, while the racialized and gendered voices of members of marginalized social groups are often assumed to be characterized by certain sonorous traits, they may in fact be much more consistently characterized by the social assumption that they are *correctable*. If this is true, we miss the mark when we understand the gendered nature of voice to be found in register, tone, or timbre, when in fact it is largely to be found in gendered practices of hierarchized receiving of gendered voices. Given the ways in which gender hierarchies have resulted in vocal injustice, we call for compensatory practices of listening designed to undermine the affective responses to gendered voices that too often serve to perpetuate entrenched forms of gender hierarchy.

Chapter 5 highlights three areas of social interaction that bear highly fraught sonorous marks of systemic injustice related to gender as well as other identity factors: maternity, childrearing, and sex. We examine the sonorous environment of the womb as one that both precedes and marks the particularity of vocal and linguistic identities, thus countering conceptualizations of the voice as prior to culture and language. We then explore a range of socially constructed sites of childbirth and their accompanying limits, expectations, rules, and interpretations of vocalized sound, and articulate ways in which birthing environments could be rendered more vocally just. We conclude with an analysis of vocalizations in sexual interaction, arguing that a more phenomenologically robust understanding of the productive role that vocalizations can play in sexual interactions troubles both the model of voice as merely a medium of expression and insufficiently intersubjective models of sexuality.

The following two chapters are the only single-authored chapters in the book. In them, we explore the ramifications of our conceptual and ethical frameworks for our respective professions. In Chapter 6, Hamel argues that long-standing practices and values of voice training and coaching can be effectively transformed by engaging with theoretical analyses of structural injustice and that doing so can ground new, and more inclusive, pedagogical approaches. Such new approaches would be grounded in deeper understandings of the classroom as a complex social field, in which the political aspects of "the natural" and "universal" have been historically neutralized. These approaches would also question ostensibly value-neutral norms (e.g., "vocal hygiene," or the assumption that sex understood as biologically determined is an accurate determination of pitch range) to determine whether they in fact perpetuate oppressive systems and further marginalize members of historically excluded social groups. Cahill then picks up the question for the discipline of philosophy in Chapter 7, analyzing two sites of philosophical activity (the conference and the classroom) for their capacities for both vocal injustice and vocal justice. Cahill argues that developing more just vocal and receiving practices in both sites is a crucial element of rendering philosophy a more diverse and just field of thought.

The final chapter of the book concludes our analysis with a consideration of contemporary vocal politics, with particular attention to how recent political and theatrical events speak to transformations in vocal politics. We track how seemingly transgressive vocal performances on political and theatrical stages have drastically different political meanings and effects; in some cases, they maintain and perpetuate existing power differentials, while in other cases, they reveal the harms and weaknesses of systemic forms of injustice. Finally, we weigh in on the politics of breath in the context of the Covid-19 pandemic, arguing that a refusal and denial of the porous, intersubjective body is mirrored by the border anxieties of the US body politic and the culture wars that arose around individual and collective public health measures.

We hope that both the theoretical frameworks that we develop in the early part of the book and the specific applications of those frameworks in the latter part of the book serve to inaugurate new conversations across and within multiple fields of study. As an embodied phenomenon central to many forms of human interaction and significantly implicated in identity and social belonging, voice as human-generated sound is a rich site for ethical and political analysis, one whose depths we have only begun to plumb here.

1

Voice

In this chapter, we develop a conceptualization of voice as human-generated sound that is irreducibly bodily and political, and thus replete with ethical relevance. Voice is marked, sonorously and politically, by the fact that it emanates from a human body, a material entity comprising multiple surfaces, cavities, textures, and physical structures of different densities, shapes, and locations. Moreover, that body is persistently situated within a specific political and social context. As we detail our understanding of the embodied, political, relational voice, we demonstrate how our analysis diverges from those offered by previous philosophers of the voice.

Thinking along the lines developed by contemporary feminist theories of the body (e.g., Alcoff 2006, Bordo 1993, Braidotti 1994, Butler [1993] 2011, Collins 2004, Lugones 1987, Ortega 2016, Weiss 1999, Wendell 1996, and Young 2005; for a detailed exploration of our reliance on this field, see Cahill and Hamel 2019) grounds our analysis in specific philosophical commitments. First, we hold that bodily practices, habits, modalities, and so on, are existentially and ontologically significant as vital and inescapable mechanisms of self-construction (and destabilization) and as necessary elements of human sociality. Ontologies of the human that fail to address the ineluctable nature of embodiment and materiality with regard to human existence, or portray embodiment as regrettable, irrelevant, or even threatening to authentic humanness are profoundly misguided and deeply implicated in systems of oppression (see Cahill 2001: 50–108).

Second, we understand human embodiment as necessarily enmeshed in and deeply marked by overlapping systems of power, signification, and relations. The physiological channels, surfaces, fibers, and the like that are involved in vocalization develop in specific historical, political, and social locations. What food voiced bodies had access to, how it was prepared, and by whom; the shape of the architectures they inhabit, and their coinhabitants; the available clothing and adornment, and the means of their production; technologies of health and well-being: all produce specific bodily shapes and capacities. More to the point, no human body unmarked by such specificity can exist.

Third, we reject dominant Western models of subjectivity privileging autonomy and self-containment, emphasizing instead the intersubjectivity of human embodiment and existence. Human bodies come into existence only within the context of complex social relations; to be human is to be-with other (human and other-than-human) beings. Human beings are thus *ontologically* relational. In addition, individual human beings are *existentially* relational, in that the particular traits, characteristics, capacities, and so on contributing to their sense of self are developed only and always in relation to human beings, other-than-human beings, built and organic environments, and so on. Even the identities possible and available under specific social and historical conditions (whether one thinks of and experiences oneself as, say, cisgender, or disabled, or a parent, or Irish-American) are inevitably shaped by social relations.

Taken together, these commitments frame our understanding of human existence as simultaneously, and irreducibly, material, political, and relational. When it comes to the phenomenon of voice as human-generated sound, its embodied quality establishes its social and political meaningfulness; that it is a persistent, although by no means universal or exclusive, medium of human interaction underscores its ethical relevance. Yet its materiality, its intersubjective quality (what we are terming *intervocality*), and its relation to identity all remain undertheorized.

The Materiality of the Voice

For the purposes of grounding the voice in bodily materiality, we begin by articulating a (simplified) Western anatomical and physiological overview of the event of voicing.[1] Voicing engages complex physiological systems, which include *all* systems of the body, most prominently the musculoskeletal system, the psychoneurological system, and the respiratory system (Sataloff 2017: 1003). These governing systems bring a great number of organs, tissues, and structures into intricate interactions, including the coordination and synchronous timing of more than a hundred muscles. Bones, muscles, mucous secretions, glands, cartilage, fibrous tissues, ligaments, dense collagen, fat, membranes, elastic fibers, nerves, cavities, blood vessels, and airway structures root the formation and functioning of the human voice. On a structural level, the skeleton (and the interweaving, connective tissues of cartilage, tendons, muscles, and fascia) provides the architecture for all of the body's major functions; its givens (genetic determinations, form, size, density) as well as its lived experience play fundamental roles in voice production. On the level of organs, the larynx (or "voice box") tends, as the primary organ of sound formation (phonation), to receive the most attention, and it is itself composed of material forms such as skeleton, mucosa, and intrinsic and extrinsic muscles (Sataloff 2017: 157). Interactions of anatomy throughout the entire body are vital in the formation of the voice which is, at its most basic level, the physical conversion of "slow-moving breath (gas) into rapid sound wave motion" (Boston 2018: 9).

This gas-to-sound conversion event is a highly complex one, during which many bodily processes seem to be functioning simultaneously, but are in fact sequenced and timed in an identifiable order of anatomical and neuromuscular events. An impulse to make sound in the brain's cerebral cortex serves as a command to the motor cortex, which then imparts instruction to motor nuclei in the brainstem and spinal cord, which then communicate via neural pathways to breath, sound, and speech structures at varying bodily locations (Sataloff 2017: 186). These instructions initiate a coordinated deployment of actions in the larynx, chest, abdomen, and vocal tract articulators and resonators (920), which cause the respiratory musculature to contract and the vocal tract to open, so that breath may enter and leave the body (Linklater 2006: 13). The power source for sound (the unified coordination of diaphragm, lungs, abdominal and back muscles) compresses air and pushes it toward the larynx (Sataloff 2017: 186), and when the right amount of air has been inspired (a vacuum effect has drawn air into the lungs' alveoli), the respiratory system reverses, and by a "combination of elastic recoil and distended tissue and by abdominal and thoracic muscle contraction" (Linklater 2006: 13–14), air is forced out of the alveoli to create a sound-producing stream. Air pressure from the alveoli is responsible for the creation of the subglottal pressure necessary for phonation.

The event of respiration (breathing) itself, independent of but coincidental with sound production, is also the event of a dynamic exchange of gases in the body. During the event of voicing, oxygen passes through air sacs into the bloodstream, resulting in newly oxygenated blood reaching every cell in the body, whilst carbon dioxide passes from the bloodstream into the lungs and is released from the body as breath and sound. The formation of sound requires that the expiring air be somewhat impeded at the level of the oscillator, or larynx. The vocal folds come together, eliminating the glottis (space between the folds) and stopping airflow (Linklater 2006: 378). At this point, the building air pressure below the folds then pushes them apart: the vocal folds' mucosal cover opens and closes, allowing small bursts of air to escape between them, separating and colliding "like buzzing lips" (Sataloff 2017: 186). As the folds are progressively pushed apart by this subglottal pressure, the Bernoulli force (the physical principle by which, for instance, shower curtains are drawn inward by the flowing stream of water) (Sataloff 2017: 264) continues to draw the folds together. The frequency at which they open and close determines the fundamental frequency of pitch, or the highness or lowness of sound.

Lastly, these puffs of air and initial vibrating sound flow into the vocal tract, the cavities of pharyngeal (throat), oral (mouth), and nasal (nose) passages, giving the vibrations space and bony surfaces through and off of which to resonate or "re-sound." The particular structures and shapes of these cavities determine the "overtones" in the harmonics of the sound released, creating the timbre (or distinct qualities) of the voice (Linklater 2006: 14). And if the intention in the sounding body is speech, the movements in the oral cavity of the various parts of the tongue and lips interacting with soft palate, hard palate, gum ridges, teeth, and uvula comprise another variety of resonance: not one that determines color or tone of voice, but one that articulates sound into phonemes, the distinct units of speech that are the acoustic building blocks for language (14). The materiality of voice as human-generated sound includes the functionings of the material human body but is not limited to it, as the materiality of the environment surrounding the voiced human being is also sonorously relevant. The acoustics of the architecture of the spatial environment is vital to the amplification and production of human sound, as are varying levels of humidity, particulate matter, air temperature, quality and porousness of adjacent surfaces, and the positioning of the listener or listening device.

It is crucial to recognize that all of the physiological dynamics that we have described so far—and the accompanying physiological dynamics that are involved in the act of receiving sound—do not occur in isolation from other sensory input, but in conjunction with them. Vocal sound may be experienced acoustically and spatially, both through the sense of hearing and as vibrations of soundwaves conducted through matter. In this way the sense of touch on the skin works in concert with vibrations conducted by the bones in the skull: sound is "felt" and "heard" simultaneously in a multisensory integration that aids in gathering consistent environmental information (Ro et al. 2013). Sound is also experienced in concert with visuality which connects sounds to the bodies that produce it and the material and "narrative" contexts in which it is taking place. Information that accrues about "what is happening" shapes the readiness to perceive and process sound meaningfully. For instance, the sound of a sudden scream when watching someone sneak up on another person in order to frighten them will hit one's body differently than it would have without that visual preparation. Oral posture, gestural movements, facial expressions, and bodily comportment of a speaker are expressive cues that inform the parsing and processing of voice from that body in ways that are highly significant to and coincidental with the experience of hearing it. The information (and bias) attached to visible identities is therefore a key component in shaping how the listener processes the vocal form and content (including accent and language) connected with those sounding bodies.

In emphasizing the materiality of voice, we are seeking to challenge the associations of voice with an insubstantial ephemerality perceived as less existentially and politically hefty than visible or tactile aspects of embodiment. We are struck, for example, by the inaptness of referring to recorded or transmitted human voices as "disembodied," a description that implies that only the visible or tactile body counts as such. Although we cannot touch the bodies we see represented in film, we do not describe them as "disembodied"; the visible body, even when not touchable, registers as present, whereas the body as sounded but not seen is portrayed as bereft of embodiment, associating it with the uncanny, the alienated, the eerie. To the contrary, we argue, voice always necessarily sounds a body. Like Roland Barthes, we hold that the grain of the voice, its sonorous texture accompanying but distinct from the conveyed linguistic meaning, is necessarily grounded in particular bodies and brimming with meaning:

> Listen to a Russian bass … something which is directly the cantor's body, brought to your ears in one and the same movement from deep down in the cavities, the muscles, the membranes, the cartilages, and from deep down in the Slavonic language, as though a single skin lined the inner flesh of the performer and the music he sings. The voice is not personal: it expresses nothing of the cantor, of his soul; it is not original (all Russian cantors have roughly the same voice), and at the same time it is individual: it has us hear a body which has no civil identity, no "personality," but which is nevertheless a separate body. Above all, the voice bears along *directly* the symbolic, over the intelligible, the expressive: here, thrown in front of us like a packet, is the Father, his phallic stature. The "grain" is that: the materiality of the body speaking its mother tongue; perhaps the letter, almost certainly *signifiance*. (1977: 181–2, emphasis in original)

Our analysis parts ways with Barthes's in some significant ways (we disagree that the embodied voice has no civil or social identity and will question the opposition between sound and social order), but share his focus on the bodily nature of voice, its reliance on and deployment of cartilage and cavities, the flesh of the surface and the interior.

Don Ihde's (2007) phenomenological analysis highlights the hefty materiality of voice. Ihde points out that beyond its capacity to fill space and interact with built infrastructure, sound also has the ability to reveal the shapes of the objects making the sounds: "At the experiential level where sounds are heard as the sounds of things it is ordinarily possible to distinguish certain *shape-aspects* of those things … At first such an observation seems outrageous: *we hear shapes*" (61, emphasis in original). While Ihde points out that not every sound provides a shape-aspect, we hold that the human voice does sound the shape of the vocalizing body; not, we hasten to add, in a way that reveals specific bodily dimensions, but rather, in a way that consistently sounds general facts of human embodiment (e.g., that breath circulates through lungs floating in a chest cavity, or that the orifices through which voice is released are located at the top of the human form).

Ihde also describes sound (in contrast to visual phenomena) as simultaneously "omnidirectional" (75), and thus immersive and even "penetrating" (76), and directional to the extent that it instantiates varying degrees of intensity or presence (77). Ihde terms this the "bidimensionality" of the auditory field: it simultaneously surrounds the hearing person while being textured in varying degrees of intensity. Moreover, this bidimensionality of the auditory field identifies important elements in human vocal interactions:

> *Both* these qualities of sound are used simultaneously in what is a most normal human activity, *face-to-face speech*. The other speaks to me in the "singing" of the human voice with its consonantal clicklike sounds and its vowel tonalities. It is a singing that is both directional and encompassing, such that I may be (auditorily and attentionally) *immersed* in the other's presence. Yet the other stands *before* me. Speech in the human voice is between the dramatic surroundability of music and the precise directionality of the sounds of the things in the environment. (78, emphasis in original)

Distinguishing face-to-face speaking from the overwhelming, all-encompassing phenomenon of auditory engulfment produced by music, Ihde highlights the persistence of the other's presence; the auditory field is thrown up by the other's voice, which focuses the auditory reception of the person being spoken to (directionality) and provides a sense of immersion that does not obliterate, but rather deploys and highlights, the distinction between the persons sharing and constructing the auditory field.

Moreover, Ihde emphasizes the penetrative aspect of sound and voice (79–81), how sound in general and the other's voice in particular does not (only) bounce off the surface of the receiving body, but takes up residence in it, revealing the receiving body's interiors (81). Unlike visible phenomena, to which human beings can close their eyes, many unpleasant or painful sonorous phenomena are not easily blocked (82), leaving the sonorous being vulnerable. The ability of the voice (and all sonorous phenomena) to breach bodily boundaries is central to its particular materiality and indicative of its potential for ethical and political meanings. Vocal interactions are bodily interactions that reveal the porousness of the involved bodies, who are simultaneously influencing and influenced by each other. That porousness raises the possibilities of harm and aid, oppression and liberation, the forwarding of flourishing or diminishment.

When we refer to the materiality of the voice, we intend to invoke the embodied and dynamic heft of the voice, the fact that it is generated and received only through bodily mechanisms and tissues situated within a specific material context. Yet we do not, as some other philosophers of voice do, contrast the embodied materiality of voice with social structures or processes of signification.

Sound and the Social Order

In highlighting the ineluctably embodied nature of voice, we are not reducing it to a biological or merely physiological phenomenon. More to the point, we reject the dominant, dualistic Western metaphysics that opposes embodiment with culture, body with mind, and so on. In doing so, we join and forward a tradition of feminist thought that has recentered theories of subjectivity on embodiment to explore the body as a social and political entity. We diverge, then, from arguments such as Linda Fisher's (2010) that emphasize the distinguishability of the material voice (understood as relatively independent of social and political structures) from the expressive voice (understood as steeped in cultural systems of discursivity and representation), arguing instead that the materiality of voice cannot be so cleanly differentiated from sociocultural forces, but is necessarily implicated in and shaped by them. Or, more precisely: the only materiality of the voice to which we have access is one that is always already marked and shaped by cultural and political dynamics.

Joshua St. Pierre's compelling analyses of the lived experience of stuttering provide rich descriptions of embodied vocalizations at once resolutely material and framed by social norms. St. Pierre argues that nonnormative voices, including the stuttering voice, disrupt humanist notions of the universal speaking subject whose access to public speech relies on the successful managing and effacement of speech's bodily requirements. The crip voice reveals the bodily indebtedness, and thus the ineffable contingency, of the speaking citizen (2015: 334). While St. Pierre resoundly rejects the medical model of stuttering (2012: 4), he consistently presents it as a bodily phenomenon, a way of enacting vocality in a political and social world that constructs certain vocalizations as contrary to both rationality and humanness in their tempo and involuntariness (Joe Biden's stutter, for example, was used by his critics as evidence of cognitive decline [Hendrickson 2020]). Such constructions, however, are clearly arbitrary and not grounded in the physiology of stuttering; their political and social meanings emerge only in highly particular contexts:

> The stutterer finds and defines herself in a context dominated by expectations of efficiency. Welded to notions of success and productivity within capitalism, expediency of both labour and communication sets the terms for participation in our socio-economic system while also enforcing the production of the sorts of subjects it requires. That is, in light of body politics, the body is itself interpreted as that which is meant and required to be efficient and productive ... In failing to conform to expectations of expediency, the stutterer herself is constructed as a faulty instrument that is inefficient and less useful. (St. Pierre 2012: 12)

St. Pierre argues that the crip voice reveals the instability of speech, an instability directly related to the fact that it is a material, embodied phenomenon (St. Pierre 2015: 336). Yet because that materiality only gains meaning within a social context, stuttering as a phenomenon needs to be understood not as an individual trait, an appropriate target for medical intervention and "fixing" (as Biden himself presents it when he uses the past tense when describing his stutter, which, he says, he has "overcome" [Hendrickson 2020]), but rather "as constructed by a hearer prejudiced against 'broken' speech as well as its speaker, and thus as a product of ableism" (St. Pierre 2012: 6).

Such a social construction theory of stuttering does not amount to pitting the materiality of the voice (whether crip or normalized) against the social order. To the contrary: the only voices sounded are those simultaneously material and framed by complex social meanings, norms, and expectations. This element of our analysis distinguishes it from other philosophical treatments opposing the sonorous voice to the social order that grounds signification. David Appelbaum, for example, criticizes Jacques Derrida for failing to attend to the sonorousness nature of voice (1990: xiii–xiv), arguing that in concealing voice's sound, Derrida conceals that which impresses its sonic reality upon our bodies without the protection of conceptual or linguistic order: "Such voice *acts* on us immediately and inescapably. Interpretation and analysis—that is, engagement of voiced signification—are by second thought. This voice that escapes the written or spoken page is deeply organic and fraught with the problem of human suffering" (xiv). Where other thinkers emphasize speech as voice's destiny (Cavarero 2005: 209), Appelbaum seeks to recover the wildness of voice, its opposition to control, logos, and propriety (as does Peter Hanly in his analysis of voice in Hegel's work [2009]). The voice of voice, he claims, is to be found in vocal phenomena that interrupt and exceed speech, jam up the mechanisms of language, and deliver to the vocalizing subject a humbling reminder that they belong to a world beyond signification. For Appelbaum (1990), the cough, the laugh, and the infant's babble challenge the dominance of speech, revealing the essence of voice in its earthy, insistent refusal to be exhausted by forces that would harness it in the name of stability, identity, assuredness, and control. Voice as voice is inarticulate and unreliable; when it is channeled by intention or language, its wildness is betrayed and undercut.

Although Appelbaum chides Derrida for concealing the sound of voice, his portrayal of voice as wild and unfettered falls neatly into a Derridean critique of presence and knowability:

> The history of erasure and the erasure of that history, of the cough (the laugh), as propounded by Aristotle, Locke, Rousseau, and Husserl, is a history denying death. The death of the meaning-intention, its absence, its lack, is voided—and life, meaning, and mental focus made eternal—by the device of refusing the cough or laugh a phonemic address. This double reversal—organic disruption = death, cognitive fixity = life—serves history by moving oblivion beyond the enclave. Without the citadel of meaningfulness, one babbles or is mad. Hence we grow protective of what we mean. (1990: 26)

For Appelbaum, sound untamed by language, significance, and/or attention is a threat to the order of language and civilization that protects human beings from the potentially overwhelming awareness of their own contingency. In placing voice-as-sound in opposition to culture, language, and power, Appelbaum endows it with an untenable romanticism and purity. We argue to the contrary that human-generated sound is not a substrate upon which the edifices of language, signification, and culture are erected, but is rather a modality that only emerges in the context of social and political institutions. Appelbaum notes that the baby's babble is preceded by the cry of need, which he describes as the "primordial economy" (1990: 74); but that cry of need is always already situated within a nexus of social relations and immediately shaped by the responses to it, which vary widely across different social contexts. Even more fundamentally, the sheer existence of that infant requires those same relations, whose sonorous aspects are experienced by the fetus in the womb (as we discuss in more detail in Chapter 5).

Related to this over-romanticization of voice-as-sound is the framing of socialization and coming to language as a necessarily limiting or oppressive dynamic. Although Appelbaum insists that his project ought not to create "the impression that cognition is inherently mischievous and given to deception" (139), his analysis is decidedly elegiac, permeated with a sense of loss and outrage for the wildness that cognition and language has stripped from voice.

While limitations entailed by language, cognition, and social norms can certainly stunt human possibilities, our more Foucauldian approach recognizes that such limitations are also both productive and amenable to transgressive deployments. To say that they are productive is not to endow their results with a necessarily positive valence; biopower produces embodied forms that conform to and sustain oppressive power structures. But it would be a mistake to understand the embodied subjects produced by networks of power as diminished, whittled-away existences, mere remnants of a complete and ideal state-of-being. To be shaped by the contingent structures of language, social order, and cognition is to be rendered capable; and although we must surely ask the critical questions about those capacities (capable of what? To what ends?), it is a mistake to frame them only as encroachments upon a wild freedom that is the true realm of the possible. Similarly, it is a mistake to overidentify those restrictions with systems of power, as if they can be deployed only to perpetuate oppression, when they can be powerful conduits of transgressive and transformative action.

Finally, contrasting the soundedness of voice with the strictures of language and social order leaves unexplorable how sound is itself implicated, *qua* sound, in that order. It is not only the logos of speech that is politically and socially meaningful; the soundings of voices, quite apart from their linguistic content, produce socially and politically meaningful experiences. As the following chapter will argue, the sound of human voices is not merely the raw material from which the structures of significance are carved, but is always already marked indelibly by structural inequalities, social norms, and political exigencies. The unintentional cough or laugh, the baby's cry of hunger, the wails of childbirth: none pierce the flimsy walls of culture to give us a glimpse of the surrounding void, but remain, like all bodily phenomena, solidly rooted in and shaped by social and political particularities.

Although Ihde's analysis centers on the demand that philosophers "listen to the *sounds as meaningful*" (2007: 4, emphasis in original), he does not extend that meaningfulness to social and political realms, and thus commits a mistake similar to Appelbaum's, albeit by omission. Emphasizing the intentionality (understood in the phenomenological sense)[2] of the experience of sound, he notes that experiences of listening and hearing frequently involve elements of focusing and filtering. To listen to or hear something often involves retracting one's auditory attention from other sounds (74–5), a habitual action that is an essential aspect of the sonorous phenomenon as experienced by the listener.

However, Ihde's analysis fails to sufficiently recognize the role of social and political dynamics in relation to that intentionality, including the role of systemic oppression. Here Ihde is limited by his reliance on traditional methodologies of phenomenology, which seek to reveal ostensibly universal structures of lived experience that persist regardless of social, political, or historical specificity; in contrast, we identify more strongly with the subfield of critical phenomenology (Weiss et al. 2019), and we consider the dynamics described by Ihde as necessarily shaped by social and political forces, and thus insufficiently explained in politically neutral terms. Experiences and practices of auditory focus and directionality are clearly influenced by systemic inequalities such as racism, sexism, and ableism, and not in a merely occasional or peripheral way. The ways in which listening bodies tune into and tune out certain kinds of human voices are central to our sonorous interactions and are consistently constructed through practices, norms, and experiences. We agree with Ihde that human-generated sound, including nonlinguistic sound, is deeply meaningful, but we argue that its meanings cannot be sufficiently understood without paying careful attention to the role of structural injustice.

Intervocality

In an analysis of truth and reconciliation commissions as vocal assemblages, Mickey Vallee describes voice as both material and "radically indeterminate" (2016: 52), always situated within a complex set of social and political relations:

Voices are thus channeled in appropriate directions in order for affects to be registered for the public record. Inasmuch as the voice, then, demarcates something ultimately discoverable, this discoverability is indeterminate, resulting from the choices people make on all sides regarding which voices speak, which voices are listened to, and which voices go on public record. We must take into account the educative tendencies of voice and voices, especially regarding the manner in which a multiplicity of repressed voices can, through such an institution as a truth commission, become historicized (in some ways that are dangerous, in other ways potent) as a singular voice. There is something ethical in the voice, if we think of the voice as a zone of potential. (54)

Vallee's description underscores the importance of understanding vocality not as a set of capacities generated within and primarily exercised by a self-contained, autonomous person, but rather as what we are terming *intervocality:* a set of capacities and modes of embodiment arising from and taking place within complex, multiple social relations.

Human voices—their timbres, resonance, prosodies, and dynamics—bear the sonic marks of how those voices have been heard, received, and responded to. Just as the details of bodily comportment are profoundly influenced by social contexts, so too the quality of an individual voice can be drastically different depending on its vocal purpose, the sonorous grammar of the situation, or the addressee(s). A careful and familiar eavesdropper may well be able to tell whether a person speaking on the phone is conversing with their child, their parent, their colleague, or their employer, without ever hearing the voice on the other end of the line. As we shall see in the next chapter, thinkers in the fields of musicology and sound studies have emphasized the intersubjective nature of sound, providing detailed descriptions of the shaping of sounds and social meanings of sonorous events by the material environment, practices of listening, racial and gender norms, and so on. In emphasizing intervocality as an existential and ontological modality of voiced human persons, we are adding a facet to these models: that voice's sound is marked by the surrounding receiving bodies. Voices, then, voice the other.

To be a voiced human being is to be intervocal, and for those human beings whose embodiment includes the capacity of voice, the use of that capacity (as well as the refusal to use it, whether completely or selectively) emanates from, and does not exist prior to, social relations. Intervocality, in short, refers to the fact that not only are voices always enacted within a context of social relations, but that sonorous qualities of voices are shaped by those social relations, including how voices are received and interpreted. To be a voiced human being is thus to be enmeshed in complex systems of intervocality that produce particular voices, particular modes of receiving voices, and sonorous aspects of specific social spaces.

Our emphasis on intervocality rather than vocality emphasizes the degree to which the material voice is never self-contained or self-defined. Here too we depart from Ihde's analysis. In detailing how sound reveals the shape of the sound-making object, Ihde notes that such objects cannot effect such revelations by themselves, but require another surface with which to interact: "I hear not one voice, but at least two in a '*duet*' of things. I hear not only the round shape-aspect of the billiard ball rolling on the table, I also hear the hardness of the table" (2007: 67, emphasis in original). In utilizing the term "duets," he refers primarily to the voices of inanimate objects:

> But individual things might well remain silent, their voices not active. Yet each thing can be given a voice. The rock struck, sounds in a voice; the footstep in the sand speaks muffled sound. Here, however, we must note that the voices of things that are often silent are made to sound only in duets or more complex polyphonies. When I strike a lectern you hear both the voice of the lectern and of my knuckle ... Here we must attend carefully to our perception. For to isolate the voice of a thing, we must listen carefully and focus on one of the voices in the duet. We can do this in making one of the voices focal—the auditory figure as it were—and the other background. (190)

Ihde's notion of the auditory duet of the voices of things carries the phenomenological reduction too far. In describing the sound of the knuckle rapping against the lectern as two voices, rather than an irreducible interaction voicing the knuckle and the lectern simultaneously, Ihde maintains a sonorous distance between the two objects, as if each had their own voice quite apart from the other, such that the listener can foreground one while affording less attention to the other.

Although Ihde is focusing here on nonhuman entities, his emphasis on the sonorous role of the other is transferable to human vocality. The phenomenon of voice as human-generated sound is fundamentally and existentially reliant on entities and materials distinguishable from, although deeply implicated with, the voiced and auditory human being. Put simply: human voicing always constitutes a *relation* among multiple bodily entities (not to mention social and political forces) and thus cannot be reduced to belonging solely or exhaustively to the voicing human being.

The phenomenon of human voicing is intersubjective across a wide variety of modalities. Its sonorous aspects are necessarily shaped by the environment into which the sound is cast: how a certain combination of breath, muscular contractions, and skeletal forms sounds depends on whether the voicing person is under water or on a mountain top, facing a brick wall or at the center of a round room with a domed ceiling. Ihde's notion of a duet suggests that this interaction sounds both the human voice and, say, the voice of the brick wall. By contrast, we hold that it is not a matter of two voices sounding together, but rather of the sounding of a voice whose acoustics are sonorously marked and shaped by its surroundings.

The material situation into which the human voice is released frequently involves other human beings as well. As social and material entities, receiving human bodies construct the sonorous qualities of the sounding human voice, at least as experienced phenomena. The sound of a human voice as experienced by an auditory human body is limited by what that particular human body is capable of perceiving sonorously, capacities framed by a wide scope of factors, ranging from the physiological (whether an eardrum is intact or perforated) to the environmental (whether the receiving body is in a crowded room or a hushed auditorium) to the emotional (whether the receiving body is calm or agitated) to the social (whether the sounded voice emanates from a person considered worthy of auditory attention).

The skeptical reader may pause here, and wonder if our analysis is beginning to conflate two quite different phenomena: the voice as sounded, and the voice as received. That is, is it not possible, and perhaps reasonable, to distinguish between the sonorous qualities of the voice released into a complex situation marked by both material and political realities, and the sonorous qualities of that voice experienced by the receiving body? Take, for example, the voice of an activist who is laying claim to a contested right. The sympathetic listener may experience the activist's voice as strong, compelling, even righteous, while the unsympathetic listener may experience the same voice as off-puttingly strident, harsh, and grating. Is it possible, and perhaps even likely, that the listeners are constructing different experiences out of an original released vocalization that was objectively singular? That there was one self-contained released voice, even if there were multiple received voices?

We are arguing that both the strictly sonorous qualities of the human voice and the meanings attached to those qualities are profoundly intersubjective, and that they co-constitute each other in significant ways. In an ontological sense, the material intersubjectivity of voice consists of the interactions that any given sound, including the sounds of human voices, necessarily involves. The voice only exists to the extent that it is released, and it must be released into something—there is no possibility of the void. The particularities that mark the situation and environment into which it is cast molds the sounds of the voice substantially. Thus, a voiced human does not have *a* voice, but is provided a set of sonorous, vocal possibilities by the situating material environment.

The released voice is thus intersubjective in relation to its material location, and even at this ontological level, we can see that the released voice is always, simultaneously, the received voice; how the surrounding environment receives (or reflects or absorbs) the voice is an irreducible aspect of its sonorous quality. Yet not all entities in the receiving environment function in identical ways vis-à-vis the sonorous qualities of the voice or its social and political meanings. Human beings who receive human vocal emanations participate in the shaping of those sonorous emanations in ways similar to a brick wall or the height of a ceiling; their flesh is a surface against which sound waves bounce (even as some are, as described above, absorbed), and their proximity influences how and when that bouncing and absorption occurs. But as vocal/ auditory beings, humans also receive the released voice as an experience, as something that happens to them. What that sound is *qua* experience is necessarily coproduced by the receiving body; a loud, sudden noise is a profoundly different phenomenon depending on whether the receiving body suffers from PTSD, or has sensory sensitivities, or is eagerly anticipating a finale in a fireworks display.

It would be a mistake to limit the relevance of the receiving body to merely physiological aspects, or to separate out too strictly the physiological body from the social and political body. The body that experiences sound is as marked by social and political norms in receiving sound as it is by physiological particularities. More precisely, those physiological particularities may be, and usually are, profoundly influenced by social and political realities, norms, and practices. How one's body receives and produces sound, as the next chapter will explore, is deeply influenced by vocal and auditory practices, including at the physiological level, and various forms of sonorous injustice (such as exposing workers or incarcerated persons to loud, chaotic noises) leave physiological (as well as psychological and emotional) marks. In addition, the lived experience of certain physiological realities is profoundly shaped by the social context in which those realities were generated. The hearing loss resulting from torture involving loud music is a different experience than that resulting from playing in a rock band for two decades; the hearing sensitivity of a person who has completed a week-long silent retreat is different from that experienced by someone forcibly deprived of human vocal contact in solitary confinement.

The receiving body is always already sonorously shaped, prepped by a variety of intersecting material and political forces, ready-to-receive in specific ways. The reception of a vocal emanation shapes the emanation itself (by virtue of the material fact of the receiving body) and the experience of the emanation as received (by virtue of physiological traits of the receiving body, prior social listening practices, the social context, emotional state-of-being, etc.), and, importantly, future vocal emanations. These multiple constructive influences of the receiving body are inescapable. The phenomenon of the released voice cannot be distinguished clearly from them, and so one cannot, as Ihde recommends, tune out the receiving surface (in this case, another human being) in order to isolate the singular voice of the human being generating the sound. The intersubjectivity of vocal interactions is more profound, and more fundamental, than Ihde's notion of the "duet" can capture, at least with regard to human vocal interactions.

The profound and constructive role played by the receiving body becomes more complex when considering the phenomenon of receiving one's own voice. The omnidirectionality of the audible field that Ihde describes establishes the voicing body also as a receiving body. Moreover, the released voice as received by the sounding body has additional sonorous elements not perceptible to other receivers. Rébecca Kleinberger (2018) suggests that the experience of the "inward voice" (the voice we hear when we are speaking) is distinct in several ways from that of the "outward voice" (that which is sounded in the spaces outside the body). The inward voice is carried to the ear not through air, but through bones serving as conductors for the vibration of sound. In addition, three essential filters manage the intensity, impact, and/or repetitiveness of the inner sound of our own voice. A small partition serves as a mechanical filter (9:09) that protects the inner ear, thereby adjusting the impact and strength of sounds coming from within. A biological filter in the cochlea (the part of the inner ear designed to send nerve impulses in response to sound vibrations) is made of cells that "trigger differently" depending on how often the sound is heard, resulting in a "habituation effect" (9:37). One's own voice, as the sound most heard by the speaker throughout life, becomes over time the sound *least heard*. The third filter is a "force filter," a neurological filter that shuts off the auditory cortex the moment one's mouth opens to create a sound; "you hear your voice, but your brain actually never listens to the sound of your voice" (9:50). For all of these reasons, the voice received and experienced by the sounding body is significantly different from that received and experienced by others—as anyone who has been taken aback by a recording of one's own voice can attest.

The singularity of the human vocal emanation is thus entirely illusory. While individual voices may be reliably recognizable, as Adriana Cavarero argues (2005), and while certain aspects of vocal emanations can be reliably measured, recorded, and replayed by various forms of technology, the phenomenon of the human voice is always marked by an inescapable multiplicity. As released, its sonorous elements are fundamentally marked by the materiality of its environment, including the materiality of any receiving bodies in its proximity. "The" voice that is "mine" is composed of a plentitude of sonorous experiences entwined and enmeshed with the other—other surfaces, other materials, other receiving bodies without which the released voice could not come into existence.

Vocal Identities

The embodiment of voice, as well as its centrality to many human interactions, is a meaningful site of both individual identity and group membership. The Western focus on visuality has contributed to the feminist focus on the politics of appearance, and the Western privileging of the ostensibly disembodied mind has contributed to the emphasis on the ideas behind speech rather than the physical aspects of vocalization. What is missing from either approach is an exploration of the connections among senses of self, the soundedness of voice, and the reception of voices.

As mentioned in our introduction, when addressing questions of identity—that is, explorations of what it means to have a sense of self, to identify as a particular being—we reject models that assume identity to be fixed, prior to social and political structures, and/or impervious to the profound effects of relational interactions. Yet we recognize that even senses of self that are constantly under construction are profoundly important lenses through which subjects experience the world, particularly in Western cultural contexts that endow the individual with metaphysical value and worth. In exploring the role of voice in the construction and shaping of identity, we seek to highlight an embodied modality that takes part in the construction and experience of subjective identity that itself profoundly configures lived experience.

Linda Martín Alcoff's work on visible identities is particularly helpful here. Alcoff provides a rich analysis of social identities as "deep features of the self" that nevertheless do not have "ready-made political orientations or fixed meanings" (2006: 287). Alcoff's emphasis on identities parsed primarily through visual markers reflects, as she notes, a materialist culture that strongly, and problematically, associates visibility with truth and reality. Yet Alcoff rejects the idea that aspects of identity associated with visible traits—most notably race and gender—are either existentially irrelevant (such that liberatory approaches should attempt to minimize or ignore them) or reducible to the surrounding systems of inequality, arguing to the contrary that the meanings of social identities exceed the oppressive systems that simultaneously produce and rely upon them. Visible identities matter in complex and fluid ways, Alcoff argues, to communities, individuals, and systems. Their entanglement in oppressive systems ought not be mistaken for the final word on their existential relevance, and their materiality ought not be used as evidence of their insignificance.

Alcoff's analysis could be extended in productive ways to understand how aural/vocal/sonorous identities are similarly meaningful. Like visible attributes, voice is profoundly marked by both material and social/political realities, as the next chapter will address in more detail; it is a crucial and widely recognized element of many (although not all) marginalized identities and plays an important role in the perpetuation of systemic inequalities. Aural/vocal/sonorous identities are also "deep features of the self," palpable aspects of existence that contribute (however contingently and fluidly) to the grounding and defining of identity. How vocalized subjects sound often constitutes a deeply meaningful way of both indexing and solidifying the membership of an individual in a distinct social group—a membership that may play an important role in the subject's sense of self.

The meaning of intervocality is not exhausted by its ability to be implicated in systems of inequality. Intercorporeality, the fact that human embodiment consists of a being-with other human bodies, and that that being-with is central to both bodily particularity and bodily experiences, can explain how bodily interactions with others can enhance human flourishing, sometimes even returning one's body to oneself in an affirming and positively transformative way. Similarly, intervocality can be a generative site of vocal exploration, identity, development, and affirmation. Learning to *kiai* in a martial arts class can be an important part of developing new forms of strength; returning to a linguistic community after an extended period of travel and immersing oneself in the vocal accents and rhythms of one's mother tongue can be deeply comforting (or profoundly alienating); vocal changes that accompany hormonal treatment can be a welcome, delightfully affirming experience for trans folx; shaping one's singing voice to meld or contrast with another can be an aesthetically satisfying experience. Intervocality is also an important site of resistance: it is no accident that social movements regularly rely on chants and songs to build cohesion and effect political change. Saidiya Hartman relates the story of a 1919 "sonic riot" (2019: 279), where Black women incarcerated at the Bedford Hills Reformatory for Women weaponized sound to protest the horrific conditions imposed upon them:

> It was the dangerous music of open rebellion. En masse they announced what had been endured, what they wanted, what they intended to destroy. Bawling, screaming, cursing, and stomping made the cottage tremble and corralled them together into one large, pulsing formation, an ensemble reveling in the beauty of the strike. Young women hung out of the windows, crowded at the doors, and huddled on shared beds sounded a complete revolution, a break with the given, an undoing and remaking of values, which called property and law and social order into crisis. They sought *out of here, out of now, out of the cell, out of the hold.* The call and the appeal transformed them from prisoners into strikers, from faceless abstractions secured by a string of numbers affixed to a cotton jumper into a collective body, a riotous gathering, even if only for thirteen hours. In the discordant assembly, they found a hearing in one another. (283, emphasis in original)

Functioning as a collective sonic body provided the imprisoned women with a new identity ("striker") as well as a shared objective that defined their individual and collective will. By demanding through riotous sound that they be heard—a demand that their imprisoners could not easily stifle or hide—they could no longer remain an abstraction, lacking identity, in the eyes and ears of those who witnessed them, including themselves.

Our focus on intervocality troubles the easy association of voice with the individual self, as exemplified in such metaphors as "finding my voice," which replicates the Western model of the self as autonomous and self-contained. Yet we do not reject entirely the close relationship between the voice and self; instead, we seek to emphasize the existential importance of the voice to the self as embedded and enmeshed in social relations, and to highlight the sonorous aspects of those relations. Along these lines, we have frequently referred to the "released" voice, a description that captures its directionality, the inescapable influence of the situation into which it is cast, and its too often underestimated materiality. We hold that voice could productively be understood as a bodily emanation that, in contrast to other bodily fluids (Kristeva 1982), does not become abject as it leaves the body, but rather only comes to belong to the voiced person in the releasing act. To have sonorous existence is necessarily to find oneself in relation to a surrounding material world, and frequently to other voiced and not-voiced human beings. My voice may emanate from my unique, bodily location, one marked by geography, social position, and so on. But it cannot be my voice, and it cannot be sound without the interplay between my embodied being, the material environment, and the various beings that share that environment. The voice as sounded is therefore "mine" and "not mine" as well as "here" and "there."

As we will discuss in detail in the following chapter, Cavarero (2005) closely associates voice with unique identity, noting how easily a person can be identified, often with a high degree of accuracy, by voice alone, absent any additional visual clues. While we disagree with Cavarero's reduction of the philosophical and political meaningfulness of voice to existential uniqueness (as we have already mentioned, it is also capable of revealing membership in specific social groups, thus conveying group membership as well as uniqueness), she is surely correct to highlight that voices are frequently identifiable. Yet it also matters that such recognizability is not infallible. Not only can voices fail to evoke a person's uniqueness accurately (family members may not be clearly distinguishable over the phone, or even in person, for example), but they can also, and in important ways, fail to reflect accurately a person's membership in a social group. We are not speaking here of the phenomenon of code-switching, whereby members of socially or politically marginalized groups might adopt the vocal gestures and habits of dominant groups in an attempt to mitigate the effects of structural injustice (a dynamic we will discuss in more detail in the following chapter). Such code-switching does not necessarily involve the misidentification of the speaking person, although it can do so, particularly in the case of identities that are not necessarily visible, such as membership in a particular economic class. The kind of misidentification that we are interested in here occurs when the vocal qualities of a person are received in a way that results in their being misidentified as a member of a social group.

Such vocal misidentifications, of course, have a wide variety of possible meanings. Some may be the result of intentional actions on the part of the speaker, who may not wish to be correctly identified for a variety of reasons, and who may perceive some social benefit in being so misidentified. Some—such as the racial and sexual misidentifications central to the singing and acting career of Libby Holmes, a white woman whose career included fame as both a torch singer and a performer of "blues concerts," and who was also an outspoken supporter of the civil rights movement—are ethically ambivalent as they can facilitate cultural appropriation and/or "an aural production that modeled possibilities of a nonxenophobic locality of sound through oscillation and 'moving between'—a desire for movement as freedom from the binary demarcation of the color line" (Scheper 2016: 97). Some are rooted in flawed and often oppressive listening practices; for example, African American persons who may not have vocal or sonorous traits that the white listening practices associate with Black voices may be heard as white. Attempts on the part of white persons to take up ostensibly Black vocal gestures and traits can reveal deeply racist assumptions about the sounds of Black voices, resulting in "auditory blackface," as occurred in 2020 when an audio recording of an essay written by Black scholar Regina N. Bradley was voiced by a white male reader whose affected accent constituted a vocal caricature (Beachum 2020).

While there may be examples where vocal misidentification results in concrete social benefits (African Americans who do not fulfill a certain vocal stereotype may receive significantly different responses and advice from, say, real estate agents over the phone than they do in person, which could be either advantageous or disadvantageous, depending on the circumstances), we want to emphasize here that, precisely because voice is a meaningful part of one's sense of self and because it is often, although not always, related to membership in a social group, such misidentification frequently comes at a significant and underestimated cost. That cost is clearly expressed in the Boots Riley-directed film *Sorry to Bother You* (2018), which centers on a Black character's decision to adopt a distinctly white voice to gain success in telemarketing. While the film's plot hinges on the ability of Black people to take on vocal characteristics associated with white people, and use that ability for financial gain, the film problematizes the seemingly easy separation of racial identity and vocal traits by dubbing the Black characters' dialogue with the voices of white actors, and emphasizing the dubbing by means of imperfect and thus perceivable lip syncing. The sound produced by the carefully misaligned dubbing draws attention to its own artificiality: it carries the marks of a voice-over recorded in a studio, free from the ambient traces of sound from the physical surroundings of the Black character. It is clear that the audience is never intended to believe that the white voices used by the Black characters are actually produced by those particular Black bodies (Harris 2018, Zuckerman 2018). The dub brings attention to the vocal performance as *remote* performance ("phoning it in" as they say in theatre when an actor isn't really *present*), resulting in a crisply articulated "radio announcer" voice picked up on a microphone close to the source. The dubbed dialogue of the white actor's voice is skewed to highlight a rather tinny higher nasal and sinus-y sound associated with whiteness, excluding the lower harmonics of vocal sounds resonating in the throat, chest, and torso: the sound has the quality of being not only disconnected from the speaker's body generally, but acoustically "cut off at the neck," a chilling metaphor. The Black body is muted out.

In sonically and visually highlighting the artificiality of the white voices deployed by the Black characters, Riley is confronting the audience with the existential price paid by people of color forced to navigate deeply entrenched racist economic and sonorous structures. To succeed in such a context requires Cassius Green to be someone he is not, and while intentional racial misidentification through voice is financially beneficial, the pound of flesh must be paid: in the loss of Cash's Black activist community, in a head wound that refuses to heal, and finally in the loss of his human body at the hands of a diabolical white tycoon who enslaves his workers by transforming them into horses with human capacities for speech and thought. The surrealness of Cash's transformation into an "equisapien" at the film's conclusion drives home the message of the emphasized artifice of the vocal dubbing at the film's beginning: the bodily demands that white supremacy makes of Black people target the viability of an embodied Black identity and endanger Black lives.

Conclusion

Our analysis of the material, embodied, relational voice has resulted in an emphasis on human intervocality. From this perspective, the releasing and receiving of vocal emanations reveal themselves as shimmering, oscillating, co-constituting phenomena. The speaking other, in Ihde's view, throws up an auditory field marked by both immersion and directionality, a sonorous being-with that does not collapse the difference between the vocalizing beings, but rather stretches between them ("the other stands *before* me" [2007: 78, emphasis in original]). We add to Ihde's description the insight that the auditory field shimmering between the vocalizing beings is both constructed by and constructing those beings. Their contributions to the interaction, their releasing and receiving of vocalizations, shape their respective sonorous, vocal, and receiving possibilities.

The releasing and receiving of vocal emanations are not to be understood as strictly chronological, happening one after the other in a linear progression. To participate in a vocal interaction is to be immersed in a vibrant, vibrating exchange wherein one's releasing and receiving capacities are constantly working in tandem. The vocalizations that one is receiving, and the complex mechanisms and social norms engaged in that receiving, both shape and are reflected in the vocalizations that one is releasing, and vice versa. Intervocality reveals not only the co-constitution of the released and received vocalization, but the ways in which the acts of releasing and receiving are co-temporal, while preserving a necessary distinction between them.

Intervocality also clarifies the inescapable vulnerabilities that accompany the exercise of vocal capacities (both releasing and receiving). If vocal identities are, as we have argued here, appropriately relevant to senses of self, including senses of self that are related to belonging to certain social groups—that is, if voiced beings have significant existential stakes in the sonorous game—and if the sonorous experiences and capacities that undergird such vocal identities are profoundly shaped by factors that include the ways in which other voicing beings release and receive human-generated sound, then intervocality is a necessarily ethical and political phenomenon. To sound one's voice is to render it open to transformation; it is to throw oneself into the sonorous care of the other. An understanding of the complex dynamics of intervocality, then, inevitably leads to ethical questions: what does it mean to interact vocally in an ethical way? And how does a focus on intervocality reveal structures of injustice that might otherwise go overlooked?

2

Vocal Injustice

In the previous chapter, we developed a detailed account of voice as an embodied phenomenon, with an emphasis on its relational and existential aspects. We argued that the concept of intervocality captures its irreducible intersubjectivity, and in doing so gestured toward a politics and ethics of voice that recognizes the meaningfulness of voice for identity (including membership in social groups) and the constitutive role of the act of receiving sound.

In this chapter, we turn our attention to the question of vocal injustice. We begin by establishing that dominant Western culture is marked by distinctly unjust soundscapes characterized by an unjust distribution of vocal social goods (volume and airtime, for example) and listening and vocal practices that shore up systemic inequalities. We then explore the work of three thinkers, each of whom develops a disciplinarily distinct approach to vocal injustice: Kristin Linklater (voice training), Adriana Cavarero (philosophy), and Nina Eidsheim (musicology). Although all three make important contributions to the development of more ethical practices of vocalizing and receiving vocalizations, none sufficiently recognizes the complex dynamics of intervocality. We conclude by articulating what a new model of vocal justice would require.

Unjust Soundscapes

Given that dominant forms of media consistently overrepresent white cishet men, and underrepresent women, people of color, LGBTQIA folk, and all the intersections thereof,[1] there is little doubt that such overrepresentation takes sonorous as well as visual forms. Moviegoers are bombarded with male-identified voices; according to Hanah Anderson and Matt Daniels's analysis of over 2,000 screenplays (2016), 307 had 90 percent or more male dialogue; 1,206 had 60–90 percent male dialogue; 314 had rough gender parity (within 10 percent); and 9 films had 90 percent or more female dialogue. Only four out of thirty-one Disney films have dialogue split roughly equally between male- and female-identified characters, and even in those with female-identified main characters, the dialogue from female characters never exceeds 64 percent (in six, the dialogue from male characters is over 90 percent, with a top rate of 98 percent). The 2015 Global Media Monitoring project reported that "women make up only 24% of the persons heard, read about or seen in newspaper, television and radio news, exactly as they did in 2010" (Macharia 2015: 8). The Center for the Study of Women in Television and Film (Lauzen 2020) reported that 2019 saw a significant increase in the percentage of top grossing films with female-identified protagonists (from 31 percent in 2018 to 40 percent in 2019), and even a small increase in the percentage of female-identified major characters (from 35 percent to 36 percent); yet somehow the percentage of female-identified speaking characters decreased (from 35 percent to 34 percent). Thus, moviegoers in 2019 were exposed to even fewer women's voices than in the prior year. Moreover, although recent years have seen an increase in the presence of trans and nonbinary actors (Laverne Cox, Rebecca Root, Nicole Maines, Ian Alexander, Ruby Rose, Nico Tortorella, to name a few) and a notable shift in the three-dimensionality of the characters they play, mainstream media remains solidly cis-centric.

Scholarship on the gendered nature of conversation in professional and personal contexts provides clear evidence for systemic sonorous inequality. Not only are women subject to more conversational interruptions than men, but when women do interrupt men, their interruptions are more negatively perceived than men's interruptions of women (which are sometimes not even perceived as interruptions) (Hancock and Rubin 2015). Moreover, the interrupting woman's talkativeness (measured as time spent talking) is significantly overestimated (Hancock and Rubin 2015). And lest we think the politics of interruption can be transcended once a woman has achieved a certain social standing, Jacobi and Schweers's analysis (2017) of courtroom transcripts demonstrate that even female-identified judges, including US Supreme Court justices, are subject to far higher interruption rates by male justices and attorneys than their male counterparts.

Unfortunately, there are not as much empirical data on the influence of racism, homophobia, ableism, and other forms of systemic injustice on the politics of conversational airtime and interruption. The substantial literature on the vocal phenomenon of racialized code-switching (see Young 2009, Young and Young-Rivera 2013) raises important questions about vocal injustice and the vocal practices of members of marginalized racial or economic groups navigating hostile social environments. More empirical data are needed about the distribution of social vocal goods of airtime, volume, the presumption of un-interruptability along the lines of various identity markers, and the vocal and aural practices of members of dominant groups that contribute to structures of vocal injustice. Even in the absence of such empirical data, it seems reasonable to assume that perceptions and experiences of conversational appropriateness would be deeply influenced by multiple structural inequalities.

Vocal social norms include damaging stereotypes that simultaneously misrepresent the complexity and nuances of lived experience and mark marginalized members of society as proper targets for disdain, discrimination, and violence (examples are only too easy to come by: vocal caricatures of gay men, African Americans, women, etc.). Moreover, different forms of inequality are related to the voice in different ways. Gender, for example, is an intensely vocal form of social identification in contemporary Western society, as scholars in the field of trans studies have pointed out (Anastasia 2014, Zimman 2018). At least in contemporary US culture, certain intersecting racial, ethnic, and geographical groups are more or less associated with vocal markings than others (Newman and Wu 2011). While some disabilities have little to no effect on a person's vocal or sonorous identity, others, particularly those involving certain muscular or hearing impairments, are closely associated with particular forms of vocalizing. In addition, vocal identities are markedly intersectional: recognizably racialized voices are simultaneously gendered, recognizably gendered voices are simultaneously raced, and all are also marked by class, geographically situated accents and dialects, and so on.

The fields of sound studies and musicology have addressed matters of sonic and vocal injustice in a variety of ways. Yvon Bonenfant highlighted the need for a queer theory of listening and voice, and in the process redefined listening as the "act of paying intense somatic attention to the ways that our bodies engage with the sonic stimuli around them, in order to decide which emanators of vocal sound to gesture toward, which of these to want and to seek, and in which baths of sound to swim" (2010: 78). Ryan Dohoney (2015) and William Cheng (2016) analyze the use of music as torture, and how sound's ability to be used for such political purposes reveals a sonic vulnerability undertheorized in philosophical models of the self; Cheng also articulates the subtle ways that the mandate to "sound good" in academic speaking and writing perpetuates systemic exclusion of historically marginalized groups. The history of sound reproduction has been analyzed for its gendered and racial meanings and effects (Ehrick 2015), as well as for how it relied on and produced specific social understandings (and practices) of listening, authenticity, and the value of speaking/hearing, often framed in a distinctly ableist way (Sterne 2003).

Jennifer Stoever's *The Sonic Color Line* (2015) describes deep-seated historical patterns of sonorous and vocal injustice related to racial inequality in the United States. Stoever offers a compelling description of the development of listening as a "racialized body discipline" (2015: 4) in the United States that perpetuated and deepened structures of white supremacy. Pushing back against the assumption that race, racism, and racialization are structured solely by visuality, Stoever details the deployment of the lived experience of sound to construct, justify, and maintain racial inequality, including the construction of the "sonic color line" and the "listening ear":

> The sonic color line describes the process of racializing sound—how and why certain bodies are expected to produce, desire, and live amongst particular sounds—and its product, the hierarchical division sounded between "whiteness" and "blackness." The listening ear drives the sonic color line; it is a figure for how dominant listening practices accrue—and change—over time, as well as a descriptor for how the dominant culture exerts pressure on individual listening practices to conform to the sonic color line's norms. Through the listening ear's surveillance, discipline, and interpretation, certain associations between race and sound come to seem normal, natural, and "right." (7–8)

Although neither the sonic color line nor the listening ear are limited to the phenomenon of human-produced sound (the listening ear might associate certain instrumental musical styles with specific racial groups, and the sonic color line may be instantiated by patterns of urban planning that burden communities of color with higher levels of noise pollution), Stoever's analysis highlights racialized patterns of vocalization and listening that lent credence to the ideology of white supremacy. Yet she also insists that practices of vocalization and listening have been deployed effectively by marginalized groups to resist the sonic color line and racism (33).

Stoever's "cultural materialist approach to a series of events between slavery and the end of segregation" (6) productively exposes the racial politics of sound. In addition to fine-grained descriptions of diverse sonorous phenomena, Stoever offers an understanding of human vocality as deeply immersed in and emanating from complex networks of power and meaning. Moreover, the interplay of the sonic color line and the listening ear emphasizes the fundamentally interactive quality of sonorous phenomena. For Stoever, the racialization of sound rested on listening practices that actively worked on sounds, and sounded voices, to produce social and political meanings and effects. One must listen in a highly particular, disciplined way to experience white voices as the norm, or to value Black voices only in specific contexts and registers.

Thinkers like Stoever, Dohoney, Bonenfant, and Cheng raise crucial questions about the nature of sound, the roles of social norms and technologies in perpetuating certain listening practices, and how human vocal emanations are shaped, interpreted, and produced. While they helpfully identify specific ways in which sound and voice are implicated in systemic injustice, they don't offer an overarching theory of vocal injustice. We now turn our attention to scholars whose work hews closer to that challenge. Despite the important insights developed by all three, we find that their analyses remain insufficiently informed by a recognition of intervocality.

Linklater and the Natural Voice

Kristin Linklater's *Freeing the Natural Voice* (1976/2006; referred to hereafter as *FNV*) is one of the most important and referenced methodologies for liberating, developing, and strengthening the voice. Her approach is utilized in rigorous actor training programs and workshops worldwide for people interested in unshackling the voice from the hold of unconscious habitual patterns and psychophysical tensions.

Linklater studied under Iris Warren at London Academy of Music and Dramatic Arts, from whom she learned an architecture of voice exercises for actors underpinned by psychological and physiological understandings of the voice. *FNV* documents Linklater's further development of Warren's exercises, and constitutes the first comprehensive communication of the work in written form. A radical divergence from the more formal methods of the time, it has since become a leading textbook for voice in the field.

FNV emerged from a particular socio-political-cultural context. Notions of "freedom" and "the natural" held specific meanings within the anti-racist, anti-sexist, anti-war cultural movements of the 1960s and early 1970s in the United States and Britain. The body became a site of nostalgia, a longing toward a time when bodies might have existed in a natural state, unconstrained by the rigidities of social norms and the invasive control of government and dominant mainstream culture. The hippie movement's rejection of convention produced an emphasis on self-presentation and the body through "new modes of self-presentation, involving emancipation from the old canons of fashion, and a rejoicing in the natural attributes of the human body" (Marwick 2011: 26). The anti-racist civil rights movement engendered a rejection of European standards of beauty and a reclaiming of untreated hair, thus equating a move toward the natural with empowerment and agency. A resurgence of Romanticism, carrying with it the promise of "allowing human beings to 'feel at home' in a meaningful, free and natural world" (Gorodeisky 2016) unfettered by the alienating and arbitrary powers of modernity, reached a critical height during this period, as a parallel distrust of dominant institutions' and government's ability to protect personal freedoms was on the rise.

Of course, the invocations of nature did not go entirely unchallenged. The women's liberation movement in the late 1960s included voices railing against the appeal to biology as a justification for inequality and demanded that women be given the freedom to control (rather than be determined by) their own bodies (Firestone [1970] 2003). Linklater's work is deeply influenced by both the call for a return to nature and the call for greater bodily freedom and autonomy. She advocates for the liberation and development of the (metaphorically and materially) suppressed and restricted voice, the voice that has gone into hiding but that is the authentic birthright of all human beings and, as much of her work implies, that has been disproportionately refused to women in patriarchal cultures. Her Company of Women (cofounded with Carol Gilligan) provided voice training workshops for women and adolescent girls as well as opportunities for women to play Shakespeare unbounded by the constraints of gender (Rousuck 1996). Simultaneously psychological, political, physiological, and philosophical, her vocal methodology has had a profound impact on the excavation of women's voices.

Linklater's approach to reconditioning and liberating the voice involves identifying and breaking habitual patterns largely internalized by socialization in a modern world: "to free the voice is to free the person ... the natural voice is most perceptibly blocked and distorted by physical tension; it suffers equally from emotional blocks, intellectual blocks, aural blocks, and psychological blocks" (Linklater 2006: 8). These socialized, habitual blocks (either conscious or unconscious) limit not only vocalizations but the emotions underlying them: "If we come to a point in our lives where we ... want to access the primitive sources of laughter, sorrow, anger, joy, we may find that the emotions themselves have been civilized or brutalized out of us. The nervous system impulses are blocked, rerouted, or crossed with countermanding impulses" (19–20).

To this end, both editions of *FNV* (a revised and expanded edition was released in 2006) and the accompanying text *Freeing Shakespeare's Voice* (1992) articulate a series of practices aimed at "awaken[ing] the dormant power that brings breath into every cell of the body and restor[ing] largesse of expression and stature to the human-actor-being" (Linklater 1992: 7). Essential to the work of undoing those limitations is the "vital difference between what is 'natural' and what is 'familiar'" (Linklater 2006: 7), connected to the objective of "a voice in direct contact with emotional impulse, shaped by intellect but not inhibited by it" (8). The natural voice is described as "transparent—revealing, not describing, inner impulses of emotion and thought, directly and spontaneously" (8). Importantly, "the person is heard, not the person's voice" (8).

The later edition of *FNV* builds on these fundamental precepts by adding an emphasis on the psychophysical connections between imagery, sensation, and embodiment as well as a consideration of the receptive aspects of voice, gesturing toward the relational aspects of intervocality. The importance of breath, relation, and the voice's ability to receive shifts in imagery and thought come to the fore: Linklater describes a voice communicating the "inner world of the psyche to the outer world of attentive listeners" (2006: 8) through the emanations of sound. Sound, through "invisible streams of energy," carry out to receptive bodies, bringing the speaker into the experience of being two places at once—both onstage and in the auditorium (or with "the other") at the same time (9).

Elsewhere, Linklater addresses an important paradox in actors' training: they must develop and train the voice to its potential in order "to forget about it, to sacrifice it—to let it be burned through by the heat of thoughts and feelings and moods and emotions" (2010: 43). It is not a matter of simply acquiring a skill, she writes: "Voice is identity. Your voice says, 'I am'" (43). Voice reveals not only the subtleties of shifting thought and feeling, but—through a mutually perceived "ring of truth"—authentic selfhood. The voice can "reveal the truth about its owner" (Linklater 2006: 25), who they are and the content of their experience.

Beyond the need or desire to simply be heard, Linklater posits that the revelation of truth in performance (as in life) requires the voice to be plugged into the inner life of instinct and emotional impulses, so that it becomes the channel through which thought and feeling are accurately revealed. She describes a tension between the raw materials of one's inner life and a modern persona presented to the world: a Dionysian inner life (2018) ruled by sensual, sensory, and emotional aspects of human nature is contrasted with an outer expression often ruled by the Apollonian, the rational, ordered, self-disciplined, and often limiting aspects of experience that prevent the owner of the voice from being known (2006). "'Per' and 'sona'—through sound.

My voice is exquisitely conditioned to a multiplicity of social prevarications. The question is: can I choose to drop my mask, my persona, and let my voice pick up the living impulses of who I am and what I care about in my intrinsic identity ... Whose voice am I speaking with? A teacher's voice or my own?" (Linklater 2009b).

In her later years, Linklater's work took up current findings in neuroscience, particularly how the brain functions in speech (Damasio 1995, 1999). Rejecting Descartes's *cogito ergo sum* in favor of "I am, therefore, I think" (Linklater 2010: 43),[2] she asserts that the body, the senses, and the emotions are all "vital to the intelligence of the whole self" (43) and seeks to reclaim the voice as a central site of the union of brain and body. Through the reconditioning of "the actor's quartet"—voice, intellect, body, and emotion (2006: 10)—she looks to reforge the brain-body connection by navigating the interruptions and restrictions in the pathways through which they might connect, reopening them or creating new "expressways" for thought, breath, and sound.

Linklater's work is deeply rooted in embodiment, training the subject to identify and release specific tensions, develop an increased awareness of the felt sensations of sound, and concentrate on the subtleties of causal thinking and powerful imagery that can lead to new freedoms of the voice, body, emotion, and psyche. The work requires the subject to navigate though (not around) the resistances of habit in order to develop new sensations and releases of stored-up energies; it rejects a manipulative, muscular, and/or mechanical approach in favor of stimulating involuntary processes unimpeded by voluntary controls. It fundamentally shifts the experience of sound from the subject's ear—tasked by earlier methods to compare the quality of their sound to a prescribed aesthetic standard—to a felt sensation of sound as energy moving in the body, wherein the pitch of sound becomes, in a real sense, frequency of thought. The radical notion that the voice does not simply live in the throat as an instrument waiting to be "played by" the self, but is an instantiation of self, connecting body, imagination, and emotion, is one of Linklater's most groundbreaking ideas.

Linklater's approach admirably takes on the embodied voice as both a meaningful existential site as well as a site of social (and other) injustices and restrictions. The strong focus on the individual practitioner in Linklater's approach as well as the focus on socialization primarily as a repressive, controlling force construct a model of freedom defined by an individual unlearning oppressive social norms and habits. However, in so doing, Linklater's method rests on untenable philosophical assumptions and problematically limits the scope of ethical analysis that a focus on intervocality requires.

Perhaps most basically, the claim that a natural, authentic, real voice exists underneath the accumulated effects of socialization awaiting liberation is questionable. Such a claim positions social forces as contrary to the expression of an authentic self, and authentic selves as prior to socialization. We hold, rather, that social forces don't act on authentic selves as much as they create the conditions of possibility under which selves emerge in their particularity; both specific selves and social groups are constituted by complex interactions of social, material, and political forces. This is not to say that any one individual, or a particular social group, is entirely determined by such forces, or that such forces are impervious to human influence. But it is to say that one cannot understand a human self in isolation from social and political forces, and so the authenticity/socialization dichotomy must be troubled.

Foucault's theory of power substantially influences our approach. With regard to structural injustice, power has often been understood as an essentially repressive force, one that limits the capacities and opportunities of members of marginalized groups. Liberatory strategies have thus frequently worked to eradicate power dynamics, or undo their pernicious effects. While such a model of power can illuminate important ethical wrongs, Foucault's articulation of disciplinary power (1977) reminds us that power also works in a productive mode, disciplining bodies to create subjective capacities, skills, and desires (Schlichter's analysis of Linklater's method [2014] relies on a similarly Foucauldian conceptualization of power). The productive model of power does not deny its damaging influence, but it does emphasize that power produces selves, rather than limiting or repressing them. The process of undoing unwanted bodily habits, even if the results are ultimately valued, may therefore be more complicated than Linklater's straightforward language of liberation implies, and it may involve experiences of existential loss. Such experiences should not be merely chalked up to resistance to letting go, but understood as, possibly, the loss of ways of being that have been neither superficial nor without value to those undertaking the process.

The fact that Linklater's method positions the vocal practitioner at the intersection of choice between valued ways of being and those no longer valued does not ameliorate the underlying assumption that the real, authentic self exists prior to socialization, which implies that structural inequalities such as racism and sexism primarily serve to undermine the possibilities of and for authentic selves. It can therefore frame the individual, authentic self as unmarked by social identity factors imbricated in systemic injustices, and so it becomes not raced, not gendered, not dis/abled, and so on. As stated in the previous chapter, we agree with Alcoff (2006) that social identities inextricably linked with systemic inequalities are nevertheless not reducible to them and are replete with existential meaning and value. Vocal ways of being are part of those social identities and serve to ground a person in a specific community, particularly if that community is politically marginalized. Indeed, they may be worth protecting rather than discarding, and as is discussed further in Chapter 6, a new model for vocal training is required that grounds and values the construction of social identities as an integral aspect of "authentic" voices.

Cavarero's Vocal Uniqueness

Adriana Cavarero's *For More Than One Voice: Toward a Theory of Vocal Expression* (2005) constitutes one of the few existing feminist philosophical treatments of the sonorous voice. Yet Cavarero's analysis, similar to Fred Evans's treatment of the multivoiced body (2009), is as concerned with the insight that a better understanding of voice could provide for both politics and philosophy as it is with the phenomenon of human vocalization itself. While Linklater seeks to liberate the individual self through the removal of vocal inhibitions and other forms of socialization, Cavarero aims to undo the Platonic devocalization of logos to ground a new politics and a more sonorous, just set of philosophical practices. Precisely because the voice is fundamentally embodied and marked by an ineffable uniqueness, Cavarero argues that restoring voice to philosophy will transform our political and ontological understandings by appropriately emphasizing two modes that the sonorous voice entails: individuality and relationality.

For Cavarero, the recognizability of individual voices, that is, the fact that human persons can often identify the voice of a familiar other without visual clues, points toward the importance of existential uniqueness. Cavarero grounds vocal uniqueness in embodied processes taking place within and from specific embodied forms; her approach to voice is thus resolutely materialist. When philosophy was experienced and understood primarily as a vocal practice, ideas, no matter how universal in content, were conveyed through an inescapably existentially unique medium, bearing a sonorous stamp of particularity that became irrelevant and eventually suspect as reading transformed into a silent activity and writing became philosophy's preferred medium. As philosophy lost the (its) voice, it elevated as the hallmark of philosophical excellence and truth an ostensible distance from the body and particularity; to do philosophy well was to transcend one's specificity, to speak (primarily and ideally metaphorically) from a position that was no position.

In Cavarero's analysis, this grievous and dangerous error can be corrected by a recentering of voice in both philosophy and politics, which would result in an Arendtian politics grounded in a recognition of particularity.[3] Positioning the voice as a kind of bridge across radical particularity and the universality of logos, Cavarero valorizes a politics of the local that maintains the dynamism of that bridge:

> The politics of the local, having finally been liberated from the cartography of nations and the individualist ontology, in fact avoids imposing cultural identities on the unrepeatable uniqueness of every human being. Because it is faithful to the ontology of plurality, the local puts in play uniqueness without belongings and entrusts the sense of the relation to this alone. And this, in addition to evoking a passivity, implies first of all the preliminary activity of stripping ourselves of our western, eastern, Christian, Muslim, Jew, gay, straight, poor, rich, ignorant, learned, cynical, sad, happy—or even guilty or innocent—being. Indeed, the politics of the absolute local includes as a preliminary act the deconstruction of belongings, the marginalization of qualities, and the depoliticization of the what. (2005: 205)

Cavarero's reclaiming of the voice as central to philosophy and politics simultaneously brings the body back to theorizing and the voice back to the body, two moves that accord well with our focus on the material and embodied voice. However, her emphasis on uniqueness precludes an understanding of voice as a significant site of the production of social identities and the inequities that surround them. Cavarero does, of course, note the association of the voice with femininity, an association that assisted in the exclusion of women from philosophy (2005: 6; see also Beard 2017 and Irigaray 2004); but quite aside from the symbolic association of femininity with the vocal is the question of gendered vocal registers, rhythms, and tones and their meaning in a patriarchal culture (a matter we address in Chapter 4). Moreover, as previously mentioned, identities associated with specific racialized identities, ethnicities, abilities, sexual orientations, and other identity markers frequently have vocal patterns and tendencies that are identifiable, existentially meaningful, and deployed in both perpetuating and resisting structural inequalities.

Cavarero's emphasis on particularity and uniqueness downplays, and maybe conceals entirely, the ways in which sonorous vocalizations express and construct meaningful group identities and affinities and are implicated in various forms of structural injustice. Cavarero is mostly right about vocal uniqueness and the recognizability of individual voices, and the fact that mistakes are possible doesn't detract from voice's general reliability. What her analysis misses is the fact that vocal identification involves the membership of the person in social groups (including, but not limited to, racial and gender groups), rendering it incapable of addressing the Alcoffian vocal identities that interest us or accounting for a form of vocal justice that acknowledges (and even utilizes) the importance of social identities.[4]

Ashon T. Crawley's exploration of the intellectual, aesthetic, and political meanings of Blackpentecostal choreosonics (2017) demonstrates how attending to shared soundscapes reveals insights about fundamental structures of existence, knowledge, and inequality:

> I consider dancing, singing, noise making, whooping, and tongue talking as ways to resist normative modes of theological and philosophical reflection, the same sorts of thought that produce categorical differentiation-as-deficiency such as race, class, gender, slave, and so on. I argue that the aesthetic practices of Blackpentecostalism constitute a performative critique of normative theology and philosophy that precede the twentieth-century moment. (7)

Those aesthetic practices, which Crawley describes as relying on "the always attendant and interconnected concept of movement and sound" (93), generate ways of being and collective experience that call into question the most deep-seated commitments of white supremacy (including the logic of categorical distinctions and the possibility of the self-contained subject), opening up the horizon of the otherwise (24). Reducing the philosophical and political meaning of voice to individual uniqueness, as Cavarero does, would render the meanings of Blackpentecostal breath, what Crawley names "*black pneuma*, the capacity for the plural movement and displacement of inhalation and exhalation to enunciate life, life that is exorbitant, capacious, and fundamentally, social, though it is also life that is structured through and engulfed by brutal violence" (38, emphasis in original), entirely inscrutable.

Intervocality highlights another limitation of Cavarero's focus on vocal uniqueness. If we understand the embodied voice as grounded in, emanating from, and marked by social relations, then it makes sense that particular vocalizations bear the sonorous stamps of not only the speaker, but also the addressee, as we argued in Chapter 1. Moreover, this vocal stamp of the addressee can identify not only individuals (one might be able to recognize when a friend is speaking to their parent, for example), but also, and just as importantly, distinct groups. Different tones, rhythms, speeds, and accents emerge in different social contexts; thus, my voice is both resolutely mine (a point that Cavarero recognizes) and always marked by individual and collective others (a point that Cavarero misses).

That the other is always present in the sound of the voice challenges the metaphorical association of the voice with an authentic, stand-alone self isolated from certain social norms and expectations. It also raises important questions for how we are to understand the notion of vocal injustice, and certainly complicates any simple exhortation to "find" and "speak" one's authentic voice. In addition, the intersubjectivity of sound, as we explore in more depth in the final section of this chapter, highlights the co-constitutive role of the receiving body; in Cavarero's approach, the ethical mandate related to receiving sound is limited to the ability to hear and recognize uniqueness, which is far too narrow a scope.

Eidsheim and Vocal Racialization

While both Linklater and Cavarero demonstrate a clear interest in vocal injustice regarding gender, Nina Eidsheim's work, grounded primarily in musicology, focuses on race and racism, and so overlaps in significant ways with Stoever's historical analysis. In *Sensing Sound* (2015), Eidsheim bears down on the intersubjective quality of vocalization, particularly in the context of musical performance. Her turn toward the "thick event" of sound rejects the conceptualization of sound as knowable, the fixed raw material out of which music is formed, shaped, and experienced, and the basis on which it is evaluated. Taking sound as that which exists prior to being received masks how the reception of that sound, and the material situation within which that sound is instantiated, is central to the phenomenon itself. If sound is not given, and if receiving and evaluating sound in the context of music is not a matter of comparing the givenness of the particular sound to an ideal, then listening is revealed as co-constitutive.

Moving from "the figure of sound to the practice of vibration" (Eidsheim 2015: 20) entails understanding singing (the form of vocalization that most interests Eidsheim) as more resolutely material than previous models had suggested. The sonorous quality of any sung music depends on a wide-ranging set of material conditions: the involuntary and voluntary machinations of the singer's body; the material medium into which the voice is cast (air, water, etc.);

the architectural surroundings; and the bodies, in all their complexities, of the receiving beings. Understanding music and sound as transmission brings all of these disparate elements of a sonorous phenomenon to the fore, and insists on the thickness of the event, a thickness which an evaluative focus on fidelity undermines and masks. While Eidsheim is focused on singing and performance, her insights transfer productively to a consideration of the spoken, mundane voice, whose emanations are also shaped by the presence of other subjects, the surrounding environment, and so on.

The Race of Sound (2019) connects the co-constitutive role of listening or receiving sound to the phenomenon of vocal racial injustice. Eidsheim grounds her analysis in "the acousmatic question":

> Whether the vocalizer is heard over the radio or the phone, as part of a movie soundtrack or in person—positioned far away and therefore hard to see or speaking right in front of the listener—the foundational question asked in the act of listening to a human voice is *Who is this? Who is speaking?* Regardless of whether the vocalizer is visible or invisible to the listener, we are called into positing this most basic question—a question of an acousmatic nature. (2019: 1)

Eidsheim points out that the acousmatic question seems to be predicated upon, and has largely been taken to entail, an assumption that the voice, absent visual and other sensory cues, should reveal important aspects of the speaker's identity (2019: 2–3). Yet, as she correctly notes, the acousmatic question in fact undermines the voice's revelatory capacity; for if the voice could reveal the speaker's identity purely through its sonorous qualities, the acousmatic question wouldn't arise. We ask *"Who is this?"* precisely because the sound of the voice, severed from clear indications about its source, fails to inform the listener about important elements of the speaker's identity.

Eidsheim moves quickly from the claim that the acousmatic question is motivated by a failure of the voice's identificatory capacity to the broader claim that voice can reveal neither interiority, identity, nor essence of any sort: "We ask the acousmatic question because it is not possible to know voice, vocal identity, and meaning as such; we can know them only in their multidimensional, always unfolding processes and practices, indeed in their multiplicities. This fundamental instability is why we keep asking the acousmatic question" (3). When such instability is ignored or denied, however, the acousmatic question continues to serve as an identificatory demand, and because race is constructed as a crucial aspect of identity in Western societies, that identificatory demand reveals and perpetuates assumptions about the racialization of sound. Here,

Eidsheim aims to undermine two persistent ways of conceptualizing the voice. The first way positions the voice as capable of revealing a true or authentic self, *who one really is*, the (knowable) essence of the self. The second positions the voice as capable of revealing a racialized or ethnic status. For Eidsheim, these two meanings and the haunting acousmatic question are intertwined: the voice cannot promise to reveal the racial or ethnic identity of a speaker except to the extent that we take it to be revealing of the real or true essence of that speaker. Denying the knowability, reliability, and fixed character of a speaker's voice—including its ability to express the speaker's racial or ethnic identity—is a continuation of Eidsheim's argument, begun in *Sensing Sound*, against sound as knowable.

The knowability of racialized voice—the common assumption that there are racialized timbres distinct to African American singers which reliably refer to and reflect their (ostensibly stable) racial identity—mistakenly locates the race of sound in the voice rather than in the listener:

> I propose that we examine racialized vocal timbre (and any other qualities that are understood as essential) in order to move from an analysis of sound to an analysis of *how that sound is listened to* ... Because of general assumptions regarding music and voice—that their major currency is sound and that vocal sounds are essential and unmediated expressions—readings of vocal timbre have remained impenetrable to critical investigation. In the same way that hair, body movement, dialect, accent, and style have been critically examined and thus are no longer available as ammunition for arguments about race as essence, *The Race of Sound* shows how timbre is institutionalized and internalized as a meaningful measurement of traits believed by a given society to be essential to people, and demonstrates the falsity of such correlative argument. (25, emphasis in the original)

For Eidsheim, then, countering racialized practices of listening necessarily entails dismantling both the association of voice with the real, unmediated self and the association of race with essential bodily particularities, which, when combined, require and assume that voice reveals racialized identity. The racialized voice, she emphasizes, has no grounding in either a particular history or set of experiences, or in anatomical differences, but has been shaped and produced primarily by listening practices that foist racialized meanings on vocalizations.

Many facets of Eidsheim's analysis of voice—the co-constitutive function of the listening ear when it comes to both the sonorous traits of voice and their social and political meanings, the emphasis on the role of culture and environment in shaping the sound of voices, the critique of the notion of the stable self marked by an a priori essence—overlap significantly with our concept of intervocality. Yet Eidsheim's assumption that racism is defined by essentialism, such that undoing the associations between bodily particularities and racial identity is central to ameliorating the harms of racism, is problematic. It is telling that Eidsheim occasionally, as in the quote above, compares the racialization of voice to the racialization of other bodily traits (hair, bodily comportment) to argue against biologically essentialist models of race. Fair enough; but neither race nor racism as lived phenomena is reducible to claims about biological essentialism. Race need not be understood as a biological essence for racial identity to be significant, and, as we have argued, the significance of racial identity is not reducible to the meanings ascribed to it by racist social structures. Racialized hair styles, for example, are deeply meaningful aspects of racial identity and belonging, not because they represent some biological essence, but because they have accrued significant cultural and personal valence that exceeds the meanings imposed upon them by white supremacy. "[H]air, body movement, dialect, accent, and style" may be "no longer available as ammunition for arguments about race as essence," but they have not been drained of racialized meanings. Moreover, the white gaze is not the sole means by which those racialized meanings are constructed; shared Black lived experiences and culture also play important roles and establish these bodily traits as effective sites of resistance to structural racism.

Eidsheim is surely correct that listening practices have played a central role in both the sonorous qualities and social meanings of racialized voices. However, in reducing the construction of racialized voices to the effects of such listening practices, she has given short shrift to the active marshalling of Black vocalization as a means to claim a racialized identity that exceeds and defies white supremacy. If the racialization of voice is imposed only, or even primarily, by the white listening ear, then the radical potential of a choreosonic Blackpentecostalism, as explored by Ashton Crawley (2017), would be difficult to defend, and Devonya Havis's analysis of Black Vernacular would be similarly ungrounded:

> This *blackness* was excluded from the western epistemological frame and as such, for the purposes of survival, generated its own modes of *ritual celebration* that have given rise to discursive communities of difference—communities that are a welcoming location for indeterminacy played out through unique stylizations evident in sound—orality, musicality and dance that evokes utterative gestures (i.e. step shows, kids' games). Through sound, the community comes into

existence—yet it is a coming into existence that is negotiated in the exchange of sound. Hence, to the extent that one is a musician—capable of taking up ethical and political obligations in the context of performing himself or herself through sound—one becomes more than a slave. One is located within a unique community that invents itself and as a grouping of co-equals, participants in its members' dynamic creation of *selves*. (Havis 2009: 748–9, emphasis in original)

In a similar analysis, Lissa Skitolsky (2020) argues that "hip-hop culture serves as a source of philosophical wisdom about the nature, politics, and consequences of anti-black violence, as well as a source of resistance against anti-black violence in the city and the cell" (2). The political meanings of hip-hop, in Skitolsky's analysis, cannot be separated from either its sonorous hallmarks or its grounding in Black experience:

If we focus on the form of hip-hop then we can recognize hip-hop as the political activity of interrupting, co-opting, distorting, and repeating sounds to rupture our sensibility or produce sounds, images, and melodies that shatter our linear, teleological framework for making-sense of reality ... If we think about this aesthetic disruption of linear form with the aforementioned relation between hip-hop culture and the socio-political conditions of being-black, then we can better grasp how the form distinct to hip-hop could serve to depict the type of collective suffering that "breaks" black communities and "breaks" the sense of popular narratives that reinforce moral and epistemic blindness to this suffering. (58–9)

To hear the Blackness of Pentecostal breath, Black vernacular, and hip-hop is crucial to understanding their political and social capacities to identify and resist anti-Black racism. Perhaps more to the point, the racial identities sounded in these contexts are not a function of oppressive, racist listening practices, but are grounded in Black aesthetic practices steeped in Black culture and history.

Eidsheim's suggested remedy for racialized vocal injustice—listening practices that refrain from associating any vocalizations with racial identity, opting instead to hear in them only the result of either acculturation or, in the context of professional singers, accrued expertise, as if acculturation or expertise is exclusive of racial identity (183)—implies that the ethical mandate for the anti-racist is to refrain from hearing the race of sound at all, and in doing so, to deracialize the voice. In contrast, we hold that identity markers such as race, gender, ability, and the like are implicated in but not reducible to structural inequalities and that a meaningful, although complex, relationship between identity and voice exists. As both Stoever and Eidsheim have convincingly demonstrated, voice is ineluctably marked by both material and social/political realities; it is also a vital and widely recognized element of many (although not all) marginalized identities and plays an important role in both the perpetuation and challenging of systemic inequalities. As "deep features of the self," aural/vocal/sonorous identities are palpable and powerful aspects of existence that contribute (however contingently and fluidly) to the grounding and defining of identity. What is needed is not a delinking of voice and identity, or a draining of vocal meanings related to membership in specific social groups (including, and maybe especially, marginalized social groups), but a recognition of vocal identity as a complex site of one's embodied, relational sense of self, as well as a site where structural injustices can be instantiated, perpetuated, and challenged.

Note that in saying that aural/vocal/sonorous identities are deep features of the self, we are not arguing that the self is reducible to vocal identity, or that one's vocal identity exhausts the meaning of one's self (a claim that would be of particular concern to Eidsheim). Nor are we arguing that being-voiced is necessary to any identity, or that it is a privileged site of embodiment when compared to other modalities. Our claim is more modest, but still places us in opposition to Eidsheim: the sonorous nature of one's voice (albeit constantly in flux) *matters* to one's sense of self (and hence deserves philosophical attention), and the ways in which it matters likely include the relation of that sonorous nature to membership in social groups. We hold that the connection between vocal identity and marginalized social groups is neither inherently problematic nor reducible to structures of systemic injustice. To experience the voice of oneself or another as racialized or gendered is not necessarily to perpetuate racism or sexism; to the contrary, it can be a profound act of affirmation, recognition, and even liberation.

To sum up: while Linklater, Cavarero, and Eidsheim all share an understanding of human vocal emanations as embodied, material, and implicated in important ways in systemic injustice, their approaches fail to reflect or respond effectively to the complex dynamics of intervocality. Linklater remains mired in a notion of individual liberation; Cavarero requires a rejection of vocality understood as positively related to group membership; and Eidsheim argues against both an existential connection between the voice and self and any positive possibilities in understanding vocalizations as sonorously marked by historically marginalized identities. What is needed is an ethical framework that values a multiplicity of vocal ways of being (including those that are gendered and racialized), resists the ways in which vocal capacities are deployed by hegemonic power structures, positions human vocality as emanating from interlocking and complex relations, and recognizes the meaningfulness, including the political and existential meaningfulness, of human-generated sound.

Toward Intervocal Justice

Our explorations of these three different conceptualizations of vocal injustice have demonstrated that developing a theory of vocal justice requires attending simultaneously to the material, social, political, and existential aspects of voice. In this section, we offer some preliminary thoughts on the ethical and political questions arising from a consideration of how the sonorous voice is implicated in, but not reducible to, systemic injustice, and how sonorous politics could be rendered more just.

A focus on the embodied voice should result in a more politically astute understanding of the spatiality of sound, and the ways in which human vocalizations shape social spaces. Throughout this discussion, we have frequently referred to how voices and sound are "received" rather than "heard," a reminder that, despite the cultural privileging of the ear as the aural receptacle, in fact, receiving sound requires a dynamic interplay and integration of multiple senses, bodily surfaces and interiorities, specific physical acoustic spaces, and narrative contexts.

As a broader concern than vocal justice, sonic justice requires a recognition that continued exposure to damaging levels and kinds of sound are frequently associated with economically and socially disadvantaged groups (incarcerated people, for example, or socioeconomically disadvantaged communities whose housing is more likely to be close to factories or airports). In terms of vocal justice, the spatiality of voice can be interrogated along somewhat different lines. We might ask about the politics of volume: whose voices are allowed to take up the most sonic space? How are different volume levels received and/or interpreted depending on the identity of the person speaking? (Unsurprisingly, volume is an insistently gendered phenomenon; see Silva 2015.) Are booming male-identified voices considered appropriately commanding, even appealing, whereas the same volume levels coming from a female-identified voice experienced as presumptuous and overbearing? How might we understand the ways in which nonlinguistic vocal emanations—humming loudly upon entering a room, for example—might serve to claim space and vocal centrality? Similar questions could be raised about the temporal aspects of voice: are different kinds of voices accorded different amounts of time?

These sorts of questions emphasize a kind of vocal equity, grounded in the ethical intuition that the sonorous specificity of a voice ought not to serve as either an advantage or disadvantage in the allocation of vocalized social goods such as volume and airtime. In some cases, we have empirical knowledge about the disproportionate allocation of these goods that can help to identify vocal situations most prone to systemic inequality. Where empirical data are lacking, it seems safe to assume that the profound influence of structural inequality extends to perceptions of vocal interactions, such that what is considered to be sonorously normal and unremarkable, particularly by members of dominant groups, is likely drastically unjust.

But vocal justice cannot be limited to vocal equity understood as equal access to vocal social goods. It must also include a consideration of how certain vocal identities are marginalized and constructed as socially inferior. The association of an accent identified as coming from the Southern parts of the United States with a lack of education or intellect; the all too easy dismissal of the worth of voices bearing the sonorous effects of age; the ableist impatience with which voices whose tempo is affected by a physical impairment are met: all these are examples of vocal injustice that must be addressed and ameliorated.

Moreover, keeping Alcoff's analysis of visible identities in mind, vocal justice requires a recognition of the existential meaningfulness of vocal marks of group identities and affinities. To suggest or require that an individual change aspects of their vocal identity, particularly to render the voice more closely aligned with dominant forms of vocality, is a potentially deeply harmful act. Rendering sonorous aspects of one's vocal identity linked to meaningful affinities with marginalized social groups problematic constructs those groups as inferior, and thus furthers their marginalization. That vocal code-switching is required by members of disadvantaged groups (but never or rarely by members of dominant groups) in order to participate more fully in social life should be recognized as an unjust tax, not just of time and energy, but of existential vulnerability. The dismantling of forms of inequality such as white supremacy, cisnormativity, ableism, and others must include greater attunement to the ability to welcome vocal identities of all sorts in social spaces currently hostile to them.

This insight about the importance of vocal identity can be applied not just to individuals, but to groups as well. The intentional destruction of indigenous languages committed by colonizing and imperializing forces constitutes not only the loss of the content of those languages—the ideas that can no longer be spoken, the metaphysics that can no longer be accessed—but also the loss of sonorous practices and abilities. In cases of complete eradication of a language, the fact that particular kinds and combinations of sound are no longer produced by human bodies irrevocably limits our understanding of human vocality. In cases of language diminishment, often to the brink of eradication (as is the case with the fewer than ten percent of indigenous languages in North America that survived the genocidal policies of European settlers [McCarty et al. 2006]), the loss of vocal familiarity with sonorous aspects of a language can constitute a significant weakening of indigenous identity—and the reclaiming of those sounds a profound challenge to oppressive structures.

The ethical and political mandate to welcome a diverse set of vocal identities in a broader scope of social sites must not, however, be grounded in an assumption that every speaker has an authentic voice unmarked by the social situation in which it is deployed. Requiring vocal code-switching as a price of social acceptability in the context of oppressive social structures is ethically problematic; deploying different vocalizations depending upon people's social, emotional, or political context is not necessarily so. Vocal injustice has harnessed intervocality for nefarious ends, and developing a more vocally just world will entail engaging voice's materiality and intersubjectivity to challenge oppressive systems and forward sonorous forms of human flourishing.

Clearly, an ethics of vocal libertarianism—a simplistic approach that would require acceptance of any and all vocalizations that individuals might choose to enact and a refusal to acknowledge harmful ways of both releasing and receiving vocal emanations—will be entirely insufficient to the task. Such an approach minimizes the centrality of relationality in vocal identity as well as the complex ways in which systemic injustices have shaped vocal and aural practices, habits, and norms. Our voices are both resolutely ours and inescapably marked by and beholden to the other. How and what we can sound out through our bodily mucous membranes and bones and the air we swim in is shaped by the architecture we inhabit, the other vocal and aural beings we encounter, the ways in which our sounds have been received and categorized and judged—and the ways in which we have received, categorized, and judged the vocalizations of others. And our voices do not merely externalize interior reality; as part of our embodied being, they are part and parcel of our ongoing material becoming, bringing into being new sensations, new possibilities, new ways of understanding and living. The challenge before us, which we take up in the following chapter, is to develop a conceptualization of vocal justice, grounded in a persistent recognition of intervocality and the complex relationship between voice and identity, that would help us to recognize, develop, and encourage just vocal interactions.

3

The Ethics of Envoicing

We have developed a conceptualization of the human voice as a complex material and political phenomenon that emerges from and within an intricate network of physiological and social forces. We have also established the irreducible intersubjectivity of voice as human-generated sound and argued that vocal capacity is better understood as intervocality, a framework emphasizing how material environments and the actions, expectations, and vocal emanations of other human subjects work together to shape voices' sonorous qualities and political meanings. Finally, we have argued that structural injustices of many sorts, including racism, ableism, and sexism, have undertheorized sonorous and vocal facets, and that existing attempts to provide theoretical models of vocal injustice have failed to account sufficiently for the implications of intervocality and the myriad ways in which voice and self are intertwined.

In this chapter, we take up the challenge of articulating a framework for vocal justice that consistently recognizes voice as an irreducibly relational, material, and embodied phenomenon. Vocal justice, we argue, is best understood by focusing on a complex process that we are terming *envoicing*: how social practices bring into being certain vocal identities, characteristics, and habits, and in so doing marshal intervocal capacities to perpetuate (or resist) systemic injustice. We argue that such a focus engenders an ethical mandate of respiratory responsibility, an obligation to be accountable for the air that we and others breathe and the ways in which the movement of that air through bodies and inhabited spaces is imbued with social and political meaning. We then turn our attention to the ethical aspects of receiving vocalized sound, exploring particular sites of envoicing (such as socially mandated racial code-switching and vocal therapy/coaching for transgender people) to identify ways in which envoicing can be enacted in more just ways. We conclude the chapter with a consideration of vocal generosity as a framework for vocal justice.

Toward an Ethics of Envoicing

An emphasis on the ethics of envoicing reveals aspects of the works of Cavarero and Linklater, analyzed in Chapter 2, worth sustaining. Cavarero's gesturing toward the existential meaningfulness of the individual, embodied voice through her emphasis on the voice's identificatory potential, while perhaps not quite as absolute as she implies, opens up possibilities for vocal justice. By rejecting philosophical traditions separating the embodied, particular voice from the privileged realm of logos, Cavarero invites attention to the philosophical and political relevance of the particularity of the embodied individual's social, political, and historical situation; ethical envoicing, as we understand it, requires an attunement to such particularity. We reconceptualize the uniqueness of voice (which Cavarero posits as opposed to membership in social groups) as an epiphenomenon of social and political location, a situatedness that can be comprehended only in relation to others, intersecting discourses of power, and specific material conditions.

From our perspective, both uniqueness and individuality can be understood as existential location, thus grounding an understanding of the individual human being as materially and bodily situated at a distinct and unreproducible intersection of forces. Understanding the human individual as existentially located emphasizes the "that-ness" of an individual's being—that they exist and act from a specific social position—as opposed to the "who-ness" of a unique, ostensibly internal essence that Cavarero invokes. While the coalescence of those forces is fine-grained enough to ensure that one's existential location could never be fully inhabited by another, other embodied beings are also being shaped and situated by those same forces, and so commonalities of experience are not only possible but certain.

The language of location risks ascribing to the individual a certain static nature, as if one's social location is not only determinable and knowable, but determinant and all-defining. To counter such connotations, we understand existential location in light of María Lugones's "world-traveling" (1987), the subjective capacity to move within and across different social worlds, which Lugones understands as complex sites of meaning-making, replete with embodied individuals, physical infrastructure, historical meaning, and so on. For Lugones, worlds construct subjective beings, and the experience of traveling between worlds is, particularly for members of historically marginalized social groups, "a matter of necessity and survival" (1987: 11). Although Lugones argues that the subject-constructing effects of different worlds result in an ontological pluralism (2003), a literal multiplicity of selves, Mariana Ortega disagrees, suggesting that the notion of ontological pluralism be replaced by existential pluralism, which entails understanding individual selves as multiplicitous, capable of and open to a wide variety of existential modalities (2016: 98).

Together, the concepts of world-traveling, existential pluralism, and existential location allow us to understand the uniqueness of the human individual, and thus of the individual human voice, as irrevocably *relational*. Any individual particularity can be grasped only by referring to the particular world in which that individual is embedded—its infrastructure, norms, and metaphysics—and the way that world constitutes the individual's existential reality. Traveling across worlds generates different subjective capacities, habits, experiences, modes of being, and, significantly, voices, all of which reflect (among other social realities) the particular social groups and organization that characterizes that world. While Cavarero animates the value of vocal (and therefore existential) uniqueness understood as a corrective to the existential salience of membership in social groups, we aim to offer a model that reveals the individual voice as multiple, embedded in and emanating from social and political contexts, and co-constituted by others.

In contrast to Cavarero, Linklater offers a nuanced understanding of how social practices have resulted in specific vocal habits. As they participate in social life, voices may mask an individual's own desires, deep affinities, and longings in order to perform personae projecting qualities or sensations other than those experienced by the individual, such as the voice of "aggressive go-getter" that "shields the frightened, insecure little boy," or the voice of a woman who "pretends weakness" vocally to find mobility in a patriarchal culture, or voices that take on "rich and deep" qualities signifying "confidence and accomplishment" where there is none (Linklater 2006: 25). And when systemic, institutional, and interpersonal relationships require a highly specific voice as the price of legibility, thus creating unjust vocal systems, Linklater's practical methods can help voicing individuals resist those systems by unlearning vocal habits and strengthening the voice in desired ways. The result is a vocal discipline that focuses on empowering, releasing, sensitizing, and engendering a feeling of freedom, which can forward personal, and even social, change.

However, the philosophical foundations of Linklater's method are steeped in the problematic tradition of liberal humanist thought that presumes the capacity of the human subject to "undo" the effects of socialization, and in doing so flattens difference and perpetuates the myth of the voice unmarked by systemic inequalities as an ideal. These foundations also assume that we are born free, and so the individual's task is a return journey (akin to Grotowski's *via negativa*[1]) (Grotowski [1968] 2002) to reclaim the birthright of a free voice—unconstrained by socialization and unmarked by language—capable of expressing the full range of an individual's emotions: a voice connected to "primary impulses" not yet "supplanted by secondary or 'learned' impulses" (Adaire et al. 2018: 347). As detailed further in Chapter 5, we reject the notion that every child is *born free*, a rejection borne out by new studies in several areas: the attachment theory of social neuroscience, postulating that every child is born with an innate attachment behavioral system that takes into consideration both environment and relationship (Vrtička 2017), recent psychological studies asserting that impulses themselves are relational (Frijda et al. 2014), and the work of social historians and sociolinguists suggesting that emotions are socially constructed (Richardson 2016, Eckert and McConnell-Ginet 2013). One's desire to develop, change, and grow one's voice is a key part of self-construction—a project that may include rejecting (or embracing) dominant vocal paradigms and might be well served by Linklater's detailed and intuitive training methods. From the point of view of intervocality, however, wherein habitual patterns can no longer be considered merely an outcome of one's individual socialization (nor seen as simply antithetical to "natural" involuntary processes), a clearer ethical and philosophical framework is required.

Voice is a fundamentally interactive event. Vocal emanations do not exist as self-contained, self-defined phenomena, but always vibrate between and among entities (human bodies, built and found infrastructure, etc.). The meanings and evaluations of those vocal emanations—whether they are viewed as disruptive, or impressive, or shrill, or beautiful—are never inherent to the emanations themselves, but are the products of power and value discourses masquerading as natural or given. An ethics of envoicing thus entails a recognition of responsibility for how both individual and collective practices produce certain kinds of voices and receiving practices. Where previous philosophical approaches to the human voice have frequently focused on its mine-ness, its irreducible association with the unique individual, here we are emphasizing the ways in which voiced human beings are responsible for each other's voices, individually and collectively, sonorously and politically.

To say that voiced human beings are responsible for the qualities and meanings of the vocal emanations of others is not to argue that any individual voiced person, or collection of voiced persons, is in a position to fully determine how a particular voice sounds or its social meanings. Intervocality is a matter of irreducible in-betweenness, a shimmering of sonorous vibration and meaning-making that entails the active contributions of both the producer and receiver of human-generated sound. While marked ineluctably by the other, individual voices are not reducible to the other, and the receiving body is not totalitarian within the context of a vocal interaction. Yet it is our position that the ethical contributions of receiving bodies to the phenomenon of intervocality have been significantly undertheorized, and that existing theories of vocal justice have not sufficiently recognized the ethical significance of processes of envoicing.

Respiratory Responsibility

In keeping with our emphasis on the material aspects of voice as human-generated sound, we hold that an ethics of envoicing necessarily entails a sense of respiratory responsibility. Air, and its form as human breath, is a promising first site from which to explore the ethics of envoicing. Described by Linklater as the "prima materia" (Linklater 2009a: 101), breath is the foundational material of the voice itself, and yet, as Irigaray has argued, has been overlooked by a Western metaphysics overly "founded in the solid" (Irigaray 1999: 25). Breath lives in the in-between, at the places where margins are created and destroyed: that which is around the body moves into the body, merges and melds with the body, and is released from the body, carrying with it bodily material. As Magdalena Górska notes, breath dissolves the clearly demarcated borders of where bodies end and other spaces begin, as it

> problematizes the distinction between concepts such as "inside" and "outside" by troubling notions of corpomaterial boundaries in the worldly metabolization of oxygen; it complicates notions of self, other, and environment in challenging individualistic concepts of humanness and articulating its transcorporeal character that defies bodily and subjective boundaries of the self; it also problematizes human exceptionalism by embedding humans in the intra-actively constitutive atmospheric, material, and social dynamics of living. (2018: 250)

This exchange of breath, the air taken into and released by the body, is always political in nature. The polluted, toxic air of New York City in 1970 was materially distinct from the air in that city in 2017 (Dwyer 2017), thanks to the creation of the Environmental Protection Agency. The air that any human takes in is replete with the residue of social practices (is tobacco available? Is cooking done inside the home, over an open fire? Is the use of perfumes socially required or frowned upon, and for whom?) and political values (is clean air viewed as a human right or a privilege of the wealthy? Should corporations be held responsible for the pollution created by their factories?). Not only the content of the air but its movements, how it flows around, among, and through built and found environments, are the result of social and political decisions, as can be witnessed in the poorly ventilated detention center and new "airtight" homes manufactured to maximize energy efficiency.

Social and political practices and norms also construct specific kinds of breathing bodies. Disproportionate levels of air pollutants, for example, as well as other factors, result in high rates of asthma and asthma morbidity among members of lower socioeconomic classes (Forno and Celedón 2009). Different breathing bodies interact with a host of social and political practices, some profoundly marginalizing. Limited access to needed medical care can transform a treatable disease such as asthma into a life-threatening one, and bodies suffering from allergies bear the brunt of an ableist epistemic suspicion that burdens them with the responsibility of convincing skeptical others that, yes, the mere dust from a few peanuts could in fact induce a potentially fatal onset of anaphylaxis. Conversely, the breathing body that aligns well with existing social and political practices regarding air and breath moves unfettered through a variety of environments, often with little if any attunement to the complexities of the content or the movement of air. This breathing body is invoked when a situation or phenomenon so common as to be difficult to perceive is described as "the air that you breathe."

One's capacity to breathe, right to breathe, and quality of breath are in a constant state of material becoming. And given the necessary relationship between breath and voice, and the more contingent but richly meaningful relationship between voice and identity, the sonorous, vocal aspects of identity exist and emerge in the context of a respiratory world constructed by an interweaving set of social and political norms, standards, decisions, and practices. Thus, the possibilities for intelligibility, recognition, and communication are continually recreated. As Górska puts it: "breathing can thus inspire diverse analyses of relational natural and cultural as well as material and social scapes that are dispersed across diverse spaces, times, geopolitical relations, ecosystems, industries, and urbanization while being situated in their phenomenal specificities. Considering such simultaneously common and differential enactments of breathing it is, hence, necessary to work with a nonreductive understanding of it" (2018: 248). Linklater describes the breathing apparatus as an "image of a tapestry woven around the inner walls of the body" (Linklater 2009a, 107), pointing out that "the root of the word 'text' (as in the text of a story) is the same as the root of the word 'tapestry': both words originate in the Latin 'tessere' which means 'to weave'" (Linklater 2009a: 107). We extend this metaphor of the tapestry to include an interweaving and circulation of sociocultural influences, material body, environmental spaces, and shared air.

On a fundamental level, then, part of the ethics of envoicing is a recognition of respiratory responsibility, a sense that precisely because no one individual body can fully control or determine the content of the air that the body takes in, or the flow of the air in the inhabited space, we all bear collective responsibility for each other's breath. The voices that emerge within the context of intersecting human communities will bear the sonorous marks of the decisions, conscious or unconscious, that those communities (and most likely the more powerful and privileged elements of those communities) have made about both air and breath. Moreover, respiratory responsibility extends beyond the responsibility for the content of the breathed air to responsibility for social and economic situations that preclude or forward access to stress-free, easy breathing. Just as living with polluted air transforms the experience of breathing (and indeed the organ of breathing itself, as in a coal miner with dusty lung syndrome), so too does living with anxieties that emerge out of social power relations (Górska 2018). Cherríe Moraga (1983) describes the CR (Consciousness-Raising) breathing techniques of second-wave feminism having actually resulted in diminished access to a free breath for all women present when in mixed racial company. As race became the unspoken pink elephant in the room, women of color bore the disproportionately allocated responsibility for managing white women's anxiety (and held breath) in the presence of difference in order to maintain a nonconfrontational space that allowed white bodies to proceed with a feeling of fluidity and ease. The weight of this labor is bodily tension, reduced access to breath, and the loss of a full respiratory release, effecting a social suffocation. The capacity "to breathe deeply and to laugh, moan, and cry, all of which compress and extend the airways" (Tremblay 2019: 95) emerges, then, as a matter of privilege.

This politics of breathing is scalable, rendering some spaces—and some lives—more or less breathable than others. The power relations at work, for instance, when a Black man is pulled over by a white police officer in the United States charges the respiratory scene with danger. As Górska points out, it is not at all surprising that the phrase Eric Garner repeated eleven times during his assault in 2015—"I can't breathe"—became a prominent slogan for the Black Lives Matter movement (2016: 23); the slogan reemerged even more strongly and urgently after police officer Derek Chauvin killed George Floyd by kneeling on his neck while Floyd pleaded for his life, saying "I can't breathe" more than twenty times (Oppel and Barker 2021). This political refrain reminds us that breathability is not merely symbolic, but a lived bodily enactment with life-or-death stakes.

The Receiving of Vocality

The notion of respiratory responsibility establishes that vocal traits or gestures that are all too easy to reduce to individual traits or choices (the rasp of the long-time smoker, the wheeze of the allergic body, the panicked gasp of the startled PTSD sufferer) are in fact the effects of broader social and political forces. The ethics of envoicing extends beyond the quality and flow of air and breath, however. How receiving bodies respond to and take up the vocalizations of others plays a crucial role in the sonorous qualities of voices. Voices are sonorously marked by the particular other to whom they are directed; deference, intimacy, professional standing, familial status, community belonging, and a host of other necessarily relational positionalities can be, and frequently are, sounded vocally. How does this sonorous intervocality relate to the ethics of envoicing?

Below, we address, with differing levels of detail, multiple sites of envoicing: the social construction of the stuttering voice, racially mandated code-switching, and voice therapy and coaching for trans folx. Exploring these sites individually fails to sufficiently recognize that these phenomena are co-constituting: voiced trans people of color navigate racialized vocal politics that are also gendered, and stuttering may be framed differently in different racialized contexts. More empirical and phenomenological research is needed on these and other sites, particularly regarding the ways in which they intersect with each other; here we seek to establish merely the ethical responsibilities associated with the many ways in which voices, marked as they are by a host of identity factors (more than we address here), come into being.

On a most basic level, the fact that the other sonorously marks the voice of the sounding human being entails a co-responsibility for the qualities of the sounded voice. The vocal deference of a restaurant server, for example, must be understood not as an accurate reflection of their current mood, but as a more or less coerced performance produced by an economic framework that ties most of their earning potential to tips that customers are free to bestow or withhold. Underfunded schools may include spaces with poor acoustics that shape the vocal emanations of both instructors and students in ways unconducive to learning. The other, whether that other is an individual, an institution, or a social dynamic, shapes the sounded voice.

Perhaps even more important to an ethics of envoicing is a heightened attunement to the ways in which receiving bodies ascribe meanings to other voices, meanings that are often understood to emanate solely from the qualities of the voices themselves. Joshua St. Pierre has argued persuasively that

> Stuttering as a communicative action is a distinctly social phenomenon that cannot properly be reduced to the physical difficulty of producing sounds, but must be situated within its social fabric. Paralleling the way in which speech has no meaning outside of an interpretive context involving a hearer, so stuttering cannot be understood apart from expectations of "normal" hearing. What if we saw stuttering as constructed by a hearer prejudiced against "broken" speech as well as its speaker, and thus as a product of ableism? Would this allow us to dismantle the myth that stuttering is an individual defect and responsibility? (2012: 6)

The "broken speech" of the stuttering voice is constituted as broken by being received in a certain way; yet the responsibility for its social meaning (as defective, problematic, in need of medical or therapeutic attention) is mystified by ableist political structures, which construct the receiver of the broken speech as neutral, and the stuttering body as the sole generator of the stutter *qua* stutter.

In addition to the pathologization of certain forms of vocalizing, aesthetic evaluations of voices are also frequently understood as politically and ethically neutral responses to inherent qualities of certain voices. To experience a particular voice as shrill, or grating, is to establish that voice as unpleasant in and of itself. Yet an understanding of vocal phenomena as inherently intersubjective would conceptualize the vocal quality of, say, shrillness, as emerging between vocalizing and receiving bodies steeped in usually unconscious vocal and aural practices. It does not take much in the way of critical reflection to realize that shrillness is a profoundly gendered quality, one rarely ascribed to male-identified voices (except to question or undermine their masculinity, framing the speakers—and not in a friendly way—as queer). Given the unlikelihood of shrillness being reduced to vocal qualities only ever instantiated by other-than-normatively-masculine voices, it's clear that the experience of shrillness arises from gendered vocal mandates requiring the use of soft, dulcet tones on the part of female-identified persons. Shrillness happens, at least sometimes, when a receiving body that expects (and constitutes itself as having the right to expect, and the right to have that expectation fulfilled) female-identified voices to be marked with a certain gentleness finds their expectations dashed. In an important way, then, the receiving body produces the shrillness of the voicing body.

So far, we have noted two modes of intervocality, which by and large we have been treating separately: the ways in which both receiving bodies and environments shape the sonorous traits of human vocalizations, and the ways in which receiving bodies ascribe value or meaning to certain vocal traits. The two modalities, however, do not function in isolation from each other. The circulation of the values and meanings that accrue to vocal traits or gestures and the enforcement of vocal social norms work to shape the sonorous qualities of voices in particular ways. Hillary Clinton's voice on the presidential campaign trail was repeatedly described as off-putting, unfeminine, and, yes, shrill, criticism that probably led to significant conversation among her advisors. But the effect didn't stop there; the drumbeat also telegraphed clearly to other female-identified persons with public aspirations what standard would be applied to their own vocal performances, and even those without public aspirations were being schooled. Public spaces that do not accommodate wide varieties of aural and vocal capacities (such as airport gates that provide only audible announcements, often over poorly designed public address systems) actively preclude the inclusion of certain voiced and unvoiced bodies from public life, and the impatience and derision that nonnormative or disabled voices routinely encounter in public and private spaces makes those voices less likely to be sounded.

Socially mandated racial code-switching is a paradigmatic example of an unethical form of envoicing that demonstrates the sonorous effects of widely circulated and consistently enforced vocal social norms. The code-switching that people of color frequently perform should be addressed not as an action undertaken by self-contained vocal agents, but rather as an interaction between racialized bodies, each positioned differently and immersed in structures of white supremacy. The white listening ear described by Jennifer Stoever (2015) co-constitutes the dynamic of code-switching insofar as it calls forth the code-switched voice, invoking it as a necessary price of admission to and intelligibility within the shared world. The demand for code-switching is an embodied practice that instantiates and perpetuates the white supremacist refusal of the Black body in its blackness as a full and equal member of the body politic. In addition, it establishes the aural/vocal comfort and ease of the racialized white body as the pertinent element of the social interaction, that which must be accommodated in order for the Black embodied voice to achieve (a degree of) intelligibility and social belonging. The vocal gestures, traits, and tones that code-switching requires of Black subjects constitute a denial of their racialized identity, a sonorous whitewashing that establishes the social inappropriateness of the recognizably Black voice. Importantly, the emphasis on the dynamics of envoicing places a significant ethical responsibility on the white listening ear to counter demands for racialized code-switching. Without such a lens, it would be all too easy to assume that the solution to the ethical harms of mandated racialized code-switching is to encourage Black bodies to refrain from engaging in it, as if it were the Black voice rather than the white ear that should bear the burden of effecting vocal justice.

As we will discuss in more detail in the next chapter, voice is a highly gendered phenomenon, and transgender memoirists have written compellingly about the importance of voice to their gender identity and its social recognition. Casey Plett describes the pressure to change her voice from recognizably male to recognizably female as one of the last phases of her experience of physical transition, one undertaken with no small amount of ambivalence:

> I practiced along to their videos and I recorded my voice on my iPhone, but when I listened to my voice I always sounded male, or, I sounded like a caricature of a female voice, (breathy, pinched, sing-song-y) or, I sounded neither male or female, genderless.

> That's where I'm at now. The best internal reaction I hope for from strangers is, "Whoa, that chick sounds weird." The shape of my female voice always sounds too alien, even coming through my own ears. It doesn't sound like a voice that I, Casey, would talk in, and my old male voice, which does, sounds awful now too because I don't want to sound like a guy. I have hated every word of speech coming out of my own mouth in the last few months. At best, I try not to think about it. My iPhone was stolen a month ago and I haven't recorded my voice since, though I own a voice recorder. I don't want to do it. I've fallen off of practicing too. Part of me knows this affects how I pass—and when people are up close and spend more than a few minutes talking with me, I generally don't—and part of me's hit a wall and stopped caring. It's too hard and it's too complicated and I'm fucking sick of it. So I don't talk as much, not in public, not with strangers. (2011)

Deirdre McCloskey (1999: 242–5) describes her fairly torturous experience with multiple surgeries aimed at feminizing her voice (McCloskey's memoir is written in the third person):

Surgeons don't know reliably how to make a voice feminine. With her original, presurgery voice her many sessions with her speech therapist in Rotterdam would probably have worked better. It's better to have the range of your natural voice, she explained, which you can train feminine. Get a tape recorder. Turn off part of the male instrument, a viola acting as violin. Place your voice forward. Speak in your head instead of your chest. Articulate more clearly. No harsh onsets. It took years to get these. The man who loved her would have to put up, too, with something other than a mellifluous woman's voice. ***Still, sexy when you hear it right.*** (245, emphasis in the original)

Plett's and McCloskey's descriptions of developing and living a trans voice illuminate just how much one's vocal emanations, *as experienced by others*, are vital to not only moving through mundane social interactions with varying levels of distress or ease but also to the forging of intimate, romantic partnerships. Research in voice studies on the experiences of transgender people confirms the relation between satisfaction with the gendered quality of one's voice and overall life satisfaction (Hancock et al. 2011, Oates and Dacakis 2015, Watt et al. 2018). Both the highly charged social responses to trans voices and the particular surgical, hormonal, and therapeutic interventions available to voiced trans people in different cultures amount to ethically relevant forms of envoicing.

Vocal challenges for transgender people vary widely, as do degrees of access to different forms of interventions. Virtually all of the scientific and social scientific research on vocal aspects of gender transition is focused on subjects portrayed as transitioning from one binary to another (hence, even very recent research refers to MtF [male-to-female] or FtM [female-to-male] persons, and almost never refers to gender nonconforming, genderqueer, nonbinary, or agender persons). Researchers frequently note that testosterone therapy has physiological effects that masculinize the voice in effective and recognizable ways (Nygren et al. 2016, Cler et al. 2020, Cosyns et al. 2013, Irwig 2017: 306), whereas estrogen therapy has little to no effect on aspects of voice that are associated with femininity (Bultynck et al. 2017), leaving transwomen more likely to seek out intervention and assistance. Timing of transition also matters; the vocal apparati of transwomen who experienced "male puberty" (Bultynck et al. 2017: 2803, Hancock and Helenius 2012) have been irreversibly marked by testosterone, unlike those of transwomen who underwent transition prior to puberty and used puberty-blocking hormonal treatments.

Given that voice is a bodily modality frequently utilized in social interactions and deeply marked by gender, it is not surprising that transgender people, perhaps particularly those whose gender identity maps more or less clearly onto the socially dominant gender binary, seek vocal therapy and/or surgeries as part of their transition process. Surgeries available for transwomen are expensive, with outcomes that are mixed and insufficiently researched (Kelly et al. 2019). Voice or speech therapy or training is frequently more accessible and less risky, and while initial research has indicated its generally positive results, the small sample sizes and lack of control groups call for further study (Davies et al. 2015). We will address here the phenomenon of voice therapy for transgender persons, focusing less on its specific techniques in favor of a conceptual analysis of how such therapy can be understood (by both practitioners and clients) and framed.

A common, and perhaps seemingly liberatory or progressive, understanding of voice therapy for trans persons might be framed in this way: a trans person assigned a gender identity at birth contrary to their sense of self has been vocally disciplined along incorrect gender lines. Continuing to utilize vocal traits resulting from this disciplining is contrary to their actual gender identity and results in deepened dysphoria. Because trans persons were not socialized into the vocal characteristics of their actual gender, they find professional assistance in developing a voice that aligns with their gender identity helpful.

In many ways, this common understanding of voice therapy for trans folx echoes our own approach to intervocality and the notion of voice as the result of both relationality and physiology. Gendered voices, as we will discuss in more detail in the next chapter, can be understood here as achievements and products, not as natural or pre-social phenomena, and as such, engaging in the process of developing a specific gendered voice may be seen as similar to learning how to choose and purchase clothes from a set of options different from those associated with the gender previously, and mistakenly, assigned. And because gendered vocal gestures and traits are perceived and experienced as more natural and pre-cultural than, say, clothing, vocal transformations require attending to physiological mechanisms and unconscious habits that can be identified and understood only with professional assistance.

Assisting a transgender person in the process of developing vocal habits and traits that facilitate a social existence more conducive to their flourishing clearly has the potential to serve as an example of ethical envoicing. However, care needs to be taken—and, if recent research is any indication, is increasingly taken—to ensure that such therapy or training is not imbued with essentialist or uncritical assumptions about the relationship between gender and voice. Kate Bornstein's performance art piece "The Voice Lesson"[2] raises precisely these questions. As Bornstein transitioned from the male gender they were assigned at birth to a female gender (they now identify as gender nonbinary), they encountered a speech therapist who taught them to speak "like a woman," that is, using a high, breathy voice, consistently accompanied by a smile, with the frequent and liberal use of questions at the end of sentences. After gamely trying to adopt the vocal traits, Bornstein eventually rejected them; whatever voice they were being taught was not the voice of the person they were becoming.

Now surely not all voice therapy offered to trans individuals makes the mistakes at the heart of Bornstein's narrative, which is most likely set in the mid- to late-1980s. Yet their experience is instructive in understanding how the envoicing occurring in this situation can potentially perpetuate vocal injustice. At first glance, it may seem that the mistake entails associating too strongly a distinctly feminine voice with vocal gestures associated with deference, timidity, and inferiority. Is the problem here, then, that the voice being taught to Bornstein was the voice of a gender subordinate, not the gender outlaw they were becoming?

We hold that such a line of ethical analysis should be rejected due to its assumption that the vocal gestures, tones, and habits strongly associated with femininity necessarily signify social and political inferiority. It presumes that the vocal qualities (breathiness, the use of high pitches and resonances) themselves produce the reality or impression of social inequality, ignoring the constitutive role of the receptions of those qualities, receptions that virtually always take into account the gendered body producing them. To introduce a point developed in more detail in subsequent chapters, it is not the breathiness or the high register per se that constitutes a particularly gendered body as less than equal, but a complex political and multisensory dynamic in which the receiving body is functioning (indeed, researchers have shown that the visual and aural cues regarding a person's gender interact in important ways [McNeill et al. 2008: 727–8]). We cannot say, therefore, that the ethical wrong of the vocal therapy can be found in the particular vocal gestures being taught to Bornstein.

Instead, the ethical wrong is grounded in the therapist's failure to highlight the intervocal nature of a voice in the midst of a gender transition. Doing so would entail engaging more directly and explicitly with the problematic gender norms that dominate vocal practices and interactions. Central to these norms, of course, is an overdetermined sense of how female-identified persons actually sound, a sense that belies the diversity of sonorously feminine voices also marked by age, race, region, and other identity markers. Here, then, the problem is not so much that feminine voices are associated with specific vocal gestures, but rather that they are assumed to reliably inhabit a weirdly narrow and clearly demarcated set of vocal possibilities. That assumption undergirds a set of unjust listening/receiving practices that punish or marginalize women whose vocalizations exceed that narrow set.

To counter this particular assumption, vocal therapists need to approach gender categories as complex, shifting phenomena, rather than taking them as reliable grounds determining which vocal gestures and habits their clients should adopt. In addition, therapists need to construct the gendered meanings of the sonorous aspects of their client's voice as co-constituted by the aural bodies who would receive it, whose listening/receiving practices are necessarily influenced by various forms of structural injustice. This is not to say that all aspects of those listening/receiving practices, or their ramifications, are easily predictable, nor that the goal of therapy should be to align the emerging voice neatly with these practices. Rather, the purpose of these insights would be to relieve the transitioning body of the entirety of the responsibility for the gendered quality of the emerging voice and to denaturalize the vocal social mandates imposed upon the transitioning body. Yet an emphasis on intervocality should not downplay the subjective experience of the client's own voice, which should play a central role in designing the therapy and assessing the success of its outcomes. This is so for at least two reasons; first, there is some evidence that reported quality of life correlates more strongly to the speaker's vocal self-perception than others' perceptions of the voice (Hancock et al. 2011: 553). Second, many of the vocal traits relied on as objective measures of the gendered quality of voices (particularly fundamental frequency, which affects pitch) may not be as reliable as speakers' own self-perceptions of gender as predictors of speakers' satisfaction with interventions (McNeill et al. 2008: 727, Dahl and Mahler 2020, Hancock 2017, Owen and Hancock 2010).

There is evidence that the research on voice work for transgender people is already moving in precisely these directions. In a review of the state of the research on transgender voice and communication, Davies et al. note that "our assessments of goals and outcomes have gone beyond the measurement of acoustic data to include the clients' own perception of their voice and their experiences of voice in their real lives" (2015: 119); the authors also recognize that not all transgender people identify with a binary gender (120) and that speech therapists should not insist on the development of a single voice, but instead should be open to the possibility of helping clients to develop multiple vocal possibilities (121). Perhaps most importantly, Davies et al. emphasize the need to center the therapy on the client's own goals and sense of satisfaction, rather than structuring the process around allegedly objective measures (122). The editors of the textbook considered to be the gold standard in the field of voice therapy for transgender people agree, stating that "use of a voice-related quality-of-life scale … should be administered as a key outcome metric" (Helou and Hirsch 2018: 365).

An emphasis on intervocality would clarify that the purpose of voice therapy or coaching for the transitioning body cannot be reduced, as it clearly was in Bornstein's case, to a mere matter of learning to speak as the binary gender with which the client now identifies. Instead, the goal would be to guide the transgender person in developing vocal habits and traits that facilitate their flourishing in a specific social and political context. Such a perspective would recognize both the harmful aspects of vocal politics, including overly essentializing notions of what "counts" as a gendered voice, and the diverse ways in which different clients may want to position themselves with regard to those politics. Rather than assuming that the project is to shape a voice that fits as neatly as possible within existing vocal norms and standards, therapists and clients both should understand the therapy or coaching as yet another survival technique for trans people, made necessary by a highly developed and confining social gender ideology.

A survival technique, yes, but not only that—voice therapy or coaching can play a vital role in the flourishing of the trans self. Vocal changes may help the client's colleagues, peers, and family members to more quickly recognize and affirm their gender identity, thus improving the client's quality of life substantially. Moreover, while trans persons may reject some vocal traits as ill-fitting for whatever reason, the adopting of other vocal traits may feel like an existential homecoming, a joyfully welcome set of embodied practices that replace other existentially grating practices. And there is no need to separate strictly the received voice from the generated voice here, as many trans people experience hearing their own changing voice as a deeply affirming aspect of living their gender identity more fully and clearly.

On the whole, an emphasis on intervocality should push back against the medicalizing and pathologizing notion that the transitioning vocal body generates the challenges motivating the therapy. The need for therapy does not rest in the transitioning body, but in the intersection of a transitioning body and a transphobic, sexist social world. In a more generous and vocally just environment, vocal changes occurring (or not) alongside changes in gender identity or presentation would be less fraught, situated within broader social acceptance of a wide variety of vocal ways of being in diverse bodies. Trans voices only show up as problematic in a social and political context with specific limiting norms, beliefs, and practices grounded in a flawed gender ideology that takes sex to be both binary and determinative of gender identity and presentation.

Vocal Generosity

That receiving bodies have a role to play in both the sonorous aspects and social/political meanings of vocal emanations establishes the ethical facets of intervocality, but it does not yet produce a standard of vocal justice. What do just practices of envoicing look like, and how do they counter unjust vocal practices? What are the ends of vocal justice?

Here, we take as our starting point Rosalyn Diprose's notion of corporeal generosity (2002) that emphasizes that all human beings, precisely due to their necessary embodiment, are always and already marked by corporal gifts. According to Diprose, the giving and receiving of breath and blood are not the results of human freedom and agency, but their building blocks, and so the ontology of the human being is revealed as grounded in a state of untranscendable indebtedness. Establishing corporeal generosity as an ontological fact about embodied human beings does not amount to an ethical mandate requiring any and all corporeal gifts; as embodied subjects develop in an intercorporeal context, they develop capacities and preferences for specific gifts, and they retain the right and ability to refuse to provide certain gifts under particular circumstances. Injustice, Diprose says, frequently takes the form of forcing the gift (compelling women to carry unwanted pregnancies, for example), as well as memorializing certain corporeal gifts while ignoring others. Diprose's notion of corporeal generosity explicitly and consistently pushes back against the notion of gift-giving as purely optional, altruistic, and undertaken by a fully formed, autonomous subject. In calling for vocal generosity, we are highlighting how gift-giving is baked into human ontology, including vocal ontology.

Transferring Diprose's concept of corporeal generosity to the vocal realm would involve the recognition that vocalized human beings only develop in a context of vocal and aural gift-giving and cannot be isolated from the vocal and aural gifts they have received and given; such a claim includes D/deaf, hard of hearing, and mute persons, whose specific bodily capacities do not exclude them from the sonorous world (rather, ableist political and social structures exclude them from important aspects of sociality). It could also ground a political and ethical analysis identifying which vocal and aural gifts have been marked as valuable, and which have been ignored. In addition, it provides a helpful model for understanding the complex intersection between the universal and the particular: while all voices have been engaged, by definition, in the exchange of vocal and aural gifts, the specific gifts they have received and given are necessarily particular. As we describe in more detail in the next chapter, the richly sonorous in utero soundscape is always marked by maternal prosody and phonology— rhythms, tones, and sounds—that actively shape the fetus' developing vocal and voice-receiving capacities. Moreover, while every inhabitant of the womb hears and feels the sounds of heartbeats and rushing blood, even these sounds are shaped by the bodily habits and practices of the maternal body, which are, in turn, shaped by a social and political environment.

Vocal generosity, then, highlights the irreducible relationality of the voice, bringing to the fore the existential relevance of the in-betweenness of vocal relations. It also allows us to understand how vocal norms have intersected with structural inequalities to privilege certain vocal gifts (the development, say, of tones and rhythms associated with renowned oratory) while ignoring or vilifying others (constructing certain kinds of voices as deficient and in need of correction, say, or neglecting the role of maternal vocalizations in brain development before and after birth). The framework of vocal generosity also generates new questions for the field of voice work, such as: how do the vocal gifts that have been engaged in the generation of certain kinds of voices affect what kinds of vocal gifts those voices are able or willing to give to others?

We also want to extend our understanding of vocal generosity in ways that go well beyond Diprose's original concept. Acutely aware of how structural inequalities have served to funnel broad vocal capacities into overly narrow categories of vocal identity, we seek to use the idea of vocal generosity as a call for the development not only of a multitude of vocal patterns, styles, tones, and so on, but for a deepened ability to receive that multiplicity in more consistently generous, open, and just ways.

Proliferating a wide diversity of vocal gestures and traits, particularly in the public sphere, is a central aspect of vocal justice. As the previous chapter demonstrated, the vocal soundscape of movies and television is dominated by white, male, cishet, able voices; such disproportionate allocation of public airtime trains the receiving ear to construct female-identified, queer, disabled, and/or racialized voices as out of the sonorous norm. Vocal justice requires that such voices be represented in far greater numbers in aural media forms, that they be represented in their multiplicity, and that attempts to police those voices into sounding more like the dominant voices be persistently challenged. Moreover, vocal justice would privilege the emergence of novel forms of vocalization that expand shared aural experiences and understandings of the wide scope of human vocal possibilities. Welcoming such emerging sounds, as well as subaltern, underheard vocal gifts, requires more generous listening practices than contemporary vocal norms produce.

Developing more just habits of receiving a wide diversity of vocalized sounds, particularly in a social and political context steeped in oppression, will require significant experiences of hesitation, disruption, and discomfort. Just as George Yancy (2018) calls on white people to "tarry" with narratives of racial violence and oppression and their own sense of responsibility for anti-Black racism, and Alia Al-Saji (2014) calls for the deployment of hesitation to interrupt and undermine racially oppressive ways of seeing, so too does the demand for vocal justice call for self-reflective receiving practices that pause to call into question how they are co-constituting sonorous and political elements of a given vocal interaction. Such pausing and hesitation can also be applied to vocalizations. Precisely because such habits are embodied and deep-seated, the pause and the hesitation may involve significant disorientation, but we are persuaded by Ami Harbin's argument (2014) that disorientation can be a productive element of moral agency, particularly in the context of sustained structural inequalities.

Vocal generosity, understood as both the ground and the means of vocal justice, is marked by several distinct moves. First, it necessarily involves understanding the production of human-generated vocal sound as a function of social and political relations, establishing the listening/receiving body as co-responsible for the meanings and values associated with any given vocal interaction as well as their sounds. Second, it requires an understanding of the ways in which vocal and listening/receiving practices have been deeply shaped by multiple structural inequalities, including sexism, racism, ableism, classism, and transphobia. Together, these first two moves result in an ethical mandate for receiving bodies to reflect carefully and critically on how and why they experience certain vocal emanations in certain ways. Third, it entails understanding a wide scope of vocal phenomena, interactions, and experiences as embodied, social gifts that serve to widen the scope of human possibility. An ethics of envoicing centered on vocal generosity values the development of a plentitude of vocal identities, modes, registers, and sounds, and it encourages individual and collective efforts to expand vocal capacities by resisting overly restrictive social vocal norms, particularly those that serve to establish certain ways of voicing and sounding as acceptable, normal, natural, universal, or ideal.

To envoice ethically is to adopt multiple practices that create the possibility for the reception and recognition of, and appreciation for, vocal emanations that have been unjustly disciplined and denied. Precisely because of the asymmetry of dominant and marginalized voices, such practices will require discomfort, ruptures with established norms, and predictable resistance. Generosity in the context of systemic oppression is neither easy nor stamped with a sense of self-satisfaction; to the contrary, it runs counter to the grain, is vexing, contrary, and destabilizing.

Diprose's corporeal generosity is framed as ontological, not something (only) enacted within social and political relations, but rather that which prefigures and makes them possible. Vocal generosity, in our understanding, also captures the sense in which indebtedness precedes vocal capacity, thus rendering voiced human beings as ineluctably intervocal. But moving from the ontological to the ethical requires a shift to a decidedly nonideal approach. Our notions of ethical envoicing, respiratory responsibility, and vocal justice are not grounded in transcendental ideals, but rather in a fine-grained understanding of the current state of vocal injustice. To envoice ethically is not to fulfill some abstract moral principles that happen to be focused on vocalizations, but to counter existing unjust structures in their particularity. Yet vocal generosity does not constitute an ethical mandate to experience all human vocal emanations as social gifts. Nor does it frame all forms of social limitations on vocalizations as necessarily oppressive. Some vocal emanations are downright oppressive and harmful (think of the way an abusive partner might yell at their targeted victim at close range, imposing their vocal fury in a way that seeks to terrify and dominate them, or the way that racial microaggressions can come packaged in warm vocal tones that sharpen their harms precisely by masking them), and some limitations can open possibilities.

An anecdote can help to illustrate the latter point. In a feminist philosophy class taught by coauthor Cahill, the division of conversational labor was falling along overly familiar gender lines. The male-identified students only constituted a fifth of the class, yet their contributions to class discussions were taking up at least half of the available airtime, if not more. Although their contributions were productive and focused on the class material, they were significantly limiting the amount of airtime available to the female-identified students in the class, and so Cahill asked to meet the male-identified students outside of class to discuss the situation. Unsurprisingly, they were utterly unaware of the disproportionate division of this particular vocal social good; they didn't *feel* like they were speaking too much, and the particular gendered allocation of airtime that the class had adopted didn't register as imbalanced or out of the norm (of course, it was imperceivable precisely because it was both imbalanced and the norm).

To their credit, they not only were willing to consider the possibility and indeed likelihood that their perceptions were unreliable guides when it came to vocal justice, but to work together to brainstorm possible structural solutions. They collectively developed and committed to three new rules: first, they would refrain from introducing new topics of conversation; second, they would never be the first to speak on a particular topic; and third, at least two women would have to make contributions to class discussion after a male-identified student had spoken before another male-identified student would speak. These limitations on their vocal participation in class constituted serious challenges, provoking precisely the kinds of hesitation, discomfort, and disorientation described above; their eagerness to jump in and the necessary restraint required to refrain from doing so were, at times, palpable, at least to Cahill. Moreover, the limitations (which the rest of the class was unaware of) resulted in new and unusually long pauses in the conversation. Yet those pauses were almost always broken by a female-identified student who had not been frequently speaking in class. When Cahill checked back in with the male-identified students a week or so later, they were astounded by how much more they were learning from their peers, and how many insights and questions they would have not heard if they had continued with vocal practices that felt intuitive and natural to them. In this case, limiting vocal emanations not only resulted in a more vocally just classroom, but also in a deepening of the learning of all the students in the class.

Ethical envoicing on the part of individuals positioned as socially dominant along identity factors such as race and gender often takes the form of attending to how one's deeply familiar listening/receiving and vocal practices replicate oppressive norms, and taking steps to transform them so that vocal social goods are more justly distributed. Taking steps to transform receiving and giving practices of vocal goods requires, of course, a recognition that those unequal practices are taking place. For this we hearken back to the notion of respiratory responsibility, but in a slightly different key; whereas our earlier discussion focused on individual and collective responsibility for the air that fills our own and others' lungs, here we look to the ways in which breath may play a role to foster vocal transformations. On an individual level, this may require an inhibition through breath (literally, "stopping to take a breath") of conditioned, familiar, or comfortable vocal responses that would habitually take up air and space. As new dynamics occur (such as unusually long pauses in classroom discussions), breathing happens. Respiratory generosity (to combine two of our central ideas) could also take the form of participation in or cultivation of affinity spaces in which nondominant groups are able to breathe air together, such as a post-show talkback/healing circle after a theatrical production event or wellness meet-ups such as "Black Girls Breathing" for Black women to care for their mental and emotional health through meditational breathwork (Pridgett 2020). The taking in or giving space for the social goods of breath, literally, of *inspiration* (both "a movement of the intellect" and "the drawing of air into the lungs") holds the power to transform a dynamic spatially, temporally, and bodily. It could be the difference between a suffocating moment and a breathable moment. Breath can itself become the "empty lungs" of a space awaiting oxygenation, new ideas, and new ways of being, out of which new vocal gifts may be breathed, then voiced into being, resonating in familiar spaces in new ways.

4

The Gendered Voice

In contemporary Western culture, it matters that voices are taken to be deeply, persistently, and reliably gendered. When experienced separate from visual cues (say, over the radio or phone), voices serve as crucial, although not always reliable, indications of the speaker's gender. Gendered vocal qualities substantially frame and structure vocal interactions, such that hearing an ambiguously gendered voice can produce social confusion and uncertainty.

In this chapter, we unpack how the embodied phenomenon of voice is implicated and enmeshed in gender politics. We begin with a critique of commonly held assumptions about the biological fixedness of gendered vocal traits, arguing that cultural practices and norms are integral to the construction of recognizably gendered voices. We then turn our attention to how differently gendered voices become imbued with specific political and social meanings, noting that the ancient Greek association of the feminine voice with disorder and noise not only structured the exclusion of women from political life but also the feminization of voice itself. We also emphasize that a central aspect of the gendered nature of voice is the establishing of marginal or nonideal voices as appropriately subject to policing and control. In the final section, we articulate a Butlerian notion of the gendered voice as a social achievement that remains under constant construction and explore the ethical ramifications of such a model, informed by the notions of intervocality and ethical envoicing developed in previous chapters.

Sounding Gender(ed)

The gendered nature of voice is often uncritically associated with a biological essentialism, as if there were physiological reasons that (as it is assumed) femininely gendered voices have higher pitch and so on. Yet the empirical data regarding gender and voice reveal a far more complicated story that resists both a biological essentialism and an overly reductive social constructionism. The gendering of voices is simultaneously deeply material (influenced by, for example, physiological changes that tend to occur in puberty) and relentlessly cultural, demonstrating the hopeless naivete of the shopworn nature/nurture opposition.

It is important to note that although our analysis deploys empirical evidence from multiple fields (psychology, sociolinguistics, etc.), we are aware that the epistemologies underlying those fields are often problematic. Some take the gender binary as a given (even when it is also an object of study), and some privilege quantifiable, ostensibly objective data at the risk of flattening their human subjects into merely passive targets for either biological or social forces, underestimating how those subjects actively engage such forces. Despite these caveats, we find that empirical data can produce important insights and questions regarding the gendered voice.

The anatomical structure of the larynx and vocal folds is nearly identical in size and shape in all children before puberty (Wysocki 2008). Yet there is a marked difference in the average pitches between girls and boys, wherein boys lower their voices and girls raise theirs, either consciously or unconsciously (Eckert and McConnell-Ginet 2013: 5), so that even from this early stage actual social conversational pitch does not necessarily conform to the sizes of the vocal instrument:

> Girls and boys begin to differentiate the fundamental frequency of their speaking voice. Boys tend to round and extend their lips, lengthening the vocal tract, whereas girls are tending to spread their lips (with smiles, for example), shortening the vocal tract. Girls are raising their pitches and boys are lowering theirs. It may well be that adults are more likely to speak to girls in a high-pitched voice. It may well be that they reward boys and girls for differential voice productions. It may also be that children simply observe this difference in older people … There is a striking production of mostly different pitched voices from similar vocal equipment. (9–10)

Gender differences among prepubescent girls and boys are thus produced by intervocal politics rather than anatomical differences. Research on infant vocalizations supports a similar explanation, both in terms of how those vocalizations are interpreted by adult listeners and how infants adapt their vocalizations based on the gender of those adult listeners (one study, for example, tracked an infant's use of lower pitches in the presence of the father, and higher with the mother, perhaps in a mirroring of the parental gender performance [Lieberman 1967]). Even in the absence of evidence of discernable sex-based differences in the mean fundamental pitch of babies' cries, there is evidence that how babies' cries are interpreted by adults plays a significant role in the gendering of the child. One study showed that low pitched cries were more likely to be attributed to boys and high-pitched cries to girls" and that low-pitched boys were taken to be more masculine and high-pitched girls more feminine (Reby et al. 2016: 1). In addition, adult men considered relatively low-pitched cries as expressing more discomfort when presented as belonging to boys rather than girls. One study (Rubin et al. 1974) found that adults were more likely to hear a boy's cry as angry and a girl's as complaining or fearful (Eckert and McConnell-Ginet 2013). Biases in caregiver's listening ears are likely to have implications for the children's welfare (Reby et al. 2016) and may "bootstrap the construction of individual gender identity" (11).

In cultures where language use, including vocal pitch, register, and tone, is highly differentiated by gender (Japan and South Korea are examples), cultural vocal norms regarding gender are in play at the earliest stages of vocal development (Duranti et al. 2011). Early imitative "conversations" between infant and caregiver evolve into a process of repetition between child and community, in which "revoicing" (Duranti et al. 2011)—when caregivers repeat children's speech to render it more culturally appropriate—creates and recreates vocal and verbal routines, coproducing gendered members of society. Revoicing is a mirroring of vocal embodiment: it embeds the child's ideal voice in the adult's, so that child may incorporate the adult's correction into their own vocalizations as part of a complex intervocal event. Cultural gendered practices and norms in these cases emerge from imitation, interaction, and emulation (Kyratzis and Cook-Gumperz 2008).

The gendering of voices continues through early childhood. Cartei et al. (2019) concluded that from 6 years of age (or possibly earlier), children are capable of varying the masculinity or femininity of their voice to participate in gendered characterizations and play. Overall, boys in the study spoke with a lower ΔF (vowel formant) than girls, and the percentage of difference only increased as puberty approached. In contrast with the anatomy of the vocal tract, girls' higher ΔF continued to increase even further after age 9, including girls speaking with spread lips (a smile) that would shorten their vocal tracts, supporting our claim that the differences in voices before puberty are a direct consequence of socialized gendered behaviors.

Gendered vocal differences can thus not be reduced to bare physiological or anatomical differences. Yet it is also true that the biological processes of puberty have enormous effects on the sounded characteristics of the human voice. During male puberty, increased testosterone typically causes several changes to the male voice: testosterone-related growth of the larynx; the descent of the larynx; the increasing of the length, thickness, and stiffening of the vocal folds; and facial development all contribute to the fundamental pitch of male voices dropping by about 50 percent generally compared to female voices (Cartei and Reby 2013, Owen and Hancock 2010: 273). Testosterone therapy in post adolescence also produces these changes (Irwig 2017: 306). Female changes in puberty typically include changes in facial development, descent of the larynx and, like males, an increased lung capacity through body size changes (NCVS undated), resulting in a pitch change of about three tones (Cleveland Clinic 2020). Taller body height generally and the secondary descent of the larynx in males also result in longer vocal tracts, lower vocal pitch, and a narrower ΔF, giving the voice a lower register and range (Cartei and Reby 2013).

However, how adolescents experience the interplay between vocal, physical, neurological, and psychosocial development during puberty is influenced and framed (through not strictly determined) by earlier life experiences (Bonnie et al. 2019) and their social and cultural contexts; environment, quite literally, "gets under the skin" (77). Research in the last twenty years has emphasized the "adaptive interaction between biology and environment" not only from birth through childhood, but including preconception, in utero, and, indeed, transgenerational influences (77). The emerging field of epigenetics synthesizes approaches from biological and social sciences to focus on the active deployment of genetic encoding over a lifetime; biological processes are then "not the primary causes of social outcomes," but "mechanisms with contingent effects that depend on social structures, relationships, and interactions" (79). The effects of puberty are not taken up on a blank slate, but on a vocal apparatus that already bears the sedimented effects of gendered vocal practices. Moreover, the adolescent's body is not a passive recipient of either genetically encoded data nor the effects of life experience, as is exemplified by the neuroplasticity of the brain. As the still developing adolescent brain intersects with tremendous changes in the child's "social, technological, and cultural environment" (Bonnie et al. 2019: 26), it rewires, matures, and forges new connections, creating a "window of opportunity" (37) for substantial growth and change. The future condition of the brain and body may be transformed at each life stage, rendering new bodily and vocal practices along the way not only possible, but probable.

Biological processes such as puberty are significantly implicated in social and political forces (e.g., the average age of the onset of puberty has dropped globally; leading theories for that drop center on social factors such as changes to food supplies, economic and psychological stressors, and so on [Holdsworth and Appleton 2020]; in the United States, the age of menarche has dropped at a disproportionate rate for African American girls [Reagan et al. 2012]). Perhaps most importantly, the biological changes accompanying puberty are intricately interwoven with culturally specific understandings of sex and gender identity, making isolating their influences on the gendered voice from cultural factors impossible. Gender ideologies common to contemporary Western cultures closely tie gender identity to reproductive capacity, and reproductive capacity to normative ideals of intimate relationships and kinship; in doing so, they imbue the changes that puberty can bring with enormous existential and social significance.

The lived experiences of puberty, including vocal changes, are always refracted through culturally dominant and intersecting assumptions about one's gendered identity, social standing, and relationships. Contemporary social pressures to identify clearly, consistently, and normatively with one side of the gender binary, combined with voice's central role in expressing that identity, result in a social mandate to *sound gendered*, to register sonorously as clearly either male or female; that mandate shapes how the pubescent voiced body adapts to and takes up new vocal capacities and limitations. For transgender and gender nonconforming youth, this time can lead to compounded experiences of physiological and emotional stress and destabilization around the possibility or actuality of developing secondary sexual traits (Bonnie et al. 2019: 40). Puberty-blocking medications can also have physiological and psychological effects that impact new and ongoing constructions of their voices. On a political level, cisnormativity constructs the gendered aspects of the cisgender voice as natural and biologically fated, downplaying the roles of both social factors and individual agency (conscious or not), while trans voices may be heard as the result of willful, even pathological attempts to refuse to both accept and express the sex that was (according to a cisnormative world) correctly assigned at birth.

Substantial cultural and historical differences in the sounds of gendered voices pose additional challenges to the notion of its biological foundation. A 1962 study comparing Polish and (presumably white) American males' average speaking pitch found that Polish males spoke noticeably higher than their American counterparts, a difference unexplainable by differences in physical body sizes (Majewski et al. 1972). A study examining the gendered vocal pitch differences (particularly in expressions regarding politeness and emotion) between Japanese and (British, white) English speakers (Loveday 1981) showed that the Japanese women's voices were pitched higher than the English women's voices, and the Japanese men's voices were lower than English men's voices, independent of other physiological differences. Socially constructed gender differences in Japan were emphasized, and thus sexed vocal anatomical differences were heightened. Ikuko Patricia Yuasa (2008) reports that Japanese women have increasingly been using a less feminine linguistic style in the last few decades, but continue to employ a high-pitched voice overall; though women have expressed apparently ambivalent feelings about high pitch, it has not been stigmatized generally and is connected to "esthetic value placed by societal preference" (14). American women, on the other hand, have consistently been lowering their pitch over the last century and "may intuitively recognize that individual and professional success depends on assimilation within the dominant group (i.e. male)" and "may resort to ... adopting that group's values" (Yuasa 2008: 133). There have been analogous findings among women in Australia, Canada, and Sweden, wherein research suggests that cross-generational (historical) change was likely due to psychosocial factors exclusively, including shifting cultural values and the emerging visibility (and audibility) of prominent women in the media employing lower-pitched voices (Pemberton et al. 1998).

And though evidence suggested that Japanese men spoke at a lower pitch than American men (Loveday 1981), the former were more likely to use a greater range of pitch when interacting with familiar speakers (Yuasa 2008). American men, in addition to speaking in relatively low tones, used a *narrower* range of pitch that Yuasa refers to as "an inexpressiveness associated with the classic image of American masculinity" (15). Interestingly, according to linguist Karen Kay, "When John Wayne's voice is dubbed into Japanese, he sounds like Barry White instead of John Wayne because that's his cultural image" (Liberman 2007). The further deepening of "John Wayne's" voice in a Japanese dub not only amplifies cultural performances of Japanese masculinity (and/or the interpretation of classic American masculinity for a Japanese audience), but exaggerates the already highly constructed nature of the icon of John Wayne himself, whose very name, gait, politics, and voice were cocreated by John Ford and others, and projected onto the American and global film scene as an extreme and rigid icon of American "hollow masculinity" that was itself a "by-product of nostalgia, a maudlin elegy for something that never existed" (Metcalf 2017). The fact that Kay evokes Black singer and icon Barry White—associated with "redefining the sound of masculinity" (Myers 2018)—as a paradigm of vocal masculinity points to the complex ways that cultural ideals and stereotypes are deployed along intersecting racial and gendered lines. The "masculine" in White's voice is marked as not only low-pitched, but as raced and eroticized: it is the hypersexualized male voice.

Intercultural differences between same-gendered voices as well as intracultural differences between dichotomously gendered voices have generated many well-worn stereotypes: for example, "all American men think that they are baritones, all Englishmen know they are tenors" (Meier 2008: 102). The performance of "baritone" for American men is, for better or worse, part of the dominant cultural soundscape. That any archetyping of the American male voice may exist at the exclusion of many (or most) American male-identified people doesn't preclude its power and resonance in both performed masculinities (particularly in television and film) and the dominant listening ear. Enculturated listening ears attempt to ascribe stable meaning to voices, resulting in assumptions about voices easily disoriented by difference.

In coauthor Hamel's course on "speech systems" (accents, dialects, and idiolects) for the actor, students are consistently disoriented when listening to representative samples from the American Deep South: white cismale voices, particularly those with markers of patrician social standing, are often misgendered female, and African American cisfemale voices are often misgendered male. Such mistaken impressions are most likely generated by the students' collective lack of deep familiarity with particular cultural contexts combined with their immersion in dominant listening practices that reinforce broader assumptions about what the categories of femininity and masculinity ought to sound like. That Republican senator Lindsey Graham—a representative example of a higher-pitched cismale with a southern drawl—has also consistently been deemed in the media as less than sufficiently masculine (Balcerski 2020) as well as gay and closeted (Hambrick 2007) suggests that white men on the national stage of a certain social and political standing are evaluated vocally in ways wherein expectations of power, race, masculinity, and sexual preference are deeply interconnected. That the voices and bodies of African American women may be misgendered points to the exclusion of Black women from the category of American femininity, calling to mind Sojourner Truth's famous (possibly apocryphal) question, "Ain't I a woman?" (Eko 2018).

Common assumptions (and, to a certain extent, scholarship) about the gendered nature of voice tend, precisely because of the ideology of the gender binary, to emphasize the vocal differences across gender and ignore or downplay the enormous overlap between male-identified and female-identified voiced persons. An emphasis on the effects of puberty on the gendered voice thus privileges one particular developmental stage over others when unpacking the complex relationship between voice and gender identity. While puberty is certainly a dramatically transformative stage of development, it is not the only one, and it is telling that references to women's voices almost always invoke a fairly narrow band of adulthood. It is possible that the stages where gendered vocal differences are most acute and noticeable (adolescence and early adulthood) receive more scholarly attention than is warranted, and that vocal similarities across gender categories are the norm, and differences the divergence.

Gender as Policeability

As Anne Carson's influential essay "The Gender of Sound" demonstrated (1995), Western thought and politics have deeply imbued the phenomenon of voice with gender inequality. Associating the feminine body with dangerous tendencies toward disorder, leaking, and irrationality, the Greeks positioned feminine vocalizations, and particularly public feminine vocalizations, as contrary and threatening to the masculine political order, as Robin James describes:

> So, (certain kinds of) men were thought to be capable of embodying (masculine) *sophrosyne*, that is, of comporting their bodies in accord with the order of the city, so that when they did speak, their speech contributed to social harmony and orderliness. The practice of *sophrosyne* aligns one's body with the logos of a properly-ordered society, and, indeed, a properly-ordered cosmos …Women (and slaves, and some other kinds of men) were thought to be incapable of embodying this logos, of transforming their bodies into microcosms of the well-ordered city and harmonious cosmos. Their speech would disrupt social and cosmic harmony with dissonant, disorganized material. Silence, then, is how women contributed to social and cosmic harmony: their verbal and sexual chastity preserved the optimal, most well-balanced political and metaphysical order. (2015)

Multiple dichotomies are in play here, all reinforcing and intensifying each other: language/sound, order/chaos, containment/leaking, male/female, mind/body, public/private, speech/voice, and so on. In each binary set, the ostensibly inferior element is persistently feminized, thus overdetermining the need to control, silence, or carefully contain the public use of the feminine voice. Mary Beard writes that "public speaking and oratory were not merely things that ancient women *didn't do*; they were exclusive practices and skills that defined masculinity as a gender ... A woman speaking in public was, in most circumstances, by definition not a woman" (2017: 17, emphasis in original). Of course, any identity requiring an opposite entails a dependence that must be repressed; how can one be, and know that one is, a man without the defining alterity of femininity? How can one revel in the logos of language and political order without encountering the chaos of the sounded, nonlinguistic, feminine lament of the keener? The threat must be made present, albeit in highly controlled, often ritualistic contexts, to substantiate the need for control and managed order.

Carson, Beard, and James demonstrate that the gendered nature of voice is not to be limited to the association of the feminine voice with particular (and ostensibly inferior) sonorous traits. In a dualistic and hierarchical Western metaphysics, voice in general (not just the voices that don't count as normatively masculine) as opposed to speech becomes imbued with femininity. For ancient Greek culture, according to Carson, women's "otherness" was constructed around the notion that all of her leakages (voice, bodily fluids, emotions, unedited truth-telling) define her as a creature who "puts the inside on the outside" (1995: 129). Categorically, the female "species" challenged and disrupted the very notion of a clear dichotomy between, and regulation of, the "internal" and "external" self. The incontinent nature of women's flowing vocal sounds (expressions of raw emotions such as lamentations, laughing, sobbing, shrieking) invoke the porous exchange of material inherent in voice's origins. Created and recreated at the margins of flesh, voice lets the outside in (breath) and the inside out (vibrations) in a fluid two-way gesture of breath-sound continuity that disrupts the possibility of bodily containment. Vocal sound is thus simultaneously feminized and naturalized, while speech, with its accompanying value of rational articulation through *logos*, is masculinized and associated with culture. "As Aristotle says, any animal can make noises to register pleasure or pain," Carson reminds us; what differentiates man from beast (or woman) is *logos*, "rationally articulated speech" (128). For the Greeks, women were of the species that lacked the ability to self-legislate through well-executed *logos* (essentially, they can't "think before they speak"); thus "silence," according to Sophocles, is "the *kosmos* [good order] of women" (quoted in Carson 1995: 127).

The binary is, of course, unstable: there is no speech without voice, nor voice that isn't on a continuum toward speech, and the overdetermination of women's speech (which must employ language) as unedited and "running off at the mouth" (Carson 1995: 131) exists only so that men's speech (which cannot escape vocalization) would not risk feminization. So there are two dimensions that must be attended to here—the role of voice in masculine speech and language in feminine speech—which, while promised to be mutually exclusive, are in fact ontologically enmeshed. We forget that the Sirens spoke in recognizable tongues, and that it was the function of myth-making that robbed them of their words (Cavarero 2005: 106). Linklater runs into a similar instability in the statement "Voice is universal, speech is cultural" (ALRA 2020); in contrast, we argue that there is no culturally created speech that isn't dependent upon voice, just as there is no vocal sound that is not coproduced by culture.

If voice as sound is imbued with feminine associations, rendering it a generally appropriate target for masculine control, then it stands to reason that identifiably feminine, trans, and nonnormatively masculine voices, as compared with their identifiably normative masculine counterparts, would be received as marked more by sound than by linguistic content. To put it another way, one way that voices are gendered is that the *sound* of other-than-normatively-masculine voices is experienced and evaluated more acutely. Hegemonic masculinity, associated as it is with logos, language, and order, frames normative masculine vocalizations as persistently oriented toward meaning and signification, transcending and effacing the materiality of voice. The raced and gendered listening ear leans into hear *what* white cishet men want to communicate; when marginalized bodies speak up, how they sound—and not what they say—is more likely to be perceived as an appropriate target for judgment and correction. So Senator Lindsey Graham may be teased for sounding less than normatively masculine, but the pragmatic and political import of such teasing never extends beyond a more or less gentle ribbing. His voice, while risible, is not constituted as subject to policing.

The disproportionate emphasis on and relevance of the sound of voices emanating from nonnormatively embodied subjects follows a familiar pattern of the embodied politics of oppression. George Yancy has written of the ways in which the Black body arrives ahead of itself (2012), how the inescapable meanings attached to its blackness by white supremacy shape social interactions well before the Black subject does or says anything. The white embodied subject, by contrast, does not lag behind its body, but emerges on the social stage fully present and fully individualized. In cases where vocal interactions are also visual interactions, the gendered and/or racialized voice can arrive ahead of its sound. Dominant listening practices prepare receiving bodies to experience nondominant voices as more mired in materiality; just as the feminine body bears the burden of being sexed so that the masculine body can be free to be generically human, and the racialized Black body bears the burden of being raced so that the racialized white body can experience itself as race-neutral, so too do nondominant voices bear the burden of the relevance of sound so that dominant voices are free to be defined by signification. Moreover, disproportionately weighting the materiality of the nondominant voice fosters a mode of policeability by invoking a familiar mind/body hierarchy.

Recognizably feminine, trans, or nondominant masculine voices are effectively gendered by virtue of their perceived predisposition for needing criticism, suggestions, and improvement; they are pre-heard as likely to be sonorously ill-formed, out of sync, and/or aesthetically wanting, whereas dominant voices are likely to be sonorously preapproved and exempt from sonorous management and correction. Contemporary examples of the gendered policing of perceivably feminine voices bear this point out. We are particularly suspicious of the recurring call—largely in mainstream television and radio, online and print journals, and the blogosphere,[1] as well as in some theatre training and performance practices—for female or queer-identified voices to abandon vocal fry, uptalk, and other vocal habits that (so the story goes) undermine the speaker's capacity to command respect.[2] Women, in particular, are encouraged to reject ways of speaking that have been part of their socialization as women "in a man's world" (Linklater 2006: 25) and to reclaim a stronger sense of their vocal self, with the promise that doing so will amount to being taken more seriously—and with no recognition that eschewing a palpable expression of their gender identity might involve significant loss. Such calls also tend to mask their (barely) underlying racial commitments; the women they target are almost always assumed to be white, as are the masculine norms that the women are encouraged to adopt.

Such exhortations not only reify the social and political desirability of the recognizably masculine "big and strong" voice; they also assume that the social meanings of vocal qualities are separable from the bodies from which they emanate, as if it were the bare, disembodied vocal qualities that generate the desired effects. We suspect that the connection between vocal qualities and social respect is a more complicated matter involving the relation of those qualities to gendered forms of embodiment and a patriarchal social context. Our suspicion is borne out by empirical research indicating that women whose voices register as lesbian, because they sound more masculine, are perceived as less competent and less capable as leaders (Fasoli and Hegarty 2020). To have women simply adopt (white) masculine ways of speaking is no more likely to garner respect than a female politician's pantsuit.

Vocal policing can also target the perceived lack of fit between voice and gender presentation, with the implication being that the gender presentation should be transformed (not the voice) in order to bring the two embodied modalities into alignment with normative gender expectations. The voices of gender nonconforming or transgender people are regularly received by bodies shaped by dominant listening practices that take voices as reliable, even uncontestable indicators of "real," biologically determined sex, and should other embodied aspects of gender presentation (clothes, gait, haircut, etc.) clash with the perceived gender of the vocalization, those receiving bodies may respond with hostility, anger, and even violence. Such damaging responses construct the nonvocal forms of embodiment as transgressive, deceptive, and pathological. Here, the construction of the voice as essentially and reliably sexed combines with a gender ideology mandating a determinate relationship between biological sex (taken as fixed and pre-political), gender identity, and gender presentation to apply coercive social pressure regarding nonvocal bodily traits.

Voices recognized as dominant and normative, including those associated with normative forms of masculinity, carry their own presumed authority and aesthetic value; voices associated with marginalized or nonnormative bodies, including feminine bodies, are met with a hermeneutics of suspicion, with regard both to the reliability or value of the linguistic content and to questions of vocal appeal. For example, when a male British scientist repeated verbatim the mathematical musings of a young teenage woman (captured on a TikTok video while she applied her makeup), suddenly the words that had been virally mocked for their alleged vapidness came off as the serious and profound questions that mathematicians affirmed they were (Hayes 2020, Crowell 2020).

Empirical evidence regarding responses to anger is particularly helpful here, given the centrality of vocal tone in anger expression. Barrett and Bliss-Moreau (2009) concluded that "the stereotype of the overly emotional female is linked to the belief that women express emotion because they are emotional creatures, but men express emotion because the situation warrants it" (654–5). Brescoll and Uhlmann (2008) agree and further demonstrate that women who express anger in the workplace experience a loss of status, whereas men who do so experience an increase; similarly, Salerno and Peter-Hagene (2015) found that women who express anger in group deliberation lose influence, whereas men who do so become more influential. The gendered qualities of voiced human beings, then, extend beyond sonorous elements such as pitch and timbre into how they are responded to, framed, and constructed. Associations of policeability with voices that don't register as hegemonically masculine and trustworthiness with voices that do register as such are central to both vocal gendering and the perpetuation of structural gender inequality.

Underlying the seeming appropriateness of the policeability of nondominant voices is an ascription of vocal responsibility that holds nondominant voices accountable for creating vocal interactions centering the comfort and pleasure of the dominant ear. Voice is deeply implicated in performances and perceptions of authority, and the very possibility of occupying power and voicing in ways that the dominant ear is willing and able to hear is marked by not only gender but race, ethnicity, language, and social and economic standings. There are finer and finer lines walked in the everyday negotiation of intelligibility (who can or is willing to hear whom), dynamics played out in interpersonal exchanges, high-profile public discourse, and charged institutional interactions, such as those occurring in carceral sites or hospitals. Here we turn our attention from the fact that nondominant voices are constructed as more policeable to explore the particular forms that policeability may take.

We have already noted that criticisms of creaky voice (also known as glottal or vocal "fry") exemplify the policeability of female and nondominant voices. We add to that analysis here by noting that such vocal sounds were first understood as a decidedly masculine phenomenon (Yuasa 2010), and in fact continue to be deployed regularly, and without controversy or criticism, by masculine voices. Thus, the very vocal gestures lauded or accepted uncritically within masculinity are rejected when performed by femininely gendered bodies, as they reflect back, perhaps uncannily, on the dominant listening ear. Sound with recognizably masculine tropes "rings false" or becomes "strident" to the dominant ear when it comes from differently gendered and racialized bodies: it is heard as excessive, unpleasant, forceful, and pushy, perhaps because it is unmasked not as the "natural" expression of biologically male human authority, but as wholly constructed. Like Mulvey's cinematic "return of the (male) gaze" the voice of the dominant listening ear is echoed back onto itself: it frames the dominant voice as knowable, subject to judgment and taste, and imitable. But unlike the avertable gaze, the dominant ear cannot easily or reliably block the intrusion of sound. It is the oft-described uncanny phenomenon of "hearing the sound of your own voice" writ large, in which the "knower" is revealed to himself as constructed, and the patriarchal ear is threatened, made vulnerable.

On the other end of the spectrum, sounds from nondominant bodies that do not ally closely enough with dominant voices—sounds that are high, soft, small, nasal, and so on—are equally as likely to ring in the dominant listening ear as excessive and unpleasant. This vocal register suggests an indifference toward dominant authoritative vocal qualities and arouses a deep suspicion: why wouldn't feminine and other marginalized voices not aspire to emulate big, strong, throaty, low sounds? These sorts of sounds are often criticized for being self-limiting, apologetic, and indicative of a self-imposed (possibly feigning) weakness or "attention-getting" personal insecurity (Eckert and McConnell-Ginet 2013) that could easily be corrected if the speaker would simply position themselves effectively. This stance misses the fact that such vocal devices may be employed as an attempt to solve difficulties in interactions generated by systemic inequalities in the first place (161) and assumes incorrectly that all vocal positions are available to everyone at any time.

If there were a "just right" vocal quality for the hegemonic masculine ear—the "Goldilocks" of vocal traits (in more ways than one, as it would need to skew racially white)—it would not position itself in competition with dominant masculine sound, but rather would occupy itself utterly with taking into consideration the listening ear. What is demanded is not a particular set of sounds, but rather sonic evidence that the voice is designed to please the whim of the hearer. This sound performance is rendered not only wholly relational to the dominant ear, but derivative of it, taking his "listening pleasure" as its sonic lodestar. When Ernest Hemingway overhears Gertrude Stein pleading with her lesbian lover as he waits downstairs in her home, the not-meant-for-him sounds are so disturbing that he flees, and his "friendship" with Stein is rendered wholly untenable: " 'I have to go,' I said [to the maidservant] and tried not to hear any more as I left but it was still going on and the only way I could not hear it was to be gone. It was bad and the answers were worse ... That was the way it finished for me, stupidly enough" (quoted in Carson 1995: 122).

The uninterrupted gaze signifies desire (to "gaze longingly at," for instance, implies desire toward the object of the gaze). Similarly, desire is created by the uninterrupted listening ear leaning toward the heard voice, a voice that is constructed as dismissible, inferior, and/or for the pleasure (or erotic fulfillment) of the listening ear. Nondominant voices are thus more persistently sexualized than dominant voices, and insofar as they are sexualized, either promise titillation or threaten devastation: containment and subsequent policing here become vital to maintaining order and the proper balance of "listening pleasure." The centrality of policeability and the duty to please associated with nondominant voices explains how sexualized feminine voices are, as Anne Karpf (2017) reminds us, "usually considered in relation to the desire they could evoke and never desire they could express" (31).

Within patriarchal logic, the threat inherent in women's vocal responsibility to arouse desire in men is made all the more potent by the repressed anatomic parallels between the mouth and female genitalia. Karpf argues that there is a certain bodily logic to the sexualizing of the voice, that the displacing of sexuality from women's genitals to their mouths (and throats) is "encouraged by the apparent resemblance in shape" (34) of labial folds and vocal folds, as well as the shared terminology: labia means "lips." The female body's speaking voicing lips become a visual and aural site of pleasure for the listener, mirroring the promise of what lies between the set of lips in the lower body, even as (or because) it carries with it the shadow of a "dangerous ensnaring power," such that "the concept of the vagina dentata has in a sense been extended to the mouth" (34). Engulfment isn't the only promise and threat being made, however, as the feminine sexualized voice is also eroticized via voice's ability to arouse desire by transgressing bodily borders across physical distance, and on the receiving body's inability to prevent the sexualized voice from entering. That voice and sound hold erotic potential is, of course, not ethically problematic. However, in the context of phallo- and heterocentric sexual politics, the eroticization of the feminine voice, precisely because of the play of hierarchized dichotomies such as voice/speech and body/mind, comes at the cost of a robust, non-derivatized (Cahill 2010) feminine sexuality. More specifically, whether eroticized for pleasure, or hypersexualized for denigration, casting the feminine voice in these ways obscures and renders inaudible the meaningfulness and content of the speech of nondominant persons.

That the feminine voice is related to the desire it might evoke causes it to be policeable in specific ways. The voice might serve as an entry point for bodily policing along reproductive lines: recent (Banai 2017) as well as ancient Greek (Carson 1995) studies have centered on the ability to detect hormonal changes in a maternal or pre-maternal body (such as the occurrence of ovulation), placing the ownership and knowability of fertility or pregnancy squarely in the dominant listening ear. One study ostensibly has proven that a (cis)woman's voice is "most attractive" to the opposite sex when ovulating (Fischer et al. 2011). And yet, what constitutes the "ideal" most attractive female voice has of course changed substantially over time (Karpf 2017) and is highly historically and culturally bound.

The current cultural moment in the United States has produced a particular version of an idealized feminine voice—consistent, unthreatening, warm, friendly, available—as the default for digital speech assistants such as Siri (Apple iOS) and Alexa/Echo (Amazon). These voices are designed to be the voices that support: they are on your side, they "give you stuff," they answer questions on demand, and you don't need to be concerned about being polite (no "please" or "thank yous" required; see Abbany 2019). "Siri" is a Norse word meaning "beautiful woman" (2019), and though she purports to be genderless (her response to the question of her gender is currently "Don't let my voice fool you, I don't have a gender") it is quite clear that, both in nomenclature and by the fact that the voice arrives with the image of a body, Siri arrives in our imagination as a femininely gendered body. This imagined body is a motherly one for the dominant listening ear, and sexualized insofar as her voice may be "erotically charged for nostalgia for the maternal" (Miller-Frank 1995: 3). In addition, this maternal voice sounds white, well-educated, and adult, thus serving effectively as a sonic mirror to reflect back a world organized around white supremacy. There is also evidence that Siri is more accurate in recognizing and decoding masculine voices better than feminine voices or voices with "non-standard" English dialects (Rao 2018), reinforcing the hegemonic masculinity presumed in both the primary speaking voice and the hearing body.

Though Siri (and her cousins Alexa and Echo) may have hit a "sweet spot" of most pleasing feminine voice qualities for the dominant ear as they were product-tested for their particular usages (Alexa/Echo lives with you in your living room, Siri works with you out in the world), studies on real-life female voices prove highly contradictory and inconclusive regarding what constitutes attractiveness (Zimmerman 2019). Moreover, aesthetic judgments of women's voices have consistently taken the whiteness of the vocally attractive women's voice as a given. While (white) female voices have been associated with sexuality, bodies of women of color as both erotic and devalued commodities have more often than not been equated with vocal silence in the context of the colonial and postcolonial West, a silencing borne of the near impossibility of successful vocal positioning vis-à-vis the dominant listening ear. And though a great deal of airtime and concern is given to the fact that patriarchy considers women's voices (in general) to be "uncertain, emotional, shrill, unpleasant, or redundant," "women of color get different messages about the worth of their voices and the consequences of speaking out" (Osborne 2018). From an early age, African American girls are getting the message that their voices are too chatty, too loud, too outspoken: they are two and a half times more likely to be seen as disruptive in school than their white counterparts (Epstein et al. 2017), as the option of the "well-behaved" vocal model is not available to them.

Black girls are also more likely to be seen by adults as needing less nurturing than white girls, and as more knowledgeable about sex and adult topics (2017). One strong implication here is that in "seeming more mature," the expectation is that they ought to be better at self-policing to "fit in." The other implication is that they are hypersexual and disruptive to the normative sexual order, which relates directly to their disproportionate sexualization, rates of experiences of sexual violence, and vulnerability to sex trafficking. The participation of English-speaking men in the global sex tourism industry, an industry that primarily offers sexual interactions across language barriers, exemplifies the eroticization of the sound of linguistically nonnormative voice; the dominant, English-speaking male doesn't have to listen to the words of the subjugated non-English speaking woman, whose vocalizations are seen as utterly devoid of and separate from language, thus reducing her moral status and heightening her sexual accessibility. Globally and in the United States, hypersexualization seems to be one of the few ways that the voices of women of color can register to the dominant listening ear; otherwise, they are met with an aural unwillingness or inability to hear across language or accent difference that results in a profound silencing. And in the political arena in which women of color are claiming more airspace and power, we have seen and heard them maligned, mocked, interrupted, misrepresented, and infantilized (Osborne 2018). Politically, then, the voices of women of color are subject to hypersexualization, heightened levels of policeability, and forms of silencing that thwart the communication of their ideas and perspectives.

Although policeability is disproportionately imposed on feminine voices, dominant listening practices also place limitations on the capacities of boys and men. The expectation that the male dominant voice is aligned with disembodiment, pure signification, logos, reason, and authority brings with it a set of highly specific sonorous demands. While such voices are not as susceptible to explicit correction should they fail to meet them, such demands nevertheless impose significant limitations on both vocal and emotional possibilities. In the masculine order of things, men are tasked with (no more, no less) "meaning what they say" and "saying what they mean" without the feminine "leakages" of emotion that may speak more loudly than words. While there is evidence that masculine American English speakers have a more limited vocal range than masculine British English speakers (Graddol and Swann 1989), it has also been shown that 8–10-year-old African American boys use more pitch variability than their white counterparts (Morris 1997), indicating perhaps that white boys may experience more pressure to conform to the hegemonic masculine standards of the day (Eckert and McConnell-Ginet 2013). This is not surprising, given that it may be obvious to them that certain kinds of men are the ones who are valued, who "do important things" (12), and who have power.

As we will discuss in more detail in our concluding chapter, the apparent increase of emotionality in "prestige" (mostly white) male voices in high-level contemporary American social and political life complicates the analysis we have been laying out here. Contemporary vocal politics seems to reward prestigious men both for displaying great emotionality vocally (high-pitched, loud, tearful, etc.) and for using less emotion in speech (maintaining expected norms of reason and a narrow pitch range). In the latter cases, of course, the welling up of emotion risks "the feminization of us all"—surely a sign (and a reliable one at that, given the epistemological privilege extended to masculine emotion) that there is deep disorder in need of reordering and correction: when white men can't control their voices, when they are compelled to traffic in tones that would be labeled hysterical when adopted by women, something, indeed, must be rotten in the state of our country.

As this section has demonstrated, the sound of the gendered voice is as much a matter of intervocal politics as it is a sonorous matter of pitch, timbre, and so on. Gendered practices of hierarchized receiving of gendered voices have profound ethical ramifications, particularly insofar as they reproduce intersectional systemic inequalities. How might new understandings of intervocality and the relational, material voice underpin new practices of vocalization and receiving vocalization that, contrary to dominant practices, forward vocal justice?

Ethically Envoicing the Gendered Subject

Judith Butler's theory of gender as performativity is of particular use to our analysis of the gendered voice. In *Gender Trouble* (1990), Butler argued that gender identity is not a stable essence shaping preferences, modes of being, or embodied behavior. In a reversal that became central to both contemporary feminist theory and queer theory, Butler posited gender identity as the sedimentation of repeated bodily acts undertaken across time and space within specific political contexts. While both the sense of one's own gender identity and the existence of stable, well-defined gender identities in general appear to many as natural, Butler argues that precisely the opposite is the case; their need for constant upkeep and affirmation reveals their vulnerability and contingency. Gender is not something that we are, but something that we do, and we are compelled by a specific ideology of gender to do it constantly in order to maintain the very illusion of necessity.

It is vital to note that Butler's idea of performativity does not map neatly on to notions of performativity commonly associated with theatrical phenomena or the profession of acting. While Butler's early work relied explicitly on metaphors with theatre, her later work emphasized the dangers of equating performativity with performance (Wald 2007: 13), which risks endowing performativity with a sense of control, agency, and autonomy. The performativity of gender for Butler does not entail the acting of the subject in opposition to who they "really" are (as we might understand the actor, who is performing as another person to be doing). Here, performativity refers to an ontology of gender identity that reverses the direction of causality assumed by a gender ideology committed to the idea of sex as biologically determined. That is, the performativity of gendered acts refers to their capacity to produce and then sustain a gendered identity, similar to the way that performative speech acts, as conceptualized by J. L. Austin (1962) and John Searle (1969), do not describe the world but perform actions that transform it. Just as the phrase "I find you guilty," when spoken by the right kind of person in the right kind of context, actually changes the accused's civil status, so too do gendered acts work on the social person to bring about a gendered identity.

Butler's theory of gender performativity sparked decades of scholarly debate in a wide variety of disciplines, and while there are and continue to be serious critiques of her theory of gender (including questions about how it risks reducing materiality to mere construction, and whether it is capable of producing a phenomenologically accurate account of transgender lives), it serves as a helpful framework for our analysis of the gendered voice. Like Butler, we reject the idea that the sexedness of any embodied phenomenon is ultimately reducible to a pre-political, pre-social materiality. Gendered voices are an accrual of gendered expectations and norms, a complex combination of embodied mechanisms habituated in particular ways under specific material conditions. Moreover, gender and voice are co-constitutive—voices, including vocal interactions, are an important modality of the gender identity that is constantly under construction, and constructed gender identity serves as a productive force in the creation of a specific voice with identifiable traits and resonances. Butler argues that we think of ourselves as having gender, or being a certain gender, when in fact, we do gender. Similarly, we are arguing that we think of ourselves as having a voice, or having a gendered voice because we are a gender, when in fact, we do voice, and doing voice in a gendered way creates sonorous sediments that result in a gendered voice and a materialized gender.

This is not to deny the material aspects of voice. Quite the contrary: just as the construction of gender identity requires the action of an embodied subject (one cannot simply imagine gender identity, nor is it conceptualized first, and then acted out), so too the construction of a perceivably gendered voice requires the deployment of muscles, bodily cavities, air flow, and so on. Dominant models of the gendered voice frame its gendered materiality as both prior to the phenomenon of voice itself, and as determinant; women talk like women, according to this story, because the physiological apparatuses that are used in vocalizations are biologically differentiated along the lines of a binary sex difference that precedes and grounds culture. As we have argued, such an explanation flies in the face of empirical facts about early childhood development and cultural differences. A more Butlerian approach reveals the voice, and gendered vocal identity, not as determined by biological factors, but as reliant on materiality and repeated bodily acts. Precisely because of its embodiment, the gendered voice is neither stable nor static, but must be instantiated repeatedly to be sustained; that dependence on repetition holds the possibility of transformation, transgression, gender treason, and the broadening of collective understandings of the scope of possible human vocalizations.

Voices that bear the marks of gender should thus be understood as intersubjective, bodily effects that are constantly under construction. The gendered voice is fundamentally intervocal, both in terms of the specific sonorous traits that mark it, and the social meanings that have been assigned to it. Just as a Butlerian theory of gender performativity undermines and troubles gender categories and their dominant ontologies, so too does the framework of intervocality reveal gendered voices as contingent, dynamic, and unsettled. Moreover, contrary to dominant conceptualizations of the gendered voice which assume that the gendered quality of voices refers solely or primarily to the gender of the voiced subject, intervocality reveals that the gendered voice is inherently relational, and as such refers to and reflects gendered social relations.

The inherently relational nature of the gendered voice recasts ethical questions regarding gender vocal justice in new and productive ways. A focus on ethical envoicing results in a deeper understanding of the ways in which receiving bodies influence both what sonorous traits are associated with specific genders and how social value is ascribed to or withheld from gendered voices. Emphasizing the co-constituting role of the receiving body in the production of the gendered voice illuminates the ethical flaws in interventions that might be mistaken as aiming toward vocal justice. Earlier we noted that the gendering of the feminized, queer, or nonnormatively masculinized voice includes the social production of that voice as policeable, inherently susceptible to—or even eager for—correction and intentional molding. This particular gendered set of vocal norms and practices is clearly and directly related to vocal injustice, and is yet another moment in the production of the feminine, queer, or racialized body as a social problem that cries out for the tempering, authoritative influence of white masculinity. One of the first moves required by a mandate for the ethical envoicing of human subjects who do not embody the norms of whiteness, masculinity, ableness, heterosexuality, and other identity factors is to refrain from policing, and to understand the act of policing itself as a form of vocal injustice.

We have also noted that the tendency to exhort women to, for example, avoid vocal fry and uptalk misunderstands how social value was assigned to aspects of gendered vocalization. Here we focus on a slightly different, but related, point: that encouraging women to take up the project of changing their vocal traits in order to gain social goods such as respect, prestige, or financial gain both reinscribes the femininely gendered voice as an appropriate site of disciplinary effort and obfuscates the co-constitutive role that such reinscription plays in the construction of the femininely gendered voice. An ethics of envoicing requires a dismantling of systems of vocal injustice that receive voices outside the category of white cishet men as less trustworthy and less worthy of social vocal goods, while simultaneously offshoring the responsibility of managing that vocal inequality to the voices themselves. Some of these policing exhortations come packaged as helpful advice, such as in the following experience of female-identified undergraduate students presenting at a professional conference:

> Our student-faculty panel had just presented potential reasons for the underrepresentation of women in philosophy departments. The opening response in the question time, however, was neither a question nor a comment about the content of our presentation. Instead, the audience member offered a recommendation for the two female-identified undergraduate presenters to change our voices: to speak up, to use less vocal fry (i.e., to not drop our voices' pitch), and to speak more like our male undergraduate colleague on the panel. This audience member went on to remark that vocal fry is a fitting metaphor for the way women do not feel heard in philosophy. The commenter suggested that if only women spoke up, things would improve. To our disappointment, much of the discussion devolved into us explaining why it was not our voices that were the problem. (Wilson et al. 2020: 45)

Other exhortations are more straightforward demands to produce vocalizations that are pleasing to the dominant receiving body. In implicit and explicit ways, female-identified persons are frequently instructed to keep their vocal tones "warm," gentle, welcoming and are told that doing so is central to their ability to be heard by the dominant listening ear. Note that such demands don't deny intervocality so much as they hijack it for nefarious purposes: the dominant, racialized white, masculine listening ear (which may exist in any receiving subject) is insisting that any and all vocal interactions must include sonorous evidence that their listening preferences are consistently taken into account. The absence of such sonorous evidence is reason enough to halt the interaction, or to change the subject to how the marginalized person is flouting the vocal rules, and thus is unworthy of being recognized as a viable interlocutor. This is a particularly effective strategy when the content of the speech of the marginalized person is unwelcome or discomfiting, although it is not limited to highly fraught interactions explicitly centered on topics related to systemic oppression.

The two modalities of advice and demand share similar ethical flaws. Whether one is claiming that the remedy for structural injustice is to be found in the transformation of the sonorous qualities of the marginalized voices, or that the aesthetic discomfort of the dominant listening ear is reason enough to undertake a transformation, one is persistently situating the ethical responsibility solely in the vocalizing body. Even and perhaps especially when the preferences of the listening ear are implicitly or explicitly framed as of paramount importance, those preferences are constructed as given, and devoid of ethical responsibility. Such situating not only belies a misunderstanding of intervocality; it also constitutes a harmful act of unethical envoicing.

Refraining from acts of vocal policing is thus a necessary mode of ethical envoicing, particularly for receiving bodies who are favorably positioned within oppressive systems. In addition, dismantling unjust gendered structures of vocalizing and receiving vocalizations will require developing capacities to receive nonnormatively gendered voices as valid and valuable instantiations of human vocal possibilities, a capacity that requires rejecting overly stringent limitations on what differently gendered voiced human beings should sound like. The development of such capacities does not amount to an ethical demand to receive all human vocalizations as gender neutral, or to refrain entirely from hearing gender in human vocalizations. In fact, recognizing how vocal identity can be an existentially important aspect of gender identity is central to ethical envoicing as well as creating social spaces where nonnormatively gendered voices are experienced in their multiplicity as meaningful elements of embodied being. Being able to hear gender identity—and, indeed, the absence of gender, for those who identify as agender—across a wide scope of vocal registers, tones, timbres, and other-than-vocal forms of embodiment is central to a broader ethical mandate to reject a gender ideology that recognizes only two sexes and insists on aligning biological sex, gender identity, gender presentation, sexual orientation, and vocal identity in harmfully restrictive ways.

5

Envoicing in Sex, Maternity, and Childbirth

An ethics of envoicing highlights how subjects, forces, and infrastructure shape both the sonorous elements of voice as human-generated sound and the social and political meanings of vocalizations and vocal interactions. In this chapter, we drill down into three distinct sites of vocal production and meaning-making, demonstrating how even the most seemingly natural aspects of vocalization are deeply enmeshed with social and political dynamics. Importantly, we begin the discussion in utero, challenging dominant conceptualizations of the prelinguistic voice as pre-social and untouched by the particularities of the pregnant body's material context. We then turn our attention to the envoicing that occurs during childbirth, highlighting the widely diverse social practices around voice and labor across cultures and historical periods, and critically evaluating the social meanings attached to the vocalizations of the laboring body. We conclude by considering the phenomenon of sexual vocalizations, an undertheorized and underresearched phenomenon too often framed as expressive (a more or less reliable indicator of what is happening sexually) rather than productive (bringing about or intensifying sexual sensations). The various meanings ascribed to sexual vocalizations are enmeshed in a hegemonically heterosexual politics marked by a distinct hermeneutics of suspicion regarding feminine sexuality in particular and sexual intersubjectivity in general.

All three sites are framed in the contemporary Western imaginary as largely or entirely determined by pre-political, biological forces, and as privileged sites of both human development and gender identity. Importantly, all three have vocal aspects that have been undertheorized, and thus are promising sites to deploy the concepts of intervocality and envoicing to illuminate the shaping and disciplining of individual voices, how that disciplining is persistently grounded in particular social and political contexts, and the underexplored importance of voice in identity and subjectivity.

Envoicing Before Birth

Before we engage with questions of voice and pregnancy, an explanation of our terminology is in order. Throughout this discussion, we will refer to the "maternal" and "laboring" body as the gestating body that releases a human infant into the world, and the social figure who accomplishes these tasks as the "mother" (or, occasionally, "gestating parent"). As not all maternal bodies or mothers identify as women, we will refrain from exclusive use of feminine pronouns for this figure. Of course, within the dominant Western social imaginary, the figure of the pregnant body is relentlessly feminized, and the lived experience of pregnancy is profoundly influenced by how that society conceptualizes, controls, and organizes bodies of all genders. Transmen and nonbinary people undergoing pregnancy and childbirth will thus experience social dynamics that sometimes overlap and sometimes diverge from those experienced by cisgender women. While our terminology resists the culturally dominant idea that only women experience childbirth, it matters that contemporary social constructions take the femininity of childbirth for granted.

Well before a baby releases their first cry, practices babbling, or utters their first word, they are steeped in an in utero environment of material becoming, as their development and growth proceed at a rate unparalleled in their lifetime. From the earliest cell division of the blastocyst to the moment of introducing air into the lungs, the growing human participates in a forging and shaping of being that relates to and relies entirely on the environment of the maternal body, which is itself marked by the food ingested and air inhaled, the sounds the body has generated, the bodily movements undertaken and their frequency, the quality of care received, and the surrounding cultural understandings of maternity and fetushood. The fetus' development is contingent upon all of these factors, beyond and including the influence of biological and genetic material, and sets the stage for a lifelong process of collaboratively becoming who they are, shaped by how they are spoken to, understood, and cared for, in concert with an emerging and expanding set of desires and needs about their participation in their social worlds. We suggest that their voices, as ongoing embodiments of desires, relationship, and the expression of self, are equally emergent. The practice of both doing voice, as well as of *learning* voice, begin in many profoundly significant ways in utero, and we will here attempt to give an overview of the relevant milestones of relational envoicing through birth and beyond.

As described in Chapter 1, the learning and doing of voice require the development and activation of whole-body systems: auditory, physioneurological, respiratory, and others. One of the first milestones in this effort is between gestational weeks 4–5, during which time cells in the embryo start to organize into ears, eyes, face, nose, and brain; by week 9, indentations (or "earbuds") where ears will appear begin to emerge (interestingly, well before eyes and other sense organs). By week 18, the fetus will typically hear sound, and by approximately week 26, they may begin to respond to noises, including the gestating parent's beating heart, breathing, digestion, and even the sound of blood moving through the umbilical cord. At this point, the fetus may also hear the voice of the mother, and by the third trimester, might recognize it, sometimes responding with an increased heart rate that indicates increased alertness when the mother is speaking. Recordings taken in the womb have shown that noises (including voices) from outside the maternal body are muted by about half, due to the subduing, muffling effect of amniotic fluid (see Timmons 2018 for details on these stages). One study indicates that despite the immaturity of newly formed auditory pathways, the auditory cortex in the brain of a growing fetus is more "adaptive to maternal sounds" (such as the voice and heartbeat of the gestating parent) "than environmental noise" (Webb et al. 2015: 3152). In addition to findings that show that the innate preference for the mother's voice in particular shapes the developmental trajectory of the brain (DeCasper 1980), it has also been shown that their voice plays a special role in the shaping of auditory and language areas specifically, as well as those involved in processing emotions (Webb et al. 2015). In short, the baby's capacities to hear, to feel, and to speak are developed neurologically and biologically in relationship to another's (the mother's) sounding, speaking voice. The biological here is not primary to or predictive of inevitable behavior, capacities, and identities, but is rather shaped and influenced at the very outset by the mother's own sociolinguistic and vocal qualities and patterns.

Not only will a growing fetus give more attention to maternal sounds over external environmental sounds; they will develop a preference to the maternal voice over other voices, recognizing its particular qualities and prosodic features (rhythm, melody, stress) (Kisilevsky et al. 2009). The mother's verbal rhythms and melodies are key in the shaping of the basic building blocks of language acquisition, and these rhythms and melodies are choreosonic; the movements that accompany sound production change the felt experience of the in utero soundscape (O'Brien 2013 and Vihman 1996). In this way, the gestural aspects of signed language used by Deaf mothers would no doubt also influence language acquisition for the developing fetus.

The awareness of difference between the mother's voice and native language from those of another speaker could "predispose the infant to orienting to the mother and the native language following birth which would facilitate both attachment and language learning" (Kisilevsky et al. 2009: 69). Another study showed that visual recognition of the mother's face seems to "depend on prenatal exposure to her voice" (69). There is evidence that infants keyed into prosodic features of their native language long before their own speech-like babbling sounds are uttered or first words are produced, and one study (Mampe et al. 2009) shows that babies' vocal cries are shaped and influenced by melodic contours of their mother's native tongue.

In these important ways, the unborn child is learning acoustically to recognize the sounds and sight of the mother (implying that we do indeed hear shapes and surfaces in sound, as Ihde [2007] noted), and to reflect those sounds in their own voices, so that a relationship, a common language, and indeed an identity may be established. On a neurological level, the child is becoming a specialist in recognizing and communicating with the mother, leaning away from any sort of universal field untouched by the effects of socialization and radically toward specificity, bonding, and social relationship.

Gestation is often constructed in the dominant Western social imaginary as a pre-political, biologically determined process undertaken by the fetus within a passive gestational body. In fact, the in utero gestational period is arguably the life period most shaped by relationship and most influenced by environment. Evidence that babies are born with the capacity to learn any language (Kuhl 2004: 832) is consistent with the claim that they are also deeply occupied with specializing in the mother's native tongue; indeed, an infant's ability to distinguish between all 800 or so possible units of human language sounds (phonemes) arises precisely through exposure to a specific language or languages (832). Babies are able to hear across phonetic difference, are interested in distinguishing language sounds, and are particularly keen to understand the vocal patterns and languages in which they are immersed.

In addition to cultivating a recognition of the maternal voice, the unborn child prepares to use their own voices after birth: they are busy practicing, rehearsing the ways in which they may communicate (and therefore thrive) amongst their people generally, and with their mother specifically. At around 10 weeks, the developing fetus will practice breathing by inhaling small amounts of amniotic fluid (more like a swallowing movement [Watson 2017]), and in the third trimester, they will practice "breath-like" movements involving contraction and expansion of the lungs. Research also shows that babies will attempt to cry in the womb, as early as the 28th gestational week: "an initial exhalation movement associated with mouth opening and tongue depression, followed by a series of three augmented breaths, the last breath ending in an inspiratory pause followed by an expiration and settling" (Gingras et al. 2005: 415), adding a fifth state—crying—to the previously recognized fetal states of quiet sleep, active awake, active sleep, and quiet awake (415). Fetuses may also practice communicating pain or distress facially in the absence of experienced pain, with their grimaces reflecting a maturing brain rather than the expression of an actual feeling (O'Donnell et al. 2017). The communication of a wide range of feelings, states, and needs are rehearsed by the unborn child in advance of any content to be communicated, challenging the assumption that vocality (crying, screaming, whimpering, speaking) derives from the need to express outwardly an inner need or truth. At the very outset, vocalizations are shaped and practiced as skillful actions awaiting further development, and refined as a kind of flexible duet between child and mother, self and other, sung together in a rapidly evolving score of dynamic survival, mutually constituted by and of the body, habits, sounds, and actions of the (m)other.

This emerging vocal duet is marked by socialization, inequalities, and the surrounding politics of the body. There is a risk of characterizing the material and acoustic connection between the gestational pair, both during and after pregnancy, as existing outside the social sphere, calling to mind the myth of the "cooing, singing mother" as described and/or alluded to by French feminist philosophy (Cixous 1991 and Kristeva 1984), in which the "nourishing" voice of the mother is associated with the biological: the "mothers' milk" of language as *languelait* (Cixous 1991). Repetitive exposure to the mother's body and voice certainly shapes the child's biology, including their neural pathways, and the sheer inescapability of the maternal body and soundscape play a fundamental role in development and attachment at the earliest stages. But both bodies are simultaneously biological and cultural, and the cultural context in which a pregnant mother lives, moves, and makes sound matters deeply, as do cultural ideologies surrounding the concept of the fetus and what maternal-baby communication in utero, if practiced, might consist of.

In her ethnographic exploration of pregnancy in two non-Western cultures, Tsipy Ivry suggests that investigating pregnancy as a meaningful cultural category requires attending to the "*multiple* loci of power in which reproductive relations are played out", including those between mother and unborn child

(2010: 9, emphasis in original). Ivry takes a Foucauldian approach to her analysis, identifying how power "traverses and produces things" as part of a "productive network which runs through the whole social body" (9). Rituals and practices around family life, marriage, and parenthood enact power, just as reproductive relations are "embedded in national as well as international global politics, where the globalization of Western medicine is a typical example" (9). Though both the Japanese and Israeli practices of pregnancy and childbirth are shaped by the utilization of Western biomedical technologies such as ultrasound, Ivry argues that the meanings assigned by those who experience pregnancy in concert with those technologies varied widely. In particular, distinct cultural differences in maternal-baby communications during pregnancy stem at least partially from distinctly divergent concepts of who or what a fetus *is*, its needs, and its communicative capacities. Few of the Israeli women Ivry interviewed spoke with their "babies" on a regular basis, whilst Japanese women seemed devoted to a daily conversation with their unborn children (146). Cultural differences along the axes of voice, body, and identity are evident in different framings of identical images:

> The picture of a fetus sucking his/her thumb is common to most [birthing] guides in both Israel and Japan. The caption in one Israeli best seller reads: "Already in the womb, a fetus sucking his thumb" … The Japanese caption reads: "I wonder how mommy's breasts taste" … Significantly, the Japanese title *gives voice* to the baby. While the Israeli fetus remains a remote and abstract entity generated by biotechnology, the unborn Japanese baby "jumps out of the picture," his or her *voice already fully equipped to express* human sensations and awareness of the body within which the baby dwells. This is not an abstract body: the baby recognizes it as the mother's body. (148, emphasis ours)

Most Japanese women in Ivry's study invented and used a name for the baby, inaugurated conversation with them soon after conception, and asserted that "communication became stronger and more 'mutual' as pregnancy progressed" (146). The intention behind the communication to the babies, often consisting of conversational descriptions of the outside world, was to comfort and soothe, reflective of the active cultivation of maternal-fetal bonding known as *taikyô*, which Ivry describes as a "practical theory of communication between the mother and the unborn baby" (151). The practice of *taikyô* is supported by published guidebooks, schedules, and suggested dialogues and repertoires of physical touch (such as tapping) with the unborn child, all of which stem from the assumptions that the mother and the baby are "bonded through love" and shared experience before birth (151). As a practice that predates obstetrical ultrasound, *taikyô* reflects the belief that life may be assigned to invisible objects or beings, and that the unseen, unborn baby is already part of an "interconnected social environment" (153).

In contrast to the Japanese social context, "the Israeli fetus remains an ambiguous being throughout gestation. Only after the birth process has come to an end, and the baby has proved itself alive, healthy, and visibly separate from the mother's body, does the mother start communicating with it seriously" (147). According to one Israeli mother-to-be, she would as soon speak to an unborn fetus as to a plant, and thought that the act of speaking to a fetus was going "too far too soon" (218). A culture of tentativeness around the possibility of birth catastrophe plays a role in conceptualizing and relating to the unborn: it is common for mothers-to-be to delay fantasizing about the fetus as an emerging child until close to the birth event, and to put off buying baby supplies (bottles, baby clothes) until a date in gestation significantly later than in some other cultures, such as those of the United States and Japan (219). Some mothers referred to their fetuses using the Hebrew word "*ze*," usually applied to nonliving objects, thus conceptualizing the fetus as fundamentally ambiguous (human, but not-yet-human) and indicating a conservative approach to bonding as a protective measure against possible reproductive disaster (218–9). Cultural conceptions in Israel of "when life begins" inform a pair of distinct and vivid dualities: "life" may exist in the growing fetus, but that "life" is distinct from the category of "my child" or "the baby" which emerges only after birth, specifically after the removal of the placenta (221, 223). In addition, pregnancy itself is divided conceptually into two separate, concurrent experiential tracks: that of the growing fetus, and that of the pregnant mother, who may thus experience, interpret, and voice bodily sensations (including pain) during pregnancy as wholly distinct from the growing fetus (222), in strong contrast to the Japanese construction of pregnancy as one shared experience.

If it is indeed the case that sensory experience (including external sounds, the sonorous, rhythmic, rumbling sensations of the mother's body, and above all, the sounds of the maternal voice) help to form the neurological pathways of the fetus, shaping how they lean into attachment and develop affinities, then cultures that enact divergent kinds of maternal-fetal interactions and "conversations" will shape and mark early development and growth differently. Also, the private or public environment of the pregnant mother may provide widely varying soundscapes and conditions, and may shape the foundations of relational envoicing in substantially different ways. According to Ivry, Israeli culture encourages fertility generally, but in the name of gender equality supports women maintaining productive professional work in the public sphere during pregnancy (186); Japanese culture, on the other hand, supports productivity in the public sphere generally, but encourages women to dedicate themselves to the private domesticity of the home during pregnancy, thus keeping pregnant bodies largely out of public view (133). The ways in which Japanese and Israeli women understand the gendered assignments of motherhood has a significant impact on how they perform or push against those assignments, including vocally. Ivry explains that women in both cultures negotiate their performances between two distinct polarities: Japanese women assess and evaluate themselves along the axis of "insufficiently bonded" with the baby to "overly bonded" (168), while Israeli women locate themselves on a continuum between being a "spoiled woman" (whose new needs are not justified) and a "superwoman" (who negates her new needs and proceeds as if nothing has changed) (190). The nuanced ways in which pregnant mothers make sense of their voices and bodies shape how they manage their personal, social, or even national obligations (Jewish women in Israel are, for instance, faced with a mission to cultivate future citizenry [202]) as they align with or resist surrounding cultural expectations and norms.

In contrast to the biologically essentializing frameworks often imposed upon the gestating body—which in turn often frame the voice and vocal capacities as pre-social and pre-political—we have argued here that the gestating body is an active, sonorous environment, marked indelibly by social, environmental, material, biological, and cultural factors, all of which influence the emerging fetal capacities for generating and receiving distinctly human vocalizations. The profound influence of cultural forces does not, in our view, undermine or challenge the importance of the materiality of the voice, but rather highlights both the inseparability of materiality and politics and what Sarah LaChance Adams has described as the ambiguous intersubjectivity of pregnancy and maternity (2014). The process of becoming voiced takes place in a lively, particular soundscape (and, importantly, the process of envoicing that the gestating parent is undertaking will shape their vocalizations in critical ways, invoking new maternal sounds and vocal gestures), and so theories of voice that begin with "a cry of need" have neglected significant aspects of its generation. The envoicing that occurs in utero instigates a process of intersubjective vocal becoming that persists throughout the life of a voiced human being, and it constitutes a form of corporeal generosity which is ontologically fundamental.

Envoicing at Childbirth

Expectant mothers, in concert with their respective cultures, institutions, belief systems, social structures, and medical technologies, coproduce not only the experience of pregnancy, but the event of giving birth. These mutual participations construct meanings of the ontology of the pregnant body, and how it fits into, challenges, is supported by, and/or supports those structures. By extension, the voicings of the maternal body along the entire timeline of reproductive sexuality is of ethical concern. How does vocal sound appear in childbirth, and how is it deployed to support or limit birthing bodies and/or the intersecting structures at work in this highly charged event? How are vocalized sounds of maternal labor reflective or indicative of how women's bodies are conceptualized generally (given strong social associations of childbirth with womanhood), and are there possibilities in rethinking envoicing in the birthing room such that it resists the hegemony of dominant Western medical practices and empowers those undergoing childbirth?

In contemporary Western societies, the matter of vocalization during childbirth is enmeshed with ideologies regarding the distinction between "medicalized" and "natural" childbirth, and so there are many possible voices at play in managing labor, all with varying stakes in preserving and/or limiting choices to ensure an "ideal" birth. Though we look to discuss the dynamics at work in the vocalizations of sound in a vaginal birth, and the relationship between vocal sound and the role of pain management in labor generally, we do not necessarily assume that a vaginal birth should be "regarded as automatically [more] woman-centered with midwives portrayed as helping women—in the teeth of the white-coated male establishment—to achieve the authentic experience they supposedly really want" (Glaser 2015). We suggest, however, that the kind of birth valued by an institution, and the ways in which birth attendants understand, encourage, and/or limit maternal sounds of labor in a contraction-based birth shed light on how maternal bodies are understood, how embodied sound is conceptualized at this complex nexus point of power, knowledge, gender, medicalization, technology and culture, and, lastly, how the event of vocalization may open up pathways for more just birth experiences.

As childbirth educator Beverly Pierce details, since the introduction of the controlled breathing techniques of Fernand Lamaze in the 1950s, the preponderance of childbirth education in the West has "taught the use of breathing patterns, carried out almost silently, to help a laboring woman stay 'in control'" (1998: 41). Though some approaches to breathing in childbirth have encouraged a relaxing, diaphragmatic approach (such as the Bradley birth method), a "central tenet to childbirth education has been that breath" (either purposed to exercise control or to relax) "supports a woman's mental and emotional well-being during labor" (41). Breathing techniques, typically demonstrated without vocal sound, and meant to be practiced at home in the same way, are a staple of childbirth training. Very little is said, however, about the role of *voice* in childbirth; in fact, Pierce finds, "an implicit message was conveyed that giving voice to emotion or effort in labour was not done, was perhaps a sign of being 'out of control'. Even today, some pregnant women admit that one of their fears about labour is the way they will sound. Some birth attendants, perhaps sensitive to the hospital setting, actively discourage vocalization" (1998: 41).

A wide range of childbirth classes have been offered within the last twenty years, particularly in birth centers and private childbirth education organizations, including approaches such as Hypnobirthing, Birthing From Within, the Alexander Technique, Lamaze, Bradley, and more. Yet childbirth classes specifically focused on vocal expression, such as "toning," which emphasizes the releasing of sustained sound on the outgoing breath, have been slow to catch on (despite evidence of their success)[1] and are not yet part of the standard offerings at hospitals. Many laboring mothers spontaneously express themselves vocally, as athletes might when they exert a large effort, and for them, "teaching, encouraging or enforcing silence may be counterproductive. Release of sound may help in releasing a baby" (Pierce 2001). Suggesting that standard nonvocal breathing practices attempt to control, limit, and contain feelings, Pierce questions the value, or even the possibility, of being in control in labor, and that a "letting go" through vocal sound (risking, perhaps, the perception of being out of control) may provide more "physical and emotional release, self-listening and self-confidence, bodily vibration, increased ability to cope with pain, useful forms of focus, and positive connection with a partner" (2001).

Pierce's description of vocalizations during childbirth invites an understanding of these maternal sounds as not merely reflecting an interiority (the role to which voice is so frequently, and from our perspective, mistakenly ascribed). Instead, they need to be understood as sound-as-action. These vocalizations *accomplish*, and what they accomplish is distinct from the task of expressing emotional content. They are an active, productive part of the birthing process, and as such they transmute the form and substance of the physical experience of childbirth. The voice that labors to bring forth human life is frequently (and understandably) not engaged in linguistic acts of signification, but in muscular acts of contraction and expulsion; the urge to control that voice, to silence or stifle it, is grounded in unjustly gendered vocal politics.

How labor pain is conceptualized and regulated in a particular sociocultural context is certain to play a significant role in whether vocalizations will take place, what kinds of sounds are likely, and how the sounds of the laboring mother are interpreted and responded to. In a 2017 study of labor pain experiences in the Ghanaian health system, differences in expectations about sensations of and appropriate expressions of pain varied along various social axes, including a geographical one (Aziato et al. 2017). Though all mothers in the study perceived labor pain as normal, some from the North were instructed by family members to be quiet despite the pain, and perceived other women who screamed and/or cried in pain as weak (4). Women from the South considered themselves far more expressive about pain, willing to cry or scream, as Northern women took pride in refraining from such expression (4). Some pregnant mothers fearfully anticipated the pain of labor: "I was scared, I was told labour was painful and I really experienced it … it is really painful" (12). The particularities and perceptions of pain relief measures available (herbal preparations, analgesics, chewing gum, placebos), and the degree and quality of support from family members, particularly those who reinforced religious beliefs regarding childbirth as an institution ordained by God, were instrumental in bringing some comfort (13–16). The attitude of midwives toward the laboring mothers played a significant role in the connection between vocalized sound and their experiences of pain: some midwives saw the mothers' vocal expressions as a nuisance, some asked the mothers to keep quiet when they were complaining, and others asked the mothers to limit their noise only when screaming (16).

Ghanaian mothers were frequently encouraged to refrain from using medication to relieve pain, whereas the epidural rate in the United States has increased to over 70 percent for all childbirths (White 2018). The norms and practices of any particular hospital, including the frequency of epidural use, no doubt have an overall effect on its vocal soundscape. Midwife Camille Williams suggests that women's birth sounds are silenced and inhibited by hospital settings in the United States, including by the nearly ubiquitous epidural, indicating: "[a] discomfort with, and sometimes utter disdain for, the sounds of normal, physiologic labor in hospital culture" (Williams 2016). Williams suggests that a birthing mother's own socially conditioned inhibitions and discomfort with the "primal" sounds of the laboring voice may be amplified in a setting that "dishonors women." And yet, "when faced with the forces of labor … all the inhibitions and trappings of our social selves are peeled away as our bodies thrust and heave, vomit and grunt, cry and leak. The animal is there for everyone to see" (Diamond 1996: 58).

Williams emphasizes that when the coping mechanism of expressing through a strong release of sound is limited, judged, and restrained, it creates additional stress, thereby exacerbating the experience of the original pain (2016). One easily imagines a situation in which the laboring mother is navigating tricky vocal territory, caught between a desire to make sound to manage pain and a fear of being *misheard* in a way that could trigger unnecessary or unwanted medical interventions or a mocking, shaming, or policing response.

The racialized dynamics of childbirth make the former more likely for white women, and the latter more likely for women of color, whose pain and discomfort is consistently underestimated by medical personnel and institutions (Hoffman et al. 2018), a fact made ever more obscene by the heightened rates of both infant and maternal mortality faced by women of color (Villarosa 2018). That the increased mortality rates cannot be explained by socioeconomic or educational status has led researchers to conclude that the experience of living as a woman of color under oppressive conditions weathers the body, rendering the stresses of childbirth, both physiological and cultural, more dangerous (Villarosa 2018, Braithwaite 2019). When this embodied weathering meets the physiological challenge of childbirth in the cultural context of white supremacy, the vocalizations of laboring women of color can become the target of harmful, racist policing, as in this narrative by Tressie McMillan Cottom:

> After several days of labor pains that no one ever diagnosed, because the pain was in my butt and not my back, I could not hold off labor anymore. I was wheeled into a delivery operating room, where I slipped in and out of consciousness. At one point I awoke and screamed, "Motherfucker." The nurse told me to watch my language. I begged for an epidural. After three eternities an anesthesiologist arrived. He glared at me and said that if I wasn't quiet he would leave and I would not get any pain relief. Just as a contraction crested, the needle pierced my spine and I tried desperately to be still and quiet so he would not leave me there that way. Thirty seconds after the injection, I passed out before my head hit the pillow. (2019: 108–9)

> I spoke in the way one might expect of someone with a lot of formal education. I had health insurance. I was married. All of my status characteristics screamed "competent," but nothing could shut down what my blackness screams when I walk into the room. (116)

Racialized and gendered dynamics create tensions and contradictions between what the vocalizations of laboring mothers are doing and/or reflecting and the uptake of those vocalizations, particularly by medical personnel.

Adding to the complexity of the sonorous situation is the fact that the unselfconscious vocal sounds of productive labor may "sound like a woman having really great sex," thus rendering them alarming to those within earshot on the other side of the hospital room door, who wonder, with prudish and/or prurient interest, "What's going on in *there*?" (Williams 2016, emphasis in original). That the audible vocal connection between childbirth and sexual activity could be uncomfortable, even worrisome, in hospital settings illuminates the tension between the expectation that the primary task of the female body entails containment and pain management, and the reality that the female body might instead be experiencing pleasure, power, and release. Female sexuality in general, and female self-eroticism in particular, are called into question in the vocalizations of labor, conflating and problematizing events inscribed within a stark duality in American cultural norms: the assignment of profane to sexual pleasure, and the assignment of sacred to childbirth. The sonorous birthing body troubles containment. Bodily fluids are escaping, vocal expressions are permeating thresholds, and the realms of maternity and sexuality are revealed as problematically leaky.

Williams and Diamond point to the technologicalization of modern life and Western culture's disconnect from nature as sources of collective disdain when confronted with the "primal female function" of childbirth (Diamond 1996: 57). In so doing, however, they overlook how their framing of childbirth vocalizations as primitive reinscribes maternal experiences in a nature/culture dichotomy that perpetuates existing conceptual paradigms about the disruptive nature of women's bodies and sexuality. For those proponents of maternal capacities to sound freely in childbirth—a freedom that would necessitate training mothers-to-be on one hand to open up jaws and throats, tap into deep release, and ground themselves through sound, and training caregivers and institutions on the other to support such (and all) sound making—the goal would seem to be to normalize and integrate all sounds that come with a productive labor into hospital culture. Conceptualizing those sounds as animalistic, primal, out-of-bounds, and as a result, *outside of culture*, would seem to undermine such a goal.

The vocabulary describing laboring mother's voices tends to be confoundingly paradoxical, occupying a duality of other-than-human concepts: first, the subhuman or animalistic—*baying, howling, growling, grunting,* and so on— wherein "women sound much like a growling bear or roaring lion in labor"

(Terreri 2015). And second, the beyond-human—*indescribable, alien,* or *trance-like*—wherein some are said to "make strange guttural sounds, or otherworldly noises" (Snow 1994: 32). The vocal soundscape of birth is simultaneously base and sublime, primal and otherworldly, profane and sacred. As one childbirth educator explains, "I let her *primal* sounds wash over me, I tune into my own energy and make sure it's in alignment with the *sacred*" (Baker 2018, emphasis ours). The aptness of either the "animalistic" or "indescribable" comparison also requires scrutiny; it seems obvious on an acoustic, purely vocal level that a woman in labor holds very little sonic resemblance to an animal such as a lion or bear, whose laryngeal and resonance structures are wildly dissimilar to those of human beings (would anyone, for instance, make the reverse association by hearing the sound of a roaring lion and thinking "that sounds *just* like a mother in labor"?). More likely, any such resemblance is related to perceptions of the laboring body as ferocious, frightening, and dangerous. The ill-fitting animal metaphor contributes to characterizing the laboring voice (and event) as outside the bounds of language. It is not, however, that the voice itself defies description, but the lack of an appropriate vocabulary or conceptualization by which to name it which confounds: we simply don't have the words.

Or perhaps the words are there, but typically unassigned to feminized bodies: imagine, for example, "her voice *boomed* as she pushed." In any case, by perpetuating the primal-otherworldly paradox, those allies to laboring mothers invested in liberating maternal sounds in childbirth squarely position those sounds at the extremes, strewn at the boundaries of social acceptability. The result is an othering of maternal vocalizations and bodies, suggesting that their sounds leak past the edges of normalcy even during uncomplicated, everyday births[2] that do not pose unusual challenges to either the maternal body or the baby. Here we find ourselves at the intersection of vocal injustice and gender injustice; as we explored in the previous chapter, the trope of the wild, destabilizing feminine voice that requires the controlling, corrective authority of the patriarch to ensure social stability is a time-honored one that continues to reverberate through contemporary institutions and vocal practices. We trace the intolerance for the sounds of labor in public settings back to their *feminizing* properties, and their connection to/from a body not only perceived to be female, but perceived to be engaged in that feminine activity resistant to logos and the civilizing effects of culture (even as, and perhaps precisely because, it is the activity upon which human sociality depends, and thus reveals a dependence that must be repressed and contained). And the laboring body is not the only object of the feminizing effect. The vocalizations of the laboring mother leak into space, past closed doors, into the bodies of others (some prepared to receive the sound, some not), and in doing so reveal the permeability of both the institutional infrastructure and the embodied hearer. Such permeability is decidedly gendered in the Western imaginary, and so the laboring voice renders the hearer more *like a woman* as it touches and moves into and through others' bodies, simultaneously creating and demanding relationship, community, and a sharing of the load of the experience of childbirth in ways that disrupt and challenge the isolation of the mother as well as the regulation and containment of the feminized body.

Given that widely practiced approaches to labor focus on breath and not voice, and that the volume and strength of the laboring voice remain problematized within the medical institutions housing most of the maternal laboring that occurs in the United States, it seems somewhat paradoxical that one of the more vocally extreme models of childbirth, namely, the "silent birth" of Scientology, is regularly met with much derision. We address at some length this approach despite the fact that only a small minority of laboring mothers would engage with it directly (there are no data regarding the extent to which Scientology's recommendations are followed by its laboring adherents, who are a small minority in the United States). The demands that Scientology places on laboring mothers are interesting insofar as they instantiate a distinction between gendered notions of voice and speech that reflect and refract stereotypical Western conceptualizations rooted in ancient thought.

Contrary to popular misconceptions, the primary goal of Scientology's silent birth is to limit *speech*, not (necessarily) a mother's laboring vocal emanations:

> It is labor and delivery done in a calm and loving environment and with no spoken words by everyone attending as much as possible. Chatty doctors and nurses, shouts to "PUSH, PUSH" and loud or laughing remarks to "encourage" are the types of noises that are meant to be avoided ... Mothers naturally want to give their baby the best possible start in life and thus keep the birth as quiet as possible. (Scientology Parent, undated)

And from the Scientology founder L. Ron Hubbard: "Maintain silence in the presence of birth to save both the sanity of the mother and the child and safeguard the home to which they will go. And the maintaining of silence does not mean a volley of 'Sh's,' for those make stammerers" ([1950] 2007: 196).

Note that the prohibitions against noise are not, in fact, targeted at the laboring mother, whose vocalizations are not expressly forbidden, or even mentioned. The "point of silent birth is NO WORDS" (STAND League, undated) and the most likely utterers of words seem to be everyone except the laboring mother. Words, for Scientologists, are inordinately powerful, and the fetal brain (like that of the ill, injured, and infirm) is particularly susceptible to their long-lasting and potentially deleterious effects (Hubbard [1950] 2007). Hubbard thus shares contemporary neuroscience's recognition of the influence of the in utero soundscape (191–2), but views it primarily as a field of potential threats to the fetus's well-being and prenatal survival, with words being its most potentially damaging elements. Those who find themselves vulnerable, including the infirm, children, and expectant and laboring mothers (not surprisingly, those who inhabit the feminine sphere) should be quarantined from the verbal world for their own protection. The safe use of words (*logos*) once again becomes the province solely of those who are of healthy constitution, under good regulation, and therefore fully "conscious" with a well-operating analytical mind, namely, men. The structure of Scientology's silent birth cordons off[3] the experience of labor from vocalized language, preserving and protecting the experience under good direction for the benefit of mother and child.

Such a prohibition against vocalized language, especially given that it is represented as "silence," surely has the effect of pressuring the laboring mother to refrain from generating loud noises, and so a full, released vocal expression from the laboring mother seems unlikely. But it is nevertheless significant that the explicit target of the prohibition is language, not noise, and that the effect of the prohibition is to infantilize the laboring mother and feminize the emerging child. The structure and activity of the birth event is thus neatly aligned with structures of male authority (195), and the clearly identified, gendered spheres of influence remain distinct, protected by bodily practices that maintain demarcation lines through the artful deployment of silence. Here we see patriarchal structures oscillating between two cultures and calling to each other across time and space and vastly different degrees of societal influence: Ancient Greeks and their concern for protecting men in the city-state from the destabilizing, infectious voices of women by relegating women's soundscapes to the sphere of ritual; and Scientologists' concern for protecting women (and more urgently, their unborn children) from pernicious, damaging speech that is the domain of men by keeping women insulated in silence during childbirth.

What might a productive model for envoicing in childbirth look like—one that does not merely tolerate and certainly does not actively discourage the laboring maternal voice? What would render those environments more vocally just, and how do we take up the ethical mandates of respiratory responsibility and envoicing in ways that forward the flourishing of the laboring mother? Surely one step toward such a goal is to create environments and receiving practices that support a broader spectrum of laboring mothers' sound-making in labor. Childbirth in the United States is more likely to be undertaken from a passive, prone position, rather than a semisitting one that would stimulate the breathing musculature and vocal apparatus in a more dynamic way (Kishi et al. 2010: 62); introducing a wider range of physical positions would foster a wider range of sound. What if voice coaching (not only breathing coaching) were a regular part of birthcoach's skill set? What if hospital rooms were designed to soften and contain sound—if there is a concern about disrupting other patients—so that filling a room with (and hearing) vibrations became commonplace? Pierce suggests that creating "a vibratory 'room of one's own' promot[es] feelings of safety and protection. Labouring in an unfamiliar or unpleasant environment has been shown to increase pain perception" (1998: 45). Intervocality could be engaged with more intentionally and productively if partners, birthcoaches, and doctors developed practices to sound-with, as if (or actually) vocalizing themselves with laboring mothers to support and encourage them vocally and energetically.

A recognition of the broad possibilities of productive vocalizations in labor, ranging across a wide spectrum of volume, tones, and timbre, could ground a more fine-grained attunement to the meanings and effects of those vocalizations. Such attunement would be able to better distinguish between powerful, loud, deep vocalizations engaged in the work of labor and vocalizations that signify distress or panic that might warrant intervention. Perhaps most basically, laboring vocalizations need to be recognized as experiences and actions well within the range of human experience, and valuable especially to the extent that they are pleasurable or useful to the laboring mother; if they are misheard as animal or alien, the fault lies in the listening practices.

Supporting a wide scope of laboring vocalizations and more just listening practices would allow the sharing of the load of the strong experience of childbirth, reinscribe the process as a community event, and transform the ways in which mothers' bodies in pregnancy and beyond may be othered (placed under the intense scrutiny of the Western medical machine, say, or deemed socially unreliable in innumerable ways) into a realm of sounding in spaces that are *designed to hear them.* Transforming the sonorous environment of childbirth could also serve as a powerful reminder that the voice can serve as not only an expressive tool to convey information, but as a means of creating a shared, embodied experience, even (or perhaps especially) across acute differences of positionality. Here we see important connections to the phenomenon of communal pushing, wherein individuals who are supporting find themselves "pushing with the muscles of their pelvic floor, often with held breath and red faces" (Adams and Burcher 2014: 70). This often unconscious bodily mirroring does not constitute an erasure of the bodily distinctions between the laboring subject and those in a supporting role:

> [T]he communal push represents support without a complete loss of bodily identity. That is, the body understands it is creating a shared space in which the pushing woman feels that others are focusing with her on the task that is still ultimately hers alone. The fact that the hardest pusher is always the woman herself would lend support to communal pushing being more a *sharing* than a true *transference* or role reversal. But the sharing that occurs includes a "forgetting" of place—a *partial* loss of individuality. (76, emphasis in original)

The possibility of co-sounding with the laboring mother also does not eliminate bodily distinctions. Sound, and sounded voices, cross and deploy those differences without destroying or transcending them. Preparing spaces and receiving bodies for laboring vocalizations is a form of respiratory responsibility, a recognition of the ethical mandate to envoice the other in ways that center and forward their flourishing.

Envoicing during Sex

As mentioned briefly above, the ethical and political meanings associated with vocalizations generated during childbirth are implicated with those associated with vocalizations generated during sexual interactions, particularly those generated by female-identified bodies. The previous chapter described the close association drawn by Greek thinkers between the two sets of lips that mark the biologically defined female body, an association used to defend the patriarchal need and right to control both. For now, it suffices to note that both childbirth and common forms of sexual interaction are sites where the neuromuscular connections between the throat and the pelvis (Keich 2016) can be and frequently are engaged. Although the sonorous similarities between laboring and sexual vocalizations can frame the former as illicit, troubling, and an appropriate target for silencing, insisting on a radical difference between the two does not forward vocal justice. Instead, dismantling systems of vocal injustice that imbue sexual vocalizations, particularly those generated by recognizably female or feminine bodies, with negative meanings (shame, sluttiness, a demeaning lack of physical control) is warranted.

Almost all of the empirical data regarding sexuality and vocalizations focus on questions of sexual attraction and voice (see, for example, Hughes et al. 2004 and Puts 2005), and the vast majority of that research centers on heterosexual identities and relationships, with little or no recognition of queer sexualities or the ways that other identity markers such as ability or race influence the vocal elements of sexual attraction (the evolutionary bent of much of the research is a serious limitation along these lines). Empirical data on the vocal elements of sexual experiences and interactions are far rarer and just as resolutely heterocentric (Levin 2006, Passie et al. 2003, Izdebski 2008). Feminist theorists of voice have left the topic unaddressed as well: Cavarero (2005), for instance, is surprisingly quiet about it, and Dunn and Jones's collection (1994b) has a section on maternal voices, but no mention of sexual voices. The absence is, perhaps, not surprising within the context of a somatophobic culture where sexuality is a site of intense shame and where nuanced understandings of either sexual ethics or biological aspects of sexual interactions are undervalued by dominant knowledge and power systems. And if, as we noted in our first chapter, the soundedness of voice has often been placed in opposition to the social and linguistic order, then vocalizations during sex, which are seemingly involuntary and may or may not deploy language, can appear as threateningly disordered. Hiding the shameful sounds of sex is central to the social mandate to keep one's sexual interactions private: ensuring that other people (roommates, family members, neighbors on the other side of the wall, carceral authorities, children, and so on) do not hear the sounds of sex is a common concern for sexual subjects. Alternatively, sexual subjects can delight in the way that the sounds of sex permeate surfaces and other bodies, bringing them into the sexual interaction vicariously, either consensually or not.

Sexual vocalizations can, as in the study that we discuss at length below, be taken as evidence of particular sexual sensation or experience, thus preserving the common (but, as we have argued throughout this work, misguided) understanding of voice as only a more or less neutral medium by which an internal reality or thought is externalized. A more phenomenologically astute understanding, however, highlights the ways in which releasing and receiving vocalizations can intensify, precipitate, and even squash sexual sensations and experiences. The degree and conditions under which they do so are resolutely political, even as they may also be highly individualized. Not unlike the vocalizations that occur in the context of childbirth, whether one's sexual vocalizations can produce or intensify interior and exterior bodily actions and sensations relies heavily on bodily self-knowledge and self-awareness, a general comfort with experiencing sexual sensations, and perhaps even a familiarity with and trust in the wide range of one's own vocal possibilities. Sexually repressive cultures will strive to keep such subjective capacities in short shrift, often along traditional gender lines.

Yet even in repressive, sex-negative, somatophobic cultural contexts—in fact, especially in such contexts—the fate of sexuality and transgression are so intertwined that reversal of vocal gender norms can sometimes become social mandates. Hegemonic heterosexuality offers a familiar double-bind for female-identified sexual partners of men, whose enthusiastic vocalizations during sex can be both desired and troubling, evidence of her appeal as a sexual partner and worrisome in her abandonment of appropriately feminine restraint: the contrast itself is titillating. Unsurprisingly, the sexual vocalizations of male-identified subjects under similar conditions are not beholden to such impossible demands for simultaneous gender obedience and transgression. This is not to say that they are free from any gendered social demands, as their vocalizations must remain manly, preferably avoiding high registers. But they are not compelled to transgress typical masculine vocal norms in ways that trouble the coherence of their gender identity. Instead, their sexual vocalizations, even and especially as they abandon the demands for, say, linguistic order, or limitation in range, establish ever more firmly the solidity of their masculine identity, especially insofar as they extend and deepen the right of the masculine voice to take up space.

Dominant politics of the sexual voice, then, are significantly enmeshed with the politics of gender identity and gender inequality. What would it mean to reorient the meanings of sexual vocalizations in a similar way to what we recommend above regarding the meanings of the laboring maternal voice? That is, what if sexual vocalizations were constructed not as markers of more or less successful alignment with gender norms, but as one of the many embodied modalities of sexuality that a sexual subject could explore, try out, and learn to deploy in order to heighten or broaden one's sexual experiences? Rather than asking what the sexual voice says about the sexual subject, we need to explore what the sexual voice can do, what intercorporeal sensations it can produce and enhance, and how cultural approaches to sexuality (including sex education) can contribute to sexual flourishing by broadening sexual vocal possibilities. Political structures of hegemonic heterosexuality are unlikely to be of much use here; queer and sex-positive frameworks will hold more promise, not because they are politically neutral or ethically untainted by structures of inequality, but because their well-honed critiques of established sexual norms and practices, as well as their insistence on the value of sexual pleasure, encourage the proliferation of new sexual possibilities.

Expanding the vocal possibilities of and within sexual interactions to forward sexual flourishing—that is, envoicing sexual subjects in new and positive ways—is an important element of vocal justice. Developing careful ways of studying and interpreting sexual vocalizations is also crucial, as political assumptions about gender and sexuality can frame the results of research in problematic ways. In one of the relatively few studies on the topic, vocalizations of heterosexual women during sex were found not to occur during the experience of female orgasm, but rather were more likely to be concurrent with male ejaculation (Brewer and Hendrie 2011). The authors of the study concluded that the evidence showed that vocalization were therefore under "conscious control" by the women, "providing women with an opportunity to manipulate male behavior to their advantage" (559); indeed, given the dearth of research on sexual vocalizations, it's even more striking that a significant portion of it centers around the question of whether heterosexual women's vocalizations are reliable indicators of whether an orgasm has actually happened or whether the woman is faking it (Izdebski 2008).

The interpretation of heterosexual women's vocalizations during sex as manipulative align well with multiple intersecting patriarchal assumptions about both voice and gender. Note first that the interpretation rests on a strict dichotomy between orgasm and conscious control, such that any behavior that accompanies orgasm is assumed to be instinctual, uncontrolled, and uncontrollable. This opposition is then paired with an additional, parallel one: that any behavior that accompanies or is in response to the behavior of another is assumed to be intentional, controlled, and controllable. Underlying these two parallel oppositions are a strict mind/body dualism (which allows for an understanding of specific bodily behaviors as either under or free from the mental, self-conscious control of the thinking subject) and a strict self/other dualism, with an implication that only self-generated impulses can be properly termed as unconscious or instinctual (the externality of the other is taken as evidence that responding to the other must be a matter of conscious control). Both dualisms, of course, are contrary to the philosophical commitments underlying the analysis we're developing here, and thus are cause for suspicion.

But perhaps even more fundamental to the notion that heterosexual women's sexual vocalizations are manipulative because they don't accompany a first-hand experience of orgasm is the familiar and contradictory set of associations ascribed to female heterosexuality in a social environment structured by gender inequality. As decades of feminist psychoanalytic theory have demonstrated, the sexual desires, proclivities, and behavior of heterosexual women are socially constructed as untrustworthy, destabilizing, excessive, immoral, and polluting; just as importantly, they are fakable, and thus are the site of feminine trickery and the victimization of the hapless but always authentically sexual heterosexual male.

Sexual vocalizations are embroiled in these sexual politics. The casting of the sexual vocalizations of heterosexual women as manipulation rests on the assumption that the proper use of vocalization in sexual interactions is as a by-product of an inner feeling, an externalization of what is occurring in the (assumedly self-contained) body of the sexual subject. The feminine sexual subject whose orgasms can frequently be confirmed only by means of vocalization is under particular pressure to demonstrate sexual authenticity and enthusiasm, especially in a phallocentric culture plagued in equal measure by two dichotomous possibilities: that she enjoys sexual interactions or that she doesn't. Empirical evidence that indicates that those vocalizations are not in fact reliable signifiers of female orgasm shores up the image of the heterosexual woman who instrumentalizes male heterosexuality for other (assumedly nefarious) ends.

There is, of course, another story to be told about such vocalizations. If sexual interactions are understood as more robustly intersubjective, such that the sensations and experiences of one's sexual partner are understood as co-constituting one's own sensations and experiences, then vocalizations associated with the other's orgasm no longer appear as questionable or even remarkable. Such a model of sexual intersubjectivity frames sexual interactions not as a meeting of two completely self-contained subjects, each with a preexisting set of fixed desires, preferences, and so on, but rather as opportunities for sexual co-construction (Cahill 2010: 157). It also breaks down the seeming duality between the sexual pleasure of the partners, illuminating how what one's partner is feeling and experiencing can be part of one's own erotic pleasure. From this perspective, the sexual vocalizations of heterosexual women described in Brewer and Hendrie's research are not necessarily manipulative, or any more self-conscious than any other sexual vocalizations. Instead, they can be both expressions and causes of intimacy, of being-with, of a pleasurable and erotic delight in the bodily experiences of another that heightens the sexual sensations for all involved.

The feminine body's expression of desire through vocalization during sexual interactions can be considered a vocal good that—as Kate Manne (2018) might say—a woman as "human giver" would be expected to perform in a heteronormative economy. This vocal production of pleasure may serve the purpose of expressing to her partner that he is giving her pleasure, and the vocalization is a form of gendered work, in that it is the expression of admiration and/or appreciation of his sexual prowess or virility. This vocal work may be subject to policing, held in suspicion (as reflected by the very fact of a study such Brewer and Hendrie's) that, when unmasked as a performance, can warrant revenge for having "faked it" and thereby "emasculating" or dehumanizing him: this is the moment when misogyny kicks in. Nevertheless, even the more sexist read of heterosexual women's vocalizations during sex—that they are manipulative, and likely false, and not reliable indicators of female orgasm—belies the intersubjectivity of sexuality that grounds certain common strains of male heterosexual resentment. That is, the coherence of such a narrative rests on the recognition that, even in the context of hegemonic heterosexuality, male sexual pleasure is often intensified, and in some cases, made possible, by evidence of female sexual pleasure. If that weren't the case, how would one explain how the manipulative deception of the sexual woman actually worked? Yet such a state of affairs reveals a troubling state of dependency for the hegemonically heterosexual male, whose identity (again, within a patriarchal social context) relies on being both superior to and independent of the other(ed) gender. The suspicion with which feminine heterosexuality is met is but a deflected unease with the contingency of masculine heterosexuality, which (paradoxically) prides itself on its indifference to feminine sexual experience.

Our discussion of sexual vocalization, like the empirical data with which we have engaged, has remained centered on hegemonically heterosexual experiences and frameworks, which represent, of course, only a subset of human sexual behavior. What might the queering of sexual vocalizations look like, and how might transgressive departures from dominant gender and sexual norms create new possibilities for envoicing sexual subjects? Sounding sex differently not only holds the promise of new and heightened sexual sensations, but of transformed sexual subjectivities and new existential modalities of sexual being. Developing such alternatives, however, will require further research and thought from a wide scope of disciplinary perspectives.

Conclusion

While feminist thinkers have long criticized the social phenomena surrounding pregnancy, childbirth, and sex for the ways in which they are structured along the lines of gender inequality, the sonorous aspects of these phenomena have not received sufficient attention. In this chapter, we have demonstrated how flawed and unjust assumptions about gender, human ontology, voice, and sound have resulted in deeply rooted, harmful social practices. Across all of these sites, each of which is saturated with multiple social meanings, voice does not serve as a mere channel through which meaning or intention pass unchanged. That is, the work of the sounded voice cannot be reduced to merely exteriorizing that which is interior, with varying degrees of accuracy and authenticity. Rather, the sounded voice accomplishes (or helps to accomplish) specific tasks, including the construction of fetal aural and oral capacities, the expulsion of a living human being from the maternal body, and the heightening of sexual pleasure. Moreover, as we have sought to argue throughout this book, the capacities of the sounded voice, as well as the meanings assigned to it, are the results of social relationships: a collective rather than individual responsibility. Recognizing the ineluctably intersubjective nature of human vocality, as it turns out, is a crucial tool in challenging Western social practices that seek to control and contain bodies that are all too persistently identified with the feminine: bodies that gestate, bodies that produce infants, bodies whose orgasms do not accompany the release of semen. Creating more and better ways for these bodies to sound their experiences, in relationships, communities, and spaces that are ready to receive them, is a worthy ethical goal.

6

Ethical Spotlight: Envoicing in
Voice Pedagogy

This is the first of two single-authored chapters, wherein each coauthor addresses some of the ways in which the ideas of intervocality, the ethics of envoicing, vocal justice, and others developed in earlier chapters might be taken up in our different fields. Here, Hamel takes up the sometimes fraught but also promising relationship between ethical theory and the practice of vocal pedagogy.

Theory Matters

The long-standing rivalry between philosophy and art in the Western tradition has resulted in a particular ongoing tension in the arena of the voice, causing theorists and practitioners of voice to struggle to establish common ground. Though many voice trainers make their homes in academia, there has been an historical resistance to allowing the academy to "hold a monopoly on the intellect" (Berry et al. 1997: 52). The highly specialized nature of theatrical voice training is such that insights provided by various fields (physiology, dramaturgy, neuroscience, etc.) are taken up somatically in what amounts to disciplinary alchemy: those forms, in practice, become greater than the sum of their parts. This alchemy is in many ways at odds with and perhaps mystifying to dominant academic epistemologies. Philosophers—even those writing about voice and/or the importance of the body in the construction of thought—rarely bring to their work the diversity and depth of embodied experiences that voice practitioners value and develop, privileging instead the written word and conceptual analysis. Voice pedagogy's historical anti-academic bias in the field, privileging embodied practice over purely theoretical considerations, frequently casts those concerns in an impenetrable, irrelevant, or impractical light.

The Santorini Voice Symposium (McCance 2011), organized in 2009 to bridge this gap between theory and praxis, aptly took place on a volcanic island in Greece, the birthplace of Western theatre and philosophy, as it brought philosophers and actors/voice professionals together simply to "see what happens" through the lens of Linklater's voice work (Krell 2011: 92). This week-long experiment brought up questions that might surface only when philosophers have an opportunity to comingle with performing artists, such as "Why do we elevate knowledge of the intellect above intuition, images, fantasy, and bodily intelligence?" and also, "Why do we do the reverse?" (Bernhard 2011: 80). Reflections on this shared time (McCance 2011) provide a window into the depth and complexity of transformations that might be possible with even more sustained engagement between the disciplines: one philosopher reported connecting more deeply with their emotions and feeling a greater sense of connection with others while sharing theoretical work, one actor/teacher suggested a renewal of confidence in their own intellectual capacities, and new modalities of listening and speaking were explored for artists and philosophers alike. These experiences also registered as vulnerable, new, and not without resistance to historical ways of thinking and being, and though the experiment seemed promising in opening up important questions about the voice, it was, in the words of one philosopher, "unrepeatable" (Painter-Morland 2011: 160), and many questions about a sustained relationship between these fields linger.

Voice pedagogues have argued, with no small amount of impatience, that critiques of the "natural/free"[1] approaches to voice training (Werner 1996, Eidsheim 2015, Schlichter 2014) demonstrate the theorist's lack of personal experience with the somatic aspects of those pedagogies as well as a lack of understanding of the nuanced differences between them (Boston 1997: 248). The work of theorists who seem to engage only superficially with nuanced pedagogies, or who base their evaluations of it primarily on the published texts intended either to support the practical work or to serve merely as less-than-ideal substitutes for experiential training with a highly trained teacher, is easily dismissed. Berry, Linklater, and Rodenburg's collective public response (Berry et al. 1997) to Sarah Werner's feminist critique of natural voice pedagogies (1996) is evidence of this intolerance: they were not inclined to take her analysis seriously, as Werner's own embodied understanding of voice work and her experience with working with the voices of actors read to them as less than satisfactorily thorough.

The aim of this chapter is primarily to cut through the static between these disciplines, and to urge the voice practitioner to think carefully about how to mine the tools that philosophy has to offer in order to grow our discipline in more equitable and sustainable ways. I hope to demonstrate that theorists' lack of experience does not render their insights moot, and that immersion in the practice does not constitute a sufficient counterargument to some of the more challenging theoretical critiques. To the contrary: theoretical challenges, when taken up carefully and in good faith by expert practitioners, can generate new practices even better suited to the ethical challenges of our time.

Cultural critic Henry Giroux emphasizes the importance of not only understanding the mechanics of a practice of teaching per se, but the importance of questioning through theoretical investigation the presuppositions (many of which we may not yet be aware of) that inform the work (Yousman et al. 2006). Many voice trainers feel confident that because we are in the trenches and have experienced viscerally how "the work *works*"—whatever the particular approach—we know that the work is essentially and reliably liberating. However, the ethical mandate to consider our practice from a theoretical point of view asks us to deliver the wisdom of pragmatism over to a deeper understanding of the latent traditions and ideological assumptions baked into our practices. In addition, to examine these implicit ideologies in our craft through engaging with theory, and as a result to recontextualize current teaching practices in more philosophically and ethically clear ways, does not necessarily preclude retaining essential and liberatory aspects of practical voice training.

It was through my own ethical impasse regarding the problems I believe to be inherent in the "deculturalization" of voice that can emerge from a "natural/ free"[2] approach to voice work—an impasse that shook my confidence that I was working with the most fitting set of pedagogical tools for anti-oppression practices—that prompted the philosophical investigations which are the foundation of this coauthored book. I was fortunate to have been able to enter into a sustained cross-disciplinary investigation with a feminist philosopher of the body to address this struggle in a detailed way. And so this chapter aims to highlight the ways that our ongoing considerations of voice, vocal injustice, and the ethics of envoicing may be directly applied to voice training for the actor. I wish to continue to open up a meaningful conversation about the philosophical foundations and underlying assumptions of "natural/free" voice pedagogy, and about the need to forge necessary connections between theory and practice.

Considerable attention is now being given to the challenges of speech training for the contemporary actor, including an ongoing critique of "standard speech" pedagogy, culturally exclusive accent-dialect training, and speech practices associated with privilege, dominance, and colonialism in many forms (Knight 1997, Brown 2000, Colaianni 2011, Ginther 2015, Oram 2019, 2020a, Coronel et al. 2020, and more). Contemporary voice training alone, however, has not received such close attention, and there is still work to be done to contextualize voice training methods along the lines of anti-oppression frameworks. In so doing, we can trace an evolution of voice pedagogy from *exclusionary* approaches of the mid-twentieth century (such as those privileging the "voice beautiful" to maintain an aesthetic status quo), giving way to *neutrality* approaches (including the democratic "natural/free" approaches of Linklater, Berry, and Rodenburg emphasizing individual autonomy and the capacity for self-liberation), giving way again to *multicultural* and *culturally sensitive* approaches (such as McAllister-Viel 2019), which highlight an appreciation of human sound across cultures and value a (re)centering around the distinct worldviews that they can provide, to, lastly, an emerging *anti-oppression* approach to voice (including Oram 2020b) acknowledging the presence of systemic, cultural, and institutional barriers and inequalities based on race, gender, and other socially constructed identity markers. What might this next evolution in vocal training look like, then? What would it mean to retain the many advances made by diverse and valued practical approaches to voice for actors including their emphasis on the materiality of the embodied voice, the recognition of its existential and indeed political importance, and the possibility of vocal transformation that enhances one's sense of self, sense of presence, and ability to communicate with others? And what would it mean to do so while simultaneously bringing to bear an emphasis on intervocality, respiratory responsibility, and a deepened understanding of the role of systemic injustice in the construction of identity in one's voice?

Intervocality and Pedagogical Cultures

To be a voiced human being is to be ineluctably enmeshed in complex systems of intervocality that shape particular voices, specific modes of receiving voices, and the air of specific social spaces. And so an actor in a training environment looking to develop their voice and body to be more "fit" for performance is produced as a voicing body shaped and received by a complex system of practices steeped in multiple histories, traditions, and values. These vocal practices show up in a variety of ways in training spaces: in the voices that are sounded in the room, in the voice of the teacher(s), in the principles articulated through the exercises, in the sounds a group may produce, and in the imaginative realm, including the kinds of performances, qualities, characteristics, and ways of being that are valued by practitioners in the field. Meaning created in envoicing is co-constituted in relationship, and those relationships are instructional, environmental, social, cultural, political, and material.

Training spaces place value on furthering fitness for the art form which, for actors, may include "good acting" (however defined) as well as personal and social transformation through artistic practice. Approaches to voice training contribute to such goals in many ways: releasing tension, building psychophysical awareness, honing mind-muscle attunement, removing blocks (physical, psychological, emotional), developing dexterities, and many more. *Desire* is present to move toward what is deemed valuable in the training, the expressive embodiment of material, and so on. This desire is not constituted autonomously: it happens in multidirectional relationships between instructor and student, student and institution(s), students and each other, students and society, and more. It's also constituted in relationships among instructors, and in the ways instructors take up students' desires as their own.

Desire reveals the ongoing, emerging values of students (and teachers) in embodied ways: it shows up as behavior, language, affect, dress, gestures, as well in vocal patterns, timbres, rhythms, and so on. Simply put, we engage in emulation in settings where desire for vocal and bodily transformations take place, and actors, who study behaviors, movements, and vocal patterns of other people, are as likely as anybody to pick up on ways of being of the people they seek to be "more like." Anyone who has suddenly found themselves empathetically taking up the harmonic resonances of a character on television or the dialect of a person with whom they are conversing can relate to the fluidity and empathy of one's vocal ways of being. Mimicry (conscious or unconscious) is at the heart of learning voice at the start (see Chapters 4 and 5), and mirroring back the vocal habits of others in the co-constitutive practices of envoicing in the studio is highly likely when the task at hand is indeed training one's voice, and particularly when the personal stakes (and tuition) are very high. An actor's ability to consciously take up human behaviors, to become transformational, is usually one desired effect of training. But the possibility that we are taking up and reflecting back various social prompts, sounds, and vocal qualities *all the time*—unconsciously as well as consciously—is worthy of consideration in spaces that often attempt to create a politically neutral atmosphere. Vocal cultures emerge out of emulation, and affinities toward embodiments occupying positions of power, however constituted (e.g., a teacher or an artistic role model), emerge out of a desire to move toward valued goals. That the magnetic pull of emulation takes place in a wider context privileging a dominant and sonorous "somatic norm"[3] is a topic I will return to shortly.

That unconscious emulative vocal practices show up in voices being trained in a pedagogy (such as Linklater voice) specifically designed not to prescribe a standard, norm, or end-resultant sound, but rather to retrain the mind-body-voice connection via causal thinking, indicates that there is simply more at work in the interaction of training than meets the ear. I'll offer a personal anecdote. I studied with my first singing teacher, Maria, from age 12 to 18 or so; the nature of her classical training was very technical, based on principles of *bel canto* technique and the vocal health approaches of David Blair McClosky (among others, no doubt). I recall that her approach was practical, physical, anatomical, and it asked me to pay more attention to feeling than to listening to my own sound. I loved studying with her; my singing improved; I did (and do) look up to her. Years later, in my mid-twenties, I was a graduate student in voice performance and took a sample lesson from a teacher, who, unbeknownst to me, knew Maria well. He heard me sing (scales, I think) and turned to me and said "Wait: you studied with Maria, didn't you?" I (proudly) thought he had responded to something in my embodiment of her healthy technique. He then said, "it's not your technique … it's something in your sound itself, in your 'overtones.' I hear *her.*" That I had picked up on the vocal timbre of my first and beloved teacher is not, in retrospect, surprising. That any teacher of voice– perhaps themselves trained in one of the master teacher/trainee mentorship models–may also emulate and embody values of their own teacher (even when working in a pedagogy more concerned with use than resultant sound) would also not be terribly surprising.

However, the fact that a culture of vocal values emerges based on the pedagogues' embodied behaviors (what Bourdieu [1984] calls *habitus*), and that those values take place in a social, economic, and political context, requires an *anti-oppression* approach to voice. Eidsheim rightly suggests that "structures of power are funneled into sound ideals" (2015: 144). On the level of vocal embodiment, it matters, then, who teaches, and what (and who) they care about, who is in their lives, who their own role models are, what their tastes are, and so on. That most voice teachers in my own training background (Linklater voice) are white middle-class ciswomen, that the senior teachers who mentor trainees are typically 50+ in age, that most certified teachers of this pedagogy have had the economic means to become designated teachers either privately or through tuition-based higher degree programs (both paths require a $20k or more investment[4]) speaks to a general picture of values, standards, tastes, and ideals. This is not to imply that no diversity exists within this group; but because many of the teachers in this group come from privileged demographics, their values are likely to converge as the dominant values of the pedagogical culture. These values have material implications for the ways in which their students will take up embodiment and vocal ways of being in the world.

The socially constructed space of actor training is produced by a complex intersecting network of cultural "fields" (Bourdieu 1993) beyond (and including) the pedagogical. In my own training program at Boston University, for instance, the field of "BFA in acting" is part of the "School of Theatre," which is one of three arts schools constituting the "College of Fine Arts," which is one of the many colleges in "Boston University," itself part of a network and culture of Boston, R1 universities, and so on. There are other social fields at work: affinity groups and clubs, religious groups, family, friends, social media, the list goes on and on. The values present (and repeated through ritual and behaviors) in each and every one of these fields play a role in the performed *habitus* of a student in the studio. Even the modern standard of "the empty space" (Brook 1968) is taken up by practitioners in ritualized and repeated embodiments. Similarly, "working from neutral" is not the absence of bodily comportments and behaviors, but a positive field itself, replete with values (symmetry, ease, simplicity, etc.).

The pull toward a dominant embodied norm for the student who is training in *somatic ways* is powerful, and preprofessional theatre programs feel the pull of current normative practices in the profession. The profession—the American theatre industrial complex (to use a term put into circulation by Nicole Brewer [Cox 2020]) in particular—is one which, despite recent strides toward centering marginalized voices, is still dominated by normatively white masculine bodies. Despite significant recent leadership changes in professional theatres in the United States, a majority of positions "at the top" continue to be occupied by white cis men (Tran et al. 2019), and the progress of diversity in leadership diminishes the larger (and more prestigious) the companies get. The dominant somatic/vocal norms on Broadway and off-Broadway, regional theatre, and Hollywood, in which white cismale actors, directors, and writers continue to dominate by a wide margin (Henry et al. 2019, AAPAC 2020, Jordan 2018, and Annenberg Inclusion Initiative 2020), are reflected and refracted in various ways within the walls of training environments, and thus play important roles in students' lives and professional development. Likewise, somatic norms within the institution of academia—who the students are, who teaches, who administrates, who the support staff is, who presides (and in theatre programs, who stage directs, who coaches, who teaches acting, "skills-based" work, dramatic criticism, etc.)—significantly *matters*.

Bodies outside of dominant norms inhabit these spaces differently than those who may more easily accomplish an uncomplicated "fit," what Bourdieu refers to as a "feel for the game" (1977). Dominant bodies and voices can occupy academic training environments with a feeling of ease, as a "fish in water" (Puwar 2004: 127), in ways that are profoundly different from those who are "somatically othered" (Oram 2019: 283), despite their membership in many cases with a global racial/ethnic majority. That is, not all bodies will feel equally at ease in their training, secure and safe, free from the threat of mosquito bites of microaggressions and sucker punches of macroaggressions alike. A body readying for those aggressions inhabits a room differently than a body wholly sure that none is in the offing, requiring those bodies that do not easily fit into certain norms to perform a kind of "ontological labor" (Kim et al. 2020) in the management of one's identity and/or body. This body management comes at a cost in many ways, including siphoning off valuable energy and increasing physical tension. Given that ease and relaxation are foundational components to many approaches to voice training, particularly "natural/free" voice approaches, the playing field for the "game of training" cannot be, and indeed is not, even. Nondominant bodies occupy spaces that have traditionally taken up the white male body as the norm as if "fish out of water" (Puwar 2004: 127): fish who struggle, quite literally, to find access to breath. In this way, there is respiratory responsibility required in training environments to understand the ways in which access to a "sigh of relief," that is, ease of breath, is not to be taken as an equitable given. Puwar additionally suggests that nondominant bodies feel the "weight of the water" (127); there is growing evidence of the ways that systemic and institutional oppression not only signifies certain bodies as othered, but has physical and material impact: it is a direct source of trauma.

The trap in discussing the embodied impacts and, indeed, trauma of systemic injustice is that it sounds a lot like the now conventional notion in "natural/free" voice training that the effects of socialization accrue in the body as blocks, tensions, held energies, and so on that should be identified and then released. The mythology (and asymmetry) in this thinking reveals that bodies aligning with the dominant somatic norm are positioned to be perceived as less blocked, and therefore less caught up in in the effects of socialization generally (which, we have argued, cannot be the case, as we are caught up in and emerge from social relations "from go"). The point is, however, that bodies closest to the somatic norm move through the world *as if* they were ungendered, unclassed, and unraced: they may experience social life as "just people," "normal," or "an individual" outside of the bounds of the particularity of a group identity. These bodies may well experience more ease in public spaces and move into training environments with a certain confidence that theirs are the voices and bodies which matter.

Conceptualizing the "free voice" as a matter of stripping away the effects of socialization is then unwittingly to align the notion of a "natural" voice with the "unmarked" voice of somatic norm. In short, it gestures toward privileging the norm as that which is by definition most free from oppressive constraints and cultural conditioning, and situates the hegemonic white masculine body as somatically most aligned with qualities of the natural/universal. It becomes the basis by which we evaluate the ease, freedom, and power of other voices and, as we discuss in Chapter 3, renders certain voices more "policeable" than others, and, by implication, more in need of liberation, harnessing, or developing. There is historical evidence of this way of thinking, wherein, for instance, it is assumed that "women hold themselves back in expression more than men" (Haynes 2010), who, presumably hold back less and are more connected to their "natural" impulses to speak. Voices unmarked by feminine tropes allegedly ring out, even to advocates of marginalized voices, as more universally understandable and hearable (Wolf 2015) though, as we have argued in earlier chapters, the same sonorous traits emanating from nondominant bodies do not receive the same social goods or approval. Criticism levied at well-educated, middle-class (presumably cis) women has featured prominently in public discourse: Naomi Wolf's "postfeminist" exhortation to "reclaim your strong female voice" (2015), and Flynn, Heath, and Holt's "Women, find your voice" for Harvard Business School (2014) have been recirculated and supported by well-meaning acting and voice trainers quite consistently since their publications. And though these narratives offer tools and encouragement to step into and claim personal power, they suggest that women's voices are something that have been poorly deployed by women themselves rather than produced and heard in a context of systemic misogyny.

The archetypal "strong, clear voice" (Cook 2012: 25) is simply defined as what is most hearable by the dominant cultural ear and emerges out of relationship with the somatic norm. The sedimentation in thinking that the category of "women" can/should empower their voices in the professional (i.e., "man's") world also obscures the ways in which race intersects with gender identities. Wolf's urging in particular invites young millennial women to step into all of the ways in which they are entitled to power, and, though racial considerations are not overtly stated, it is textually and pictorially clear that the prompt is aimed at *white* women. Implicitly white feminine voices are criticized for being at best self-limiting and at worst "put on" or "fake" (Wolf 2015) in contrast with masculine voices *in a (white) male world* which seem "real": men's fitting, natural, easy power and persuasiveness is that which they may come by without pretense or effort. And even when the power dynamic of patriarchal context is acknowledged, as Linklater does as she encourages societal changes to allow women to access their own "natural easy power" (Haynes 2010), the emphasis is all too often on the ways white cisgender women should vie for equal vocal rights, while the voices of other people (BIPOC, trans, disabled) remain outside of the dominant conversation. It matters significantly which bodies produce powerful voices, as a "big, strong, rich, resonant sound" from certain identity intersections (for instance, the racialized and gendered bodies of Black cis or transwomen) is neither a guarantee of expressive freedom nor an assurance of a receptive listening ear. This rings true in professional theatre spaces as well: the same vocal and physical expressivity that may characterize one actor as "transformational," "genius," and "transcendent" may in equal measure frame another as "diva-like," "unstable," "difficult," or "overly political."

Given pervasive cultural biases which favor the somatic embodied norm, we need to take care not to assume that actors in theatre training who are somatically othered in intersecting ways—the queer, disabled, economically underserved, racialized, neurodivergent, and so on—have more training to do on their bodies and voices than their white middle-class cishet male counterparts. They are neither aberrations nor exceptions, but specific instantiations of the scope of human embodied possibilities. We need to see how all students in training occupy specificity of experience, marked by a multiplicity of intersecting identities, shaped and enabled by various social and political forces, each of which may offer limitations as well as productive, useful modalities and possibly even pathways of resistance to hegemonic norms.

Embracing Performativity

The voice trainer's impulse may very well be to strengthen, empower, and "raise up" marginalized voices by using theatre and its training ground as a vehicle for social change; however, unless there is conscious consideration of what is at work in the mechanisms by which identities are themselves constructed, the work may reinforce power dynamics that sustain and reify inequalities already present. We should be critical of acts which are done in the name of women, for instance (e.g., to strengthen women's voices gone into hiding), rather than— as Judith Butler suggests—challenging the very category of "women" itself as a cultural construct (1990). Butler, as we discussed in Chapter 4, asserts that gender identity is not a simple matter of static interior essence expressed and "performed" outwardly, but in fact, very much the reverse: an accumulation of sedimented acts (including vocal behaviors) which produce identity with a feeling of coherence. Central to Butler's theory is the recognition that the dependence of normative gender roles and identities on iterative, performative acts provides the basis for the possibility of transgression: one can perform gender differently, and so generate (not autonomously, but in certain discursive social contexts) different gender identities and, just as importantly, different experiences of gender identity. In this way performativity holds existential value for the subject and may be a worthy avenue of exploration in the voice classroom to open up interesting intervocal opportunities. By rejecting any static notion of "the real you/your natural voice" that requires excavation from the encrusted (and presumably limiting) effects of socialization and/or acculturation, the voice student may instead embrace a proliferation of multiple vocal ways of being, bringing about new possibilities of identity for voiced human beings, fulfilling Butler's liberatory promise.

In order to embrace vocal performativity in this way, the "natural voice" must be understood as itself a productive modality brought about through a vocal discipline that might create, among other possibilities, an experience of a more bodily connected and expressive self. Mollie Painter-Morland (a philosopher who took part in the Santorini Experiment) does precisely this when she asks, "Is rediscovering this 'nature' not just yet another form of culture?" (Painter-Morland 2011: 149). Such reframing allows the pedagogue to unshackle voice from notions of a latent, static, interiority awaiting liberation. It also prevents the historical overidentification of nature with the universal which all too often (in liberal humanist thought) defaults to "that which is not *other*," thereby perpetuating a somatic norm. If we recognize a "natural" *experience* of voice as another form of culture, then we can see that differently positioned embodied identities are going to interface with it in dramatically different ways; by understanding various identities as constructed by intersecting systems of power, we can begin to recognize persistent patterns of asymmetry that result in the production of dominant and nondominant voices.

As we recognize the existence of a dominant somatic norm, the "naturalness" often associated with the "easy power" of certain kinds of voices must be called into question. Those bodies closest to the somatic norm, who may or may not have experienced themselves as marked by race, gender, and so on, may indeed "feel more free" or "at home" in a training environment. However, the lived experiences of white cishet male students are, of course, entrenched in multiplicity and nuance, and given that actors and artists in general may not conform easily or completely to societal standards and normative behaviors, there are many ways in which those embodying the somatic norm may also feel socially and politically "othered." It is also important to note the degree to which those students have taken up normative expectations about how their voices signal race, class, masculinity, and sexuality that may have significantly (and negatively) impacted their vocal and emotional range. As politics of identity have become more conscious among students in our universities and artistic institutions, the bodies of the somatic norm may experience heightened (and defensive) bodily responses: an activated nervous system, self-consciousness, and sense of unease have perhaps replaced a more or less uncomplicated feeling of freedom and relaxation that comes with feeling "at home." Formerly invisible "whiteness" and "masculinity" (traditionally taken up as "standard" in actor training, from which nondominant identities are trained to perform [Dolan 2001], unmarked, transparent, and even "vessel-like") now mark that student-actor as embodying a position of privilege.

A conscious awareness of race and gender identity does not arrive autonomously: it comes about from seeing and hearing others through the lens of difference. It comes from a room in which the bodies of the somatic norm are "called in" to recognize that race and gender are highly constructed categories (albeit operating through very different mechanisms) that benefit some bodies more than others. Voice teachers can invite students to reflect how they vocally sustain and/or challenge hegemonic norms, perhaps allowing them to occupy spaces of training with a new sense of accountability to the injustice and asymmetry that creates dominant and "othered" bodies. It is easy to imagine that a possible response to this emerging awareness (and responsibility) among students who are aligned with the somatic norm is a kind of tension-filled doubling-down on the vocal tropes of white cishet masculinity, amplifying the vocal behaviors associated with its historical traits. Another possible, and more productive, framing could be that there may be deep relief in opening up the category of white masculinity itself as a "playscript," as it may unburden that student from onerous gendered and racialized expectations and open up new possibilities—and empathy—that could emerge from the deeply relational aspects of envoicing.

A new model of liberation which frees the self (and voice) from unhelpful or unwanted identity scripts no longer looks like finding the "natural/real" self, but is instead an embracing of one's identity (and identity per se) as constructed, so that one may take a more active role in its production. And though one is never totally in control (some new ways of being may be open to you, others not, and certainly one can't fully determine meaning in such experiences), there can be a greater invitation to play around with and develop new habits of self that can have a desired effect on the act of envoicing. Actors understand (and are drawn to) "various identity configurations of production and reception" (Dolan 2001: 84) as they bring old (and new) texts to life through inventive and ever-changing repetitions, and they can find, in theatrical performance, a space to produce new selves and to receive others. And so the act of recognizing vocal and bodily actions as (re)enacted and performed as one continually constructs the self, may give the actor the space and time (through habit-changing methods like Alexander Technique, Linklater voice, and others) to inhibit habitual behaviors of self and suspend the unconscious playing out of prescribed (gender or other) group identity scripts.

Terri Power (2016) discusses the ways in which she explores gender-bending in performance: for her, the actor must shift their intention to become a conscious "producer of meaning" (39) wherein they invoke a preparatory state that quiets the habitual performance of gender significations and allows them to take on new imagined and embodied gender signs. In this preparatory state, like Rodenburg's "state of readiness" (2002), breath is awake and flowing, and more options shimmer on the horizon of expression as one aligns with the imaginative state of the Other. Working across difference (in this case, gender) requires the actor to "identify with a seeming Other, imagine what it must be like to be the Other," and disrupt "years of physical, vocal, and emotional conditioning to perform that Other" (Blair 1993: 297–8). The actor's job is to embody the physical and vocal possibilities of the Other of a character in an intentional way. And from a voice perspective, the actor learns quite consciously to tap into their own felt experience of *intervocality*: the shimmering oscillations between self and other(s) in relationship that participate in coproducing and recreating one's own voice and sense of self, now deployed consciously to create embodied, theatrical transformations. That they do so in the service of ultimately building a character in a dramatic performance hardly diminishes the subversive potential in this move: they learn, powerfully, to rehearse and pattern new ways of being in the world by enacting them through new repetitions. Simply put, moves can be made, shifts in pattern may be accomplished, through an embodied empathy that suggests the possibility of both unique existential location and of traveling through terrain that is neither "me" nor "not-me," but, as Rhonda Blair puts it, "not-not me" (298). Jill Dolan beautifully writes, "I am interested in how geographical and identity locations can come to mean something more for theatre studies, something in which bodies of differences (those among us and within us) tread across the performance space in a way that calls attention to their dangerous effability" (1993: 418).

It is indeed dangerous and disruptive to notice, speak, and embody difference through exposing identities as performed and by embodying performative transformations. It is perhaps why actors have traditionally occupied marginalized societal positions and elicited mistrust: revealing identity as the sedimentation of performative acts challenges conventional narratives of power, destabilizes the status quo, and calls into question historically stable identity categories defined along its contours. Actors have the potential to reveal both the capacity to hear and see oneself in others who are very different from oneself, as well as our limitations of understanding as we recognize that the Other is not completely or exhaustively knowable.

There is a common distinction, particularly in classical acting training, which distinguishes the (small "s") "self" as unique, particular, and contemporary in contrast with the (capital "S") "Self" as universal, ageless, and an aspect of shared humanity. Our vocal justice approach would suggest a reframing of the embodied subject as neither "self" nor "Self," but as *existential location*, as we describe in Chapter 3. Existential location invites an understanding of the self as situated, in a bodily and material way, at a unique intersection of a multiplicity of forces, including group identity scripts, many of which will be shared with other people. We also argue that embodied subjects are capable of both literal and existential movement ("location" of self is not static), as well as existential transformation: identities themselves may shift, change, or evolve from this location through developing different forms of relation. An emphasis on *mobility*, rather than *liberation*, from a specific situatedness then emerges as one may seek other possibilities of lived experience. Vocal performativity might then be conceptualized as "awakening my *vocal mobility*," a liberatory model quite different from "freeing my natural voice." The work of removing psychophysical (road)blocks may be understood as providing more freedom for existential travel, in contrast with an emphasis on the revelation of the inner resources of self. With mobility comes the opportunity for ongoing vocal transformations in which vocal growth is neither conflated with a static existential uniqueness nor a universalizing understanding of humanity, but performed and recreated from ever-changing particular material, social, political, cultural, and personal circumstances.

Listening Across Difference

If voice pedagogues (1) understand that human voices emerge through intervocality, a complex set of social and political relations; (2) embrace vocal mobility as the possibility of transforming vocal ways of being that may be produced out of different contexts in their kaleidoscopic multiplicity; and (3) commit to pushing back against the ways in which vocal capacities of all sorts are marshalled to reify and perpetuate various forms of systemic injustice, they will need to radicalize normative listening practices within training environments and rehearsal halls. This will require a deep reflection on the qualities of acting and voice traditionally deemed valuable, an awakening to the important role of the teacher as a substitute for the dominant listening ear of the theatre-going audience/public, and a courage to engage in meaningful sites of oral and aural misconnections, misunderstandings, and disruptions as creative acts.

As we embrace voice as a site of multiplicity, a reconceptualization of the nuts and bolts of exercises and experiments of the training room becomes necessary. For instance, if the pedagogy focuses on releasing (presumably unwanted) habitual vocal or physical, mental/emotional tensions, we can now understand that new freedoms and released energies in the voice are no less socially constructed than the unwanted habits themselves. In relinquishing responsibility to Nature in this way, we recast human sound as always already replete with both existential and political meaning, and as materially participating in shifting social and personal topology. The voice becomes unshackled, not from the constraints of socialization, but from the concept that my own voice is necessarily constrained by my very participation in human social life. Nondominant bodies who "feel the weight of the water" in institutional spaces may otherwise feel that their limitations, stemming in part from the psychosocial burdens of structural inequalities, may be particularly heavy, with the experience of freedom (on many levels) feeling very far from sight. When all ways of being are truly valued, and the student is encouraged to follow their own path toward vocal mobility (which may or may not include a full 2–3 octave range, as I will discuss later), the voice trainer can function as something of a tour guide in the existential terrain of "world-traveling" rather, than, perhaps, as a therapist or even police officer,[5] focused on the removal of pernicious or stubborn blocks. Such an approach acknowledges the highly complex role of intersecting systems in how voices are created, rather than limiting vocal liberation to the realm of inner, psychophysical work. As a result, a spirit of adventure, the thirst for travel into the vocal unknown, and a deep pleasure in the work of transformation may rise to the surface, all of which of course may have therapeutic and empowering benefits for the traveler. The duality of nature/culture is replaced with the student's animating force of desire (even wanderlust) that may mobilize their voice in any number of directions, to perform any number of identities, in many kinds of spaces. How a student pursues their own flourishing, and how one can support them as a trainer are questions that, in my experience, need constant revisiting and space to shift and grow.

In training human beings with this wider lens and by respecting multiplicity, we may also debunk the no-longer useful myth of the archetypal Actor (capital "A"): "he" who is able to allow personal habits of self to recede into the background to give way to universal truths from poets and voices of the past, and who in doing so seems, somehow, a "little more human" than the rest of us. Instead, we might invite the actor (small "a") to bring in their shimmering particularities of experience as a unique existential location from which to reflect, mirror, and amplify difference, so that we may compare and contrast the myths of the past with the stories of now as new sites of meaning-making out of deep specificity. Here, there is the potential to reinforce and encourage vocal transformations that open an actor to an embodied understanding of historical worlds (and the kinds of selves they produced) from the perspective of the current world inhabited. The embodied particularity of one's voice meeting voices of the past (as my patterns or prosody give way to the character or playwright's prosody) need not amount to an erasure of differences, but, from a more Brechtian perspective, is an invitation to live in the discomfort and tension of "worlds colliding." In this sense, of course, the actor always has multiple subjectivities as they oscillate between several worlds at once: they are both "present" in the here and now as well as in the imaginative setting of the play, no matter how fully they give over to the character's experience. The voice of the actor of "classical" texts is also not ahistorical, exempt from the particularities of existential location, but reveals by way of contrast its situatedness in the intersecting productive forces of the present, including their vivid imagination in relation to the texts at hand. And so when Rodenburg suggests that Shakespeare, for instance, "seems to be able to speak to us all over those hundreds of years and across every cultural bias and barrier" (2002: 171), I would argue that his words may excite a reason to perform them in the present by bringing to light, rather than "evaporating," cultural bias and barrier as relational, reenacted, and highly relevant. Likewise she suggests that "[h]e … understands our likenesses as well as our individuality" (171); I would add, *and what does that mean for us when we see and acknowledge difference?* Rather than train actors to vie for an "exalted state of pure understanding" (Dolan 2001: 88) of a text, we can open up how they (and audiences) hear through difference and may come to "hold respect for things [they] might never understand" (88). How do we hear voiced bodies— particularly out of various sedimented historical expectations for what classical acting looks and sounds like (perhaps equated with a kind of "transparency" or "range" or, even, as I've heard, "physical prowess")—in a way that does not suggest we are, "underneath," all the same? The notion of "transparency" holds a double-bind for actors: there is an obligation, on one hand, of letting the character "shine through" one's bodily performance, and, on the other, of making one's own self transparent, "uncolored and unflavored by anything artificial" that gets in the way of "honesty and clarity" (Rodenburg [1992] 2015: 34–5).

One Rodenburg teacher describes the voice work as a "firehose spraying all of the coating off you to work from a place of clarity" (Leavitt 2020: 100). The capital "S" "Self" and "character" are then revealed as, simultaneously, the outer, socialized small "s" "self" is rendered invisible. The danger of this image is the sense that what's "outer" does not matter, unwittingly rendering one's social identity (in terms of race, gender, ability, and so on) as irrelevant, dismissible, and extra. Difference is again effaced. According to Jill Dolan, the "humanist understanding of difference" and the practice of assimilating otherness into the self in a common humanity of "sameness … has become worn and needs to be retreaded" (2001: 88). She suggests that *misunderstanding* (rather than universal understanding) in theatre performance is productive. Dolan employs Phelan's bridge metaphor, in which "*It is in the attempt to walk (and live) on the rackety bridge between self and other—and not the attempt to arrive at one side or another—that we discover real hope. That walk is our always suspended performance—in the classroom, in the political field, in relation to one another, and to ourselves*" (89, emphasis in original). I am curious to see how intentional misunderstanding, disruption, and misfittings (by casting against ability norms, racial identity, gender expression, etc.) would shed light on, rather than obscure, identity as socially constructed. Misfitting in this way can challenge easy assumptions and collective expectations about identity norms in historical contexts and open up understandings of the plays themselves through the lens of the structures of power which render those norms valuable.

Challenging our assumptions about what is at work in understanding each other (the heart of the matter for vocal communication) requires voice teachers to consider their own complicity in perpetuating the stronghold of the dominant listening ear in both training and coaching. It asks us to recondition habitual thinking about "what translates" from stage, what "can be understood," and what kinds of performances hold meaning. The question is, of course: "translates" to whom? "Be understood" by whom? Whose voices have been internalized as "standard listening practices" for the coach or teacher? Are the presumed listening ears (un)consciously aligned with the demographic of majority white theatre-going audiences of predominantly white theatre institutions? As more BIPOC actors are being brought into those institutions, are the listening practices of the audience actually shifting, welcoming in new voices and sounds, utilizing the same capacity for adapting the ear required for Shakespearean verse or for a play performed in a Eurocentric accent? Or do they resist valuing and centering voices from Black and brown bodies? Are new vocalities in those spaces merely fetishized or dismissed? Given that bias is embedded in the practice of listening—our ears are not neutral, but, rather, finely trained, grooved, and specialized—the vocal coach can take on the ethical responsibility to care for the sonic landscape in a theatrical space, even when it risks asking an audience to work through discomfort. The listening ear of the voice coach then holds the promise to reimagine, in a highly creative and productive way, the complex dialogue between actor and audience, and new listening practices, developed in relationship to embodied voices that disrupt traditional sonic norms, may be born. When confronted with vocal multiplicity from diverse bodies, an audience's own listening *habitus* can rewire. A shift from aural passivity to an awakened, active ear and body may open up new possibilities across the "rackety bridge" between actor and audience, and new empathies may emerge both out of and through *mis*understanding.

Playwright Dominique Morisseau has created a "Rules of Engagement" for an audience to enter into the sonic space of her plays, originally developed as a program insert for the Lincoln Center Theater production of her play *Pipeline* in 2017 (Morisseau 2017). She brings attention to the audience's (respiratory) responsibility to play a meaningful and supportive role in the theatrical event through their own sound-making: "Please be an audience member that joins with others and allows a bit of breathing room. Exhale together. Laugh together. Say 'amen' should you need to" (1). Morisseau also acknowledges the theatre space as deeply intervocal, encouraging an audience to actively engage with, but not thwart, live performances of the actors. She is particularly attentive to the vocal policing which may take place among audience members, noting the role that predominantly upper-middle-class white audiences have played in silencing audience members of color who might be vocally responding to the play exactly as Morisseau had intended. Such Rules of Engagement invite ethical responsibility for predominantly white institutions and their audiences to lean into a dynamic enjoyment of the play whilst centering diversely embodied vocal experiences of audiences and artists alike.

Following Morisseau's lead, can the role of the voice coach—as caretaker and custodian of the vocal theatrical space—be reimagined to include all "actors" present, including the audience? Can they invite an audience to breathe, to make vocal sound when so moved, to engage with actors in a dynamic, meaningful way that is wholly unlike watching a two-dimensional screen? How can a voice coach (or artistic team generally) develop a "session agreement" with an audience, to warm up the space, increase receptivity, and consciously subvert the polite, quiet, even constricting atmosphere resulting from theatrical consumerism within white supremacy culture? Given ongoing political divides and imagining into a post-pandemic theatre, how can an audience be encouraged and best supported to bring their fullest, oxygenated embodiment of self to a performance space with others as they breathe shared air, welcoming all selves in their wholeness?

Practical Matters

As I shift from theoretical considerations to more practical ones, I am loath to offer anything resembling a new vocal pedagogy. My goal is to recontextualize ideologies framing established practices—particularly "natural/free" approaches—and open up new ways of thinking about the methods themselves. Established approaches in the field have much to offer, have detailed and comprehensive investigations, and have been proven to be effective in significant ways. That said, the following are a few practical points I want to suggest (primarily from the lens of my own pedagogical approach which remains deeply influenced and enhanced by my engagement with the work of Linklater and others) in the context of the theoretical ideas considered above.

Recognition as Relaxation

Relaxation, a ubiquitous and seemingly uncontroversial principle in voice pedagogy, is conceptualized as a "feeling of ease" or "release" or "letting go" or "surrender," serving to free stored energy, stimulate involuntary bodily responses, support endurance in performance, and so on. Natural/free voice work often suggests that the voicing person "allow" or "let" or "invite" relaxation and release to happen, rather than demand or command relaxation, as that might "boss the body around," resulting in more unwanted physical and mental tension.

Taking a cue from the practice of Yoga Nidra,[6] I have been working with the principle that *awareness* and *recognition* are more fundamental to relaxation than the pointed directive of "letting go" or "allowing release" itself. The principle here is that in the process of a body scan (used by various pedagogies to progressively move through the body to notice places of habitual holding and tension and then willingly let them release), the practitioner does not invite relaxation directly, but simply brings their whole attention to the sensation of each body part. The premise is that just by being noticed and feeling seen, the body will "sense" that it has permission to relax (if it wants to), and that "it's going to be ok." The script, in my teaching, has changed from "notice/feel your (body part), and allow it to let go" to "notice/feel your (body part)" without further adjustment of any kind: a response is suspended, perhaps with the prompt "*and there is nothing you need to do about that.*" The focus shifts primarily to an "atmosphere of attention" in the body rather than an "atmosphere of relaxation" (Linklater 2006: 87), per se: the feeling of being witnessed emerges as more important and powerful than undoing the work of accrued tensions directly.

From one point of view, this may seem like a minor tweak to a well-worn script. However, from an anti-oppression approach to voice training, I believe it is deeply paradigm-shifting. Resmaa Menakem's detailed work on racialized trauma and healing suggests the same attention to feeling deeply into *what is*, concentrating on developing one's ability to progressively bring consciousness to all bodily sensations as a means of settling or mindfully activating the body (as needed), and clocking the potential trap that an immediate demand for "relaxation" can be as it can override feeling and result in a numbing (2017). His work highlights the ways in which bodies respond to other bodies, and how they may experience constriction or openness that is important to assess in order for change to occur (52).

Giving students permission to sense their own daily physical constrictions in relation to others and to the shared training space (to the "water" and the "fish" in it) without rushing to "cast off the tensions of the day" is a way of honoring embodied selves marked by inequitable social conditions. A standard warm-up that invites an awareness of one's physical, emotional, and psychological condition might now also invite a felt awareness of one's identity locations, including how one is (or has been) experiencing themself as a body that is racialized, gendered, classed, and so on. "What is your experience of your physical self at this moment?" might be followed by "and what is your experience of your gender and/or racial identity at this moment?" which, given the discursive nature of identity, invites a "seeing with others" (Al-Saji 2014: 159) and a heightened sense of the embodied self as intersubjective. This invitation to awareness names group identities in the space, takes the charge out of differences left latent, unseen, and unacknowledged, removes taboo in acknowledging inequalities, and shines light on how we may experience our shared environments very differently and yet through ongoing relationship. Noticing and honoring self and others by neither immediately responding nor demanding change (even the seemingly innocuous change of "and let it go") allows for a deeper sense of the contingency (and changeability) of "what is" that can shift experience on many levels. According to Al-Saji's anti-racist phenomenology of hesitation:

> The body waits before acting; it has the time not only to perceive, but also to remember. In this sense, to feel is to no longer repeat the past automatically, but to imagine and remember it ... hesitation can thus make felt the historicity, contingency, and sedimentation of habitual actions and perceptions, as well as their plasticity ... [and] opens up routes for feeling, seeing, and acting differently. (143)

Providing space to notice, to acknowledge, and to feel may allow deeper desires in the room to surface, as students unburden themselves from the weight of the task to "access relief" through methods that fail to acknowledge the role of systemic inequalities in their lives. By noticing, feeling, *and then suspending* an immediate response, they may change their habitual bodily patterning and relations to others in non-habitual ways that open up greater possibilities for physical, psychic, social, and vocal mobility.

Vocal Social Goods: Airtime Distribution in Check-Ins and Feedback

Hesitation as an anti-oppression tool may also be deployed in the classroom in a mindful curating of unstructured conversations and/or feedback about an exercise. This requires a recognition of the ease that some bodies will have over others in sharing their thoughts in academic/training spaces, and the real possibility that those students who feel as if "fish in water" will be more likely to speak first, and to speak longer. Structurally, this would demand both an understanding that one is such a fish (i.e., that one occupies identity locations associated with privilege) and an acknowledgment, if applicable, that certain social identities may dominate the space as a result of unequal access to the institution. If left unattended to, a predominantly white space will inevitably give voice to predominantly white values, problems, and sound ideals, as an instructor might (unintentionally, in the name of encouraging "freely speaking on impulse") send already marginalized perspectives and voices into hiding. As a voice teacher, I think it is incredibly challenging to resist any thoughtful, sensitive student who feels deeply and has a lot to put on their voice. However, by hesitating (breathing) before necessarily giving the green light to dominant-bodied students to speak, we can open up space to center nondominant voices that might emerge in that moment. If students and instructors do the work of identifying and understanding their social identity locations, how those locations afford them various privileges, and how those identities show up in their voices, they can be tasked with holding increased responsibility for the airtime in (often very meaningful) unstructured conversation. Giving over or taking airtime can be framed as an embrace of ethical envoicing, so that listening—a crucial component of intervocality and fundamental to the construction of all voices—is understood as fundamental to one's "voice work." If a student occupies identity locations resulting in a high degree of privilege, their task might be to lean into strengthening the "listening" of voice work as their first port-of-call. If a student occupies identity locations associated with a low degree of privilege, they might be welcomed to lean into the "speaking" part of the work, to practice centering their feedback and shifting the dynamic around which experiences are shared first and with most frequency.

George Yancy calls upon white bodies in particular to *tarry*:

> …to render unstable that familiar white sense of being-in-the-world. The process of tarrying encourages forms of courageous *listening*, humility, and the capacity to be touched, to be shaken … (2015: 26, emphasis mine)

> …whites must learn when and how to be silent … silence and the dynamism of tarrying can create spaces of openness; create important moments of vulnerability, of being wounded, of coming to admit, though painfully, that they thought they knew themselves in ways that they have now come to realize that they were mistaken. (28)

Voice work (indeed the work of theatre generally) is perhaps most importantly about those very promises: to create "spaces of openness," "moments of vulnerability," and deeper understandings of the self as veils are pulled back revealing latent truths. Listening, then, as a vocal modality—one to be cultivated in training—has a far more vital role to play in the art form than has as yet been given truly proper attention.

The Individual and the Intervocal Ensemble

Natural/free voice work—particularly as codified in print—has tended to focus on an individual's capacity to free themself from habitually accrued tensions in order to recondition their voice. A highly notable exception is Linklater's "Sound and Movement" sequence, which investigates the deep relationality of the voice, and comes closest, to my mind, to radicalizing the pedagogy of the individual: it creates a space to explore the felt experience of Lugones's "bodies in relation, touching and being touched, moving across social and bodily geographies together" (Dolan 2001: 87). Framing the voice as intervocal, as cocreated wholly in relationship with a variety of "others" at work, I have been investigating how actor voice and text work may be adapted to include relationality in a deeper way. One example of such an adaptation is "mirroring" an individual vocal exploration by use of a group "Chorus." I have borrowed here from Richard Armstrong's open investigations of sustained vocal sound (the "orange work") emphasizing the evolution (and coexistence) of the moments of "solo," "duo," and "chorus," as well as from the Jon Lipsky's (undated) conceptualization of the actor's warm-up not *only* as an individual's personal voice and body work, but consciously created in relationship with particular individuals and with the ensemble as a whole. When sharing a prepared monologue/speech, I have invited the ensemble to occupy a dual position in relation to the individual speaker: they become both the "mirror" (the chorus) to the speaker by taking on their energy, gestures, breath, and perceived intention (as if they were also making sound, although they do not, themselves, come onto voice), as well as "encouragers" to the speaker by staying connected to their own appetites for where they want that speaker to "travel to" moment to moment. In this way the chorus reflects back to the speaker their own embodied sense of what they are receiving, and the speaker sees themselves reflected in the chorus, feels their power to affect the chorus, and senses how the chorus—through deeply empathetic listening—is encouraging and supporting them to move in any number of expressive directions. The traditional actor-audience dichotomy is upended, and an active and receptive model for audience participation is embodied. There are sometimes ruptures and disconnects: the group may kinesthetically encourage performances that are resisted by the speaker, and it's also possible that the speaker's expressions fail to have the desired effect on the group. However, discomfort has a creative role to play as the speech event unfolds through connections, disconnections, and desire, and I consistently find that some of the actors' most courageous and transformational work is the result.

Patsy Rodenburg's "Second Circle" is a highly useful framework for coming into an experience of presence and focused energy through relationship: it "brings forth what is within each individual and connects this vital energy to something specific outside of the self—a scene partner, a text, an audience" (Leavitt 2020: 10). These connections, I would add, shimmer in relationship, and they move in multiple directions dynamically. And though Rodenburg also values ensemble explorations, I do not agree that their purpose should be to "bring out our sameness, our common humanity, instead of our difference" (10). Rather, the benefit of ensemble work is "to see according to others" which "is not to see through their eyes or to assimilate them to my vision; it is to find the perceptual field to have been reoriented by others" (Al-Saji 2014: 161). In the reorientation of working with others, I feel my multiplicity rather than the collective, cohesive, unified force of sameness; I see myself as constituted in relationship with individuals and a group, who are themselves inhabiting multiple consciousnesses (both "mirrors" and "encouragers," for instance). Difference is acknowledged, plasticity through mutual discovery is encouraged, and the sensory field around me opens up for new vocal, emotional, or imaginative possibilities.

Rethinking Pitch, Reframing Anatomy

As we understand better the diverse ways in which sexed and gendered identities are lived, there are basic assumptions about vocality that should be revisited. A previously uncomplicated gender binary has divided many vocal exercises into explorations roughly one octave apart in pitch. As we know more about the way bodies come to be sexed and gendered, we must interrogate the assumption that sex assigned at birth determines the pitch range within which a person will feel the most relaxed and "at home." A complex arrangement of genital, chromosomal, and hormonal factors render "assigned sex" a far from simple category, irrespective of gender identity or expression. That said, notions of "starting pitch" for exercises have largely centered around comfortable, easy pitches for adult cisfemale white-European bodies, and thus need to be reconsidered. As voice is a deep feature of identity, and as vocal pitch in particular plays a constitutive role in gender expression, we might do well to take a cue from the ways voice work has started to be reimagined and expanded for trans and gender nonconforming people generally and actors specifically[7]. Rather than framing "nonconforming" gender identities as exceptional or as a special category of embodied identity requiring a tailored approach to training, we can embrace gender diversity as a *starting point* from which to train all students. Honoring any and all students' desired expressive outcomes with the same respect as must be done for a trans/nonconforming student would begin to acknowledge the complexity of gendered selves and sexed bodies. Hearns and Kramer (2018) suggest that truly "gender-conscious voice training dispels any associations between pitch range and gender" (105) despite historical associations between the two. I would suggest that just as a trans person's voice range goals (if applicable) are central to "actively defining their own natural voice" (104), so too might any student's goals be centered in order "to discover a voice that feels as though it truly belongs to them and that it expresses who they are" (104). Anatomy, though structural, is simply not the whole picture on a material level in vocal development; I've certainly had many students who are most at ease physically and vocally well outside the established binary contours of pitch that have been traditionally assigned from an anatomical and/ or acoustic viewpoint. New approaches in the training room, such as more self-selection of pitch by the student—in concert with a sensitive teacher and the sustaining techniques they might provide—should be investigated. The practice of having diversely gendered and sexed groups work in unison of pitch (and not the typical octave apart), as exemplified by Richard Armstrong's extended voice approach, may well also find a home in what we've been calling natural/ free voice pedagogy should it loosen its conception of the anatomical/natural inevitability of vocal pitch.

Rethinking "Vocal Health"

As we understand the systemic and structural inequalities which render some voices more policeable than others, there is a call for voice pedagogues to become increasingly conscious of the ways in which we might unwittingly perpetuate oppressions and privilege dominant norms of experience in the name of "empowering voices." As trainers in a somatic arena, we need to take special care that systems of knowledge about the body (vocal anatomy, body mechanics, nutrition, trauma and the nervous system, etc.) are not marshalled against nondominant bodies in ways that reify and perpetuate social injustice. Along these lines, voice teachers should specifically consider abandoning the long-standing use of the term "vocal hygiene" and embrace the notion of "vocal self-care" to acknowledge the deep materiality of the voice and its embeddedness in social, cultural, and political contexts that extend beyond (but include) the resiliency of the tissues of one's vocal folds.

The term "vocal hygiene" conjures a particular sense of keeping the voice pure and free from disease, contaminants, and pollutants. A critique of this term in no way undermines the importance of caring for the physiological aspects of voice; attending to the material well-being of the many bodily systems involved in the production of voice is crucial to developing the skills that voice training fosters. However, framing that care as "hygiene" is both problematic in terms of anti-oppression and contrary to the fundamental commitments of the profession. Voice care does not involve "cleaning the voice" any more than it involves "cleaning the self," and to frame a well-functioning expression of voice (which involves, as we discuss in Chapter 1, all systems of the body) as "clean" undermines the existential aspects of voice as a deep feature of the self. As I have argued above, the liberatory aspects of vocal mobility would likely include a transgressive, border-crossing, messy quality to new vocal ways of being that may themselves open up existential possibilities. Messages of "purity" and "anti-pollution" have no business in the arena of voice understood as a product of emotional, physiological, social, cultural, and political forces.

In our time of the Covid-19 pandemic, demands for "hygiene"—more than ever—have the risk of being deployed in service of white supremacy and xenophobia. People of color are getting sick and dying of Covid more than white people, inviting a dangerous (but not at all new) conflation between marginalized populations and the hygienically "risky." Frontline workers are cast as the "dirty" people, perforce, as their bodies are more in the path of the virus, and once again the underserved and vulnerable are dismissed as expendable human capital at literal and metaphoric borders of power. The suppression and marginalization of already disadvantaged bodies can all too easily masquerade as vigilance against contamination, and it is no accident, I think, that an emphasis on hygiene *others* both systemically oppressed bodies as well as historically feminized body parts, as the term typically only modifies "the oral," "the vocal," and "the feminine." As we discuss in Chapter 4, the infectious, leaky, and threatening parts of feminine bodies in particular—the "two sets of lips" of the mouth and female genitalia, as well as the vocal folds which highly resemble the latter—are, according to dominant patriarchal attitudes, best kept under good regulation and control.

A pivot away from "vocal hygiene" toward "vocal self-care" is an invitation for the embodied vocal subject to be taken up as necessarily complex, and would invite such care to include well-being along many axes of life (emotional, physical, psychological, etc.) in a more self-determined way. "Vocal self-care" could be imagined as an essential component of "self-care as a societal movement" (Tygielski 2019), embracing its political aspects that resist the effects of oppression on the body (Smith 2020). And given that "self-care" in many dominant iterations is resolutely apolitical (of the manicure/glass-of-wine—or even the "wellness"—variety, both associated with white privilege), it is important to note that I'm referring here to the mindful aspects of caring for self in a way that pushes against the somatic effects of inequality in social/political life and seeks to renew and rejuvenate the voice as instrumental both in resisting hegemonic oppression and in healing its traumas.

We should also question how the deployment of concerns about "health" is related to the power dynamics of policing. Voice pedagogues may find themselves cast as guardians of many kinds of health: vocal, physical, emotional, psychological, and more. That certain kinds of vocal sounds (vocal fry, for instance) are deemed more "unhealthy" (vocally, psychologically, and emotionally) *in certain bodies* is worthy of sustained attention (vocal fry is a meaningful sound in quite a few languages[8] and is performed in many masculine bodies without perceived limitations). Thinking into voice as material and embodied, we might consider other ways that bodies historically have been policed (even out of ostensible concern) in the name of health. It is now well known that "fat-shaming" and "body-shaming"—even at the level of "concern" (Vogel 2019)—have deleterious effects on the mental and emotional well-being of the person who is being "helped" by such concern. Performances of "concern," however well-intended, are problematic: they can all too thinly mask attempts to control and police, and although one can believe one is acting out of concern, one is not always in a position to have accurate insight into one's own motivations.

Just as many theatre training programs (though surely not all) move away from a "body-normative" attitude toward a more "body-inclusive" one, inviting a greater diversity of bodies onto the theatrical stage, we need to make the same move vocally. That is not to say that the demands of performance won't require highly specific vocal usages that must be sustainable for the actor as they relate to an audience; it is only to say that we can consciously invite in the "hesitation/pause" before we encourage a vocality to exist "in the name" of anything (health, relatability, intelligibility, etc.) other than an actor's creativity as it meets the intersecting artistic needs of the project at hand. By embracing the theoretical frameworks of intervocality, respiratory responsibility, and vocal mobility, voice trainers can allow a "voice-normative" approach (one relying on traditional, historical sonic norms in theatrical performance) to yield to a more inclusive "voice positive" approach to envoicing, and in so doing invoke the same level of care and attention to the voice as to the more visible aspects of embodied identity on stage.

7

Ethical Spotlight: Envoicing in/and Philosophy

Like Chapter 6, this chapter is single-authored (this time by Cahill). It focuses on the discipline of philosophy, and how an attunement to intervocality and vocal justice can generate new, and more inclusive, forms of philosophical practice. We return to our coauthored voice in the concluding chapter.

As Chapter 2 demonstrated, Adriana Cavarero (2005) argues that the expulsion of voice from philosophical practice exemplified a vilification of embodiment that persists in Western philosophy. Moving from understanding philosophy as a primarily vocal practice (oral dialogue or the reading aloud of written text) to a primarily written one was, for Cavarero, an epistemological, political, and ethical misstep. That so much philosophical scholarship on voice focuses on style or tone in writing, as opposed to human soundedness, seems to substantiate Cavarero's point. Yet two sites of contemporary philosophical practice either challenge Cavarero's characterization of philosophy as unvoiced or provide robust examples of how her call to return voice to philosophy could be (and maybe is being, although in insufficiently recognized and valued ways) heeded. This chapter highlights the processes of envoicing occurring within the context of the classroom and the conference.

Neither site is unique to the discipline of philosophy, and thus my analyses may transfer, with varying degrees of accuracy, to other areas of study, particularly within the humanities; further exploration by scholars and instructors of those fields would be needed to identify overlaps and divergences. My point here is that important philosophical work is being done at each, and that each relies on voice as human-generated sound to accomplish that work; yet their reliance on vocality has been underexplored. By and large, the vocal sounds of philosophizing are taken to be irrelevant by the discipline itself. Given the ways, as detailed in earlier chapters, that intervocality can be deployed to perpetuate multiple forms of structural injustice, this failure to take such sounds seriously constitutes yet another way in which the discipline enacts oppression. In turning my attention to the sound of explicitly philosophical voices, I seek to trouble and expand upon the traditional objects of philosophical analysis (à la Dotson 2012) in order to more fully understand how dominant ways of doing philosophy replicate oppressive norms and behaviors, and how these underappreciated modes of doing philosophy hold promise for resisting those norms and behaviors. In order to maintain the focus on the vocal sounds of philosophy, I will thus refrain as much as possible from attending to the ideas that philosophical speech seeks to convey (although there are surely rich and profound ways in which the two co-constitute each other).

Philosophical Classrooms

The material conditions and pedagogical approaches framing philosophical teaching vary widely among different countries, communities, and institutions. For the purposes of this discussion, I focus on contexts common to contemporary higher education in the United States, recognizing that those contexts represent different class sizes, levels of institutional investment, and pedagogies.

Naming philosophical classrooms as sites of meaningful philosophical work is somewhat unusual. Contemporary philosophers distinguish starkly (if often implicitly) between *teaching* philosophy (transferring philosophical knowledge to students) and *doing* philosophy (producing original, usually single-authored, published works). Thus, the current atmosphere all too often constructs teaching as the professional activity that one must undertake in order to earn the right to dedicate time and energy to one's "real" philosophical work: writing. Such a hierarchy, among its many flaws, cruelly heightens and perpetuates deep patterns of inequality within the profession. For instructors with enormous course loads and class sizes, setting aside time for one's own research is virtually impossible; given that achieving tenure usually requires some publication record, and that institutions that value scholarship tend to offer far better remuneration and benefits to their tenure track and tenured faculty, such instructors are significantly limited in both their earning potential and their ability to achieve the job security and academic freedom that tenure affords. Crucially, the most precariously employed philosophers, those employed as adjunct or part-time instructors (often at multiple institutions) or visiting instructors, frequently without health benefits and almost always without the dependability of multiyear contracts, undertake a sizeable proportion of the teaching in the discipline and are more likely to be members of historically marginalized groups than their tenure-track colleagues (Zheng 2018, Kim et al. 2020).[1]

Structurally, scholarship serves as the primary metric of professional success for philosophers, such that how *little* one teaches serves as an indication of one's status in the field, with the most prestigious figures teaching one or two classes a year, with frequent research leaves that temporarily free them from almost all teaching responsibilities. Moreover, only those instructors on permanent, full-time employment tracks have even a chance of framing their jobs as including both teaching and research. Precariously employed philosophers who continue to apply for permanent, full-time positions experience enormous pressure to maintain a scholarly agenda to remain competitive in an exceedingly bleak job market, usually without institutional support of any kind.

Using research as the primary metric of professional success within philosophy, and constructing teaching as a necessary burden, has a host of negative ramifications. In addition to heightening the inequalities mentioned above, it underestimates the rich and productive exchanges among instructors and students, exchanges that illuminate philosophical controversies, inspire unexpected insights and novel readings of texts, and forward conceptual understandings. Moreover, such a prioritization devalues the very activity that most employed philosophers spend most of their time doing, framing it as an intellectually uninteresting set of demands to be avoided whenever possible. When "doing philosophy" stands in for "doing philosophical research" and excludes teaching philosophy, the philosophers for whom teaching makes up the bulk of their professional activity—that is, the vast majority of us—labor under unnecessarily alienating conditions.

The disciplinary privileging of the written word over the spoken word, where the former is associated with philosophical progress and achievement and the latter with either a degree of intellectual not-yet-doneness or rudimentary exposition, is surely related to the devaluing of the persistently vocal site of the classroom. In most philosophy classrooms, of course, lectures or discussions focus resolutely on written texts, and so the written word continues to hold sway. Yet, with the possible exception of online courses relying solely on text-based communications, philosophy classrooms explore those texts primarily through vocal interaction. Cavarero's recommended revocalization of philosophy could thus imbue the classroom with the philosophical prestige it deserves; yet careful and critical work would be required to render it a vocally just site.

Although some philosophy instructors challenge the authoritarianism of the "sage on the stage" (see Weston 2018 for a step beyond the "guide on the side" development), the lecture remains a dominant form of classroom instruction, particularly in classes large enough to make discussion formats virtually impossible.[2] Decades of research criticizing lecturing as the paradigmatic example of the "mug and jug" or "banking" approach to learning (Regmi 2012) have failed to undermine its status as a default pedagogy. Merely on the basis of airtime alone, then, and given philosophy's demographics, the reliance on lecturing acclimates students' receiving bodies to associating certain kinds of bodies (white, male, heterosexual, cisgendered, and able-bodied)[3] with philosophical expertise. Yet such ascription of expertise is not independent of the identity markers of the lecturers; that is, instructors identified with historically marginalized social groups may be experienced by students as inappropriately arrogant, whereas instructors who identify as members of historically dominant groups may be perceived as wise and knowledgeable. Enhancing the sonorous justice of the philosophical classroom, then, requires transforming the receiving practices of students so that they can better engage with the voices of philosophers of color, nonmale philosophers, trans philosophers, and/or disabled philosophers as experts.

Attending to the vocal politics of the philosophical classroom also requires moving beyond noting the allocation of airtime along the lines of perceived authority and the resulting perpetuation of existing systems of inequality. An emphasis on intervocality and envoicing leads to a heightened attunement not only to who gets to speak, how frequently and for how long, but on how the sounds of the speaking participants' voices are shaped, generated, and received. Here, it's important to note that the lecturing voice is frequently constructed as unmarked by the particularities of the receiving bodies. Its distinct tone of authoritative elucidating communicates confidence and learnedness; it rarely struggles (if and when it does, it most likely registers as a failing lecturing voice). Even this traditional lecturing voice is not unmarked by intervocality, insofar as it assumes (sometimes contrary to all available evidence) an audience of students at least willing to receive the lecture (or, even worse, perhaps an imaginary audience of colleagues, in which case the presence of the listening student body is ignored entirely). However, its intervocality is limited by the presumedly generic quality of those receiving bodies. If an instructor teaches multiple sections of a class, they may aim to present lectures as identically as possible, which would include maintaining a sonorous similarity across their vocalizations. Sonorously, the lecture neglects the co-constituting relevance of the receiving aural body, and the ways in which that receiving body is marked by engagements with social and political phenomena, including systemic inequalities. In this way, the dominance of the lecture model habituates students and instructors alike to a set of unjust vocal and aural practices.

Pedagogical critiques of the effectiveness of the lecture, as well as the ways in which lecturing perpetuates hierarchical models of education, have encouraged the development of approaches that center students' voices in a variety of ways. Yet those approaches tend to focus on the quantitative matter of airtime and/or the types of content that student voices can contribute, without attending to what classroom voices sound like and how they are received. How can attending to the sonorous qualities of classroom vocalizations and the degree to which various pedagogies invite or discourage different kinds of sounded voices, enhance an attunement to vocal justice beyond the merely quantitative and content-based?

I offer below several pedagogical approaches designed to transform the sonorous aspects of the philosophical classroom by more consciously deploying the possibilities of intervocality to forward the goals of vocal justice and pedagogical effectiveness. Of course, different institutional situations will allow for different practices, and individual instructors will have varying levels of comfort with pedagogical experimentation. Even more importantly, instructors who identify with historically marginalized groups are likely constrained by how racism, sexism, ableism, and other systemic inequalities intersect with creative pedagogies. Finally, what follows is certainly not a comprehensive list, but rather just a few examples of the kinds of pedagogical possibilities that an attunement to vocal justice might inspire.

Just-in-time Lecturing

My critique of the lecture does not amount to a denial of instructor expertise. Although students bring their own proficiencies to any scholarly inquiry, the instructor should bring to the collective enterprise a depth and breadth of subject matter knowledge exceeding that of the students, and there are times when sharing that expertise directly in a lecture format is enormously helpful to students' progress. Deploying lectures in a "just-in-time" mode, however, departs from traditional lecturing in ways likely to show up in the sonorous qualities of the lecturer's voice.

"Just-in-time" lectures are deployed when conversations become stalled such that an intervention by the faculty can be productive. In my experience, these "just-in-time" lectures are relatively short, rarely more than fifteen minutes. They serve as emergent curriculum responding directly (and, ideally, immediately, although there's no reason they couldn't be provided in a subsequent class) to the students' learning process. Reversing the common chronology of lecture classes that offer some form of discussion, where the lecture precedes the question and answer period or small group discussion, this approach begins with student discussions that identify both students' specific interests and gaps in their understanding. The lectures should aim to have the students deploy the knowledge they gain from them immediately as they turn back to their discussion. The emergent and focused nature of the lecture—that it is directed to a particular group of students as they grapple with a particular text or concept— would influence the prosodic features of the lecturer's speaking voice.

Just-in-time lectures challenge some of the sonorously unjust aspects of the traditional lecture by centering the students' particular learning process and encouraging the instructor's voice to be sonorously marked by the specificity of the students (both individually and collectively) receiving it. The lecture that is provided on the instructor's schedule, and that precedes substantial and specific student engagement with the text and ideas, *sounds different* than the just-in-time lecture that emerges from, responds directly to, and forwards the particular progress that the students are making in a class; the students can hear themselves, and their relevance to the work being undertaken in the classroom, in the sonorous qualities of the just-in-time lecturing voice.

I hasten to reiterate the point I made above: like the other approaches that I will describe here, this one will not suit every pedagogical situation and every instructor. Some instructors find the prospect of giving a short lecture on a topic that they were not prepared to speak on that day impossible, and for good reason. But there are many variations on the just-in-time lecture, including: preparing a variety of short lectures, and having the students decide which one would be most helpful; identifying a certain gap in one class meeting, and then presenting the corresponding lecture in the following class; and developing a set of frequently needed lecture modules that can be provided with little to no preparation time.

Provide Opportunities for Students to Adopt Vocal Roles Usually Reserved for Instructors

An emphasis on merely allocating more airtime during class to students does not necessarily entail troubling the vocal roles commonly assigned to students and instructors. Changing assignments so that students use their voices differently, particularly in ways that are consistently reserved only for instructors, can envoice students in productively different ways. For example, classes that rely heavily on discussion can adopt the practice of having the last person who spoke choose the next speaker, rather than having the instructor always serving as the conversational conductor. Such a practice encourages students to attune themselves to patterns of participation and enlists them in efforts to create an equal and inclusive division of conversational labor. Presentation assignments, which rarely position students as sources of meaningful instruction, could be replaced by assignments that require students to teach their peers (e.g., the content and structure of exams could be determined by what and how the students teach each other; or, perhaps even more radically, the teaching students could be evaluated by assessing the learning of their peers). In such assignments, the expertise of the instructor is deployed not only by helping the teaching students to understand the course material, but also by helping them design student- and learning-centered lesson plans. Teaching material in a way that centers the learning experience of their peers will most likely result in more engaging, sonorously textured vocalizations than those characterizing typical student presentations.

Experiment with Varying Levels of Noise within the Classroom

Large class size is surely a leading reason for the continued dominance of the lecture as a pedagogical approach. While there are significant empirical data that large class sizes impede student learning (Monks and Schmidt 2011; the authors also note the deleterious effects of large student loads across multiple classes), the sonorous influence of such class sizes has been insufficiently explored. Having hundreds of voices speaking simultaneously could well be overwhelming and chaotic (this is true even if such a sonorous dynamic may be experienced as pleasant, even invigorating, in a different social context such as a party or even a workshop). Classrooms have been constructed, through infrastructure (architecture, seating arrangement, use of technology, etc.) as well as social practices, as sites of vocal control that carefully and predictably orchestrate the sonorous contributions of their inhabitants. Acclimating our receiving bodies to the possibilities of wider ranges of volume and simultaneous vocalization would encourage the development of pedagogical innovations that would otherwise register as unproductively out of control.

Yet expanding individual and collective capacities to experience a wider range of soundscapes as amenable to pedagogical goals will not constitute an unqualified or immediate step toward a greater degree of intervocal justice. Louder and less vocally focused classrooms will present significant and difficult to resolve challenges to students and instructors with various forms of hearing loss and sensory sensitivities. Teresa Blankmeyer Burke describes how moving from an institutional setting where small-scale, fairly polite classroom conversations were the norm to one where loud disagreements and overtalking were common made her participation as a hearing-impaired student much more difficult:

> It wasn't until I experienced my first seminar in graduate school that I realized the limits of the speech-reading strategies I had honed as a mainstreamed student sitting in the front row of the classroom, eyes locked onto the professor's face as I scrawled notes across my neatly lined paper. The shift from small seminar courses at a women's college, with eight to ten students who deliberately took turns and drew in quiet classmates, to the aggressive "verbal brawling" of male-dominated graduate philosophy courses was an adjustment, to say the least. In order to speech-read, one must first locate the speaker, which most people do via listening, not looking. Measured seminar discourse with hand-raising, turn taking, and pauses to ensure that the speech-reader has made eye contact, is much more effective for speech-readers than discourse where impassioned speakers talk over one another in order to gain the floor (and one surmises, to assert dominance). (Burke and Nicodemus 2013)

Finding ways to organize the activities and/or the learning space in ways that render the classroom experience maximally accessible to all students will require innovation and creative problem-solving on the part of instructors, some of whom will have limited support from their institution in devising such approaches. Moreover, philosophy instructors will not always be aware of the auditory status of all of their students, who are under no obligation to disclose that status. Should such disclosure occur, instructors must take their students' auditory status into account when shaping the sonorous environment of the classroom.

Perfect and perfectly equal accessibility with regard to any aspect of the classroom, including its sonorous aspects, will, of course, remain beyond any instructor's reach. Contrary to the implicit promise of the Universal Design model, spaces, activities, infrastructure, and so on cannot be designed in a way to render them equally accessible to all bodies (indeed, as Aimi Hamraie [2016] argues, to the degree to which Universal Design has been developed in isolation from vital commitments and insights emerging from critical disability studies, it tends to reproduce ableist norms and structures). That promise belies the many ways that accommodating for one set of bodily particularities can result in decreasing accessibility for another. The same classroom may include participants whose ability to learn and participate is greatly increased by engaging in handcraft, such as knitting, and participants for whom the visual and sonorous stimuli associated with handcraft creates excruciating and incapacitating discomfort. Because learning engages a wide range of bodily capacities, and because there is no neutral, universally shared set of bodily capacities, there is no set of pedagogical choices that can guarantee perfectly identical and equitable access. Yet attending to how those choices affect accessibility is preferable to merely and uncritically reproducing the pedagogical status quo, which is not itself ethically or politically neutral.

Allowing Students to Hear Instructors Think

The sonorous qualities associated with the lecture format, including the stereotypical droning of a monotone or the vocal booming that brims with confidence, often indicate that the instructor has already worked out (and worked over) the presented content. If the lecture is particularly well presented, those receiving it may experience some surprise at its twists and turns—but the instructor knows what lies ahead (and, unlike the actor, is not trained to speak from the moment *as if* one does not know what lies ahead). The lecture thus offers to students the finished product of an instructor's thinking process. What it cannot display for the students is the development of philosophical insight and knowledge in real time, and if the purpose of the philosophical classroom is not only to transmit knowledge, but also to develop philosophical skills, failing to model grappling with texts and ideas is a significant omission. Such grappling would, for most instructors, entail an entirely different set of vocal gestures from those typical of the traditional lecture. There would be hesitations, false starts, pauses, perhaps even nonlinguistic expressions of frustration, enthusiasm, or puzzlement. Unlike the lecturing voice, this voice would struggle. The alive-ness of the questions posed by both students and instructors—the fact that they are asked precisely because the answer is not predetermined or prefabricated— would be sounded, producing a simultaneously vocal and philosophical mobility that emanates from the relation with the students and their embodied particularity. The instructor who allows the students to witness the development of their own thought will share in the discussion's potential for uncertainty and surprise, and that uncertainty will, if deployed effectively, imbue the classroom with a compelling sonorous vibrancy that would normalize the confusion that many students experience when reading and discussing philosophy.

Utilizing Podcasts as Listening Assignments

So far, the suggestions I have made regarding pedagogical approaches to envoicing in the classroom have focused on vocal discussions of the class material, with the implicit assumption that the assigned texts under consideration are written. The ever-increasing availability of podcasts, however, provides philosophy instructors with a new source of texts marked from the outset as sonorous and vocal (care would need to be taken to ensure that the material was also available in formats accessible to D/deaf students). Podcasts offer opportunities to render the philosophical classroom more diverse and inclusive, both in terms of the ideas presented and the kinds of sonorous voices that can be received; the comparatively modest start-up costs associated with podcasting have allowed podcasters to produce and share their production without ties to an established media corporation (Berry 2006), thus mitigating, although not obviating completely, the unequitable allocation of representation found in mainstream media (Bottomley 2015: 181).

Podcasts instantiate intervocality in a variety of ways. Certainly podcasters design their products for far more specific audiences than mainstream radio, a focus detectable in their content and sonorous characteristics. As Lars Nyre describes, where radio is designed "for anyone-as-someone" (2015: 282)—the listener receives the product directly, and thus has the experience of being individually addressed, but is also framed as generic—podcasting is designed "for-anyone-as-interested" (283). Moreover, the material conditions under which podcasts are consumed are significantly controlled by the listener; mobility, platform choice, and on-demandedness is central to the genre. Podcast listeners can easily transform at least some of the sonorous qualities of any given podcast, opting, for example, to listen at twice the normal speed, or to eliminate pauses (such capacities, however, need to be understood within the context of capitalist consumerism; see Morris and Patterson 2015). Even the choice of hardware has significant impact on the experience of listening: earbuds penetrate the body's social borders, implying intimacy and directness; headphones include a sense of cushioning, but can also become physically uncomfortable after long periods of time; and not using either would allow the sound of the podcast to extend to larger spaces, either private or shared.

Philosophical podcasts also have the potential to capture intervocal exchanges between and among thinkers, allowing their consumers to eavesdrop on philosophical conversations that envoice the participants in particular ways. Of course, not all philosophical podcasts include exchanges; some are little more than recorded lectures or musings provided by a single individual. But the medium is more amenable to exchanges, and certainly to extended vocalized exchanges involving two or three interlocutors, than either academic journals or the classroom; in addition, the exchanges they can facilitate are often more in-depth and extended than those in a question and answer part of a conference presentation. And while radio and other audio media have the ability to capture intervocal exchanges, they rarely focus on specifically philosophical exchanges; podcasting's low barriers to entry make it more welcoming to interests that are not necessarily culturally dominant. Including podcasts within the assignments of a philosophy classroom, then, can serve to return voice to philosophy, just as Cavarero suggests, and potentially ameliorate the exclusion of marginalized perspectives that more traditional media entail.

The vocally unjust practices likely to be perpetuated in the traditional lecture format, particularly in a discipline with disproportionate levels of white, male, cishet practitioners, are yet another reason to seek out pedagogical alternatives. Engaging carefully and creatively with the sonorous classroom, along the lines of the possibilities I have offered here, can envoice both instructors and students in ways that forward both student learning and vocal justice.

Philosophy Conferences

Just as there are a wide variety of types of philosophy classrooms, not all philosophy conferences are organized in identical ways. Some encourage participants to read papers ahead of time (presumably silently), reserving the meeting time entirely for discussion. The vast majority of philosophy conferences in the United States, however, consist of individual presenters, sometimes arranged in groups or panels, reading prepared papers aloud. The gathered audience listens and is eventually invited to pose questions or comments; the ensuing discussion is usually shorter than the time dedicated to the reading of papers. Occasionally, but less commonly, an author will not read the paper word-for-word, but instead present the ideas more extemporaneously, often in conjunction with visual elements and/or a handout. Not infrequently, papers are followed by comments prepared and delivered by other participants; in such cases, the comments are usually shared in advance, and the author has the opportunity to prepare a response.

While recognizing that the purposes of a conference extend well beyond the presented papers—conversations over dinner or coffee or drinks are often just as valuable as attending the scheduled talks—it still seems reasonable to understand the presented paper, and therefore the voice, as central to the conference experience. To attend a philosophy conference is to be promised a fairly rare experience in our daily lives: to hear philosophy spoken in real time, to be steeped in philosophy-as-sound, philosophy-as-voice, to engage ideas and their creators in a shared, and carefully constructed, sonorous environment. Philosophy conferences thus seem to recognize the importance of our intervocality.

Yet voice is also strangely devalued within philosophy conferences. While the conference is a carefully organized sonorous environment, with clear (at least to those well versed in the cultural context) rules about when and how different voices emerge, the vocal prosodies encountered at a philosophy conference are both extremely limited and considered peripheral to philosophical practice. The voice that philosophers bring to the task of reading papers is almost always a measured voice, unmarked by changing rhythms or tempos, lacking in expressivity and inflection. Although there are certainly exceptions to this rule, it seems that philosophers' reputations for droning monotones is well earned.

Moreover, despite the importance of conferences to scholars, philosophy as a profession puts little to no time or energy into developing its practitioners as speakers—and, just as importantly, as listeners. As speakers, we are encouraged to sharpen our ideas, plug up the gaps in our argument, develop a philosophical insight; as listeners, we are encouraged to listen intently for accuracy, originality, and, if we're honest, mistakes. But when it comes to sharing those ideas in public, in the company of other scholars whose responses we value, we pay almost no attention to the bodily complexity of generating and receiving sounded voices. The paper is finished once it is written, and any rehearsal is aimed almost entirely at time management. Our preparation to hear a philosophical paper is even more paltry, limited perhaps to gathering our focus and silencing our phones.

The voice privileged at a philosophy conference is a reading voice, not a voice animated by emergent thought and the feelings that thought inspires. Its monotone is grounded in the fact that it is relaying meanings that have been set, fixed in advance, worked out and worked over (not unlike the lecturing voice). Now it is true that not every reading voice has this quality of being-done; there are real pleasures in being read to, when the reading voice is expressive, dynamic, and actively interpreting the work that is being read. But in philosophy conferences, such vibrant reading voices are remarkably rare. More varied vocal tones and tempos tend to emerge in the question and answer period, where the voice is engaged in more spontaneous meaning-making, and where the speaker's voice is often directed at an individual person, responding to a specific question, comment, or challenge. Such a voice brings intervocality to the fore, insofar as it is marked in both sound and content by the particularity of the other persons in the room.

Related to their failure to engage in a wide range of intervocal possibilities are the myriad ways in which typical philosophy conferences enact multiple forms of vocal injustice. I will explore just three potent examples here, although there are surely others worthy of analysis.

The temporal organization of voice typical to philosophical conferences represents a set of conversational norms that are common in predominantly white social spaces: the silent, still audience who withholds most or any vocal responses to the presentation until the question and answer period, the individualized turn-taking of questions, and so on. Such norms preclude the sort of vocal affirmations or disagreements that, in some US communities of color, communicate respect by letting the speaker know that the audience is paying appropriate attention. Sonorous environments that would perceive such spontaneous and repeated responses to the presentation as rude, untoward, and unwelcome require aural code-switching on the part of participants accustomed to different vocal norms; they also can leave similarly situated speakers confused and uncertain as to how to interpret the silent passivity of the audience, which can seem to communicate either disapproval or indifference.

D/deaf or hard of hearing participants in philosophy conferences regularly find their access to presentations nonexistent, significantly limited, or achieved only after expending enormous amounts of time, emotional and cognitive labor, and persistence. Signed language interpreters are not provided as a matter of course; such accommodations must be individually sought after, even at the largest of conferences that attract upwards of a thousand participants and thus are likely to include D/deaf or hard of hearing individuals. When interpretation services are requested, conference organizers not infrequently balk at the cost, implying or stating outright that they are unwilling or unable to provide the services; even when there is the willingness and financial ability to support the presence of an interpreter, ensuring that those interpreters have the disciplinary knowledge necessary for interpreting philosophical papers and conversations is challenging (Burke 2017, Burke and Nicodemus 2013). As Burke points out, the majority of the labor involved in identifying whether an accommodation such as an interpreter is legally required, and then insisting that organizations meet that legal requirement, falls on the part of the deaf participant (2017: 274); such additional forms of labor are required and expected for participants with a wide variety of disabilities (Tremain 2013). For participants who have hearing losses of various degrees, amplification systems are often inadequate, and while the sonorous norms are slowly changing on this front, too often audience members are convinced that they "don't need the mic"—perhaps precisely because they are accustomed, as the previous section detailed, to embodying the privileged position of the lecturer! Such unjustified confidence in their ability to articulate and project their voices sufficiently excludes participants who experience the speakers' vocal contributions as hopelessly muddied and/or muffled.

Finally, the persistent monolingualism of philosophy conferences in the United States, particularly combined with the classism and lack of socioeconomic diversity within contemporary academia, marginalizes participants whose vocal identities are enmeshed with languages, dialects, and accents other than those associated with so-called Standard English. Such marginalization encourages the development of a philosophical ear ill-equipped to engage with vocal diversity; although to my knowledge no empirical studies have been conducted along these lines, it seems likely that, just as instructors are penalized on student evaluations for having a perceivable accent (Gill 1994, Subtirelu 2015), presenters who have a nonnormative accent (a category which, in the field of philosophy, would not include British accents, which would probably enhance credibility) are perceived as less scholarly, less intellectual, and less philosophically impressive.

The philosophical conference is a crucial site of professional development where arguments are honed prior to publication, collaborations are instigated, friendships among scholars are deepened, and academic reputations are nurtured (or tarnished, or torpedoed). Exclusion from full participation in conferences harms philosophers' professional and intellectual prospects. The sonorous environments typical of philosophical conferences are obviously not the only forms of exclusion that are at work; the high financial cost of attendance, the ubiquity of racist, sexist, classist, transphobic, heterosexist, and ableist microaggressions, not to mention pernicious patterns of sexual harassment, all serve to perpetuate existing forms of structural injustice. Yet if the discipline and profession of philosophy is to address long-standing patterns of exclusion and marginalization, it must include the sonorous sphere in its attempts at transformation and seek out models for more ethical forms of envoicing.

The Association for Feminist Ethics and Social Theory (FEAST) has been holding biennial conferences since 2001. The 10th FEAST, held in October 2019, included two keynote addresses that challenged and disrupted dominant sonorous practices of philosophy conferences. As a specific genre of academic speech, keynotes are potent ways to honor a scholar's contributions, and so invitations to provide keynote addresses are reserved for accomplished and widely recognized figures. In addition, it is common (although certainly not universal) for keynote addresses to either not have question and answer periods, or only to have very brief ones. Although the two keynotes at FEAST 2019 retained the practice of recognizing highly esteemed and respected scholars, they departed from the status quo in structure, format, and sonorous qualities.

The first was billed as a "Keynote Conversation" between Kristie Dotson, professor of philosophy at Michigan State University, and Brittney Cooper, associate professor of Women's and Gender Studies and Africana Studies at Rutgers University. Dotson and Cooper had been provided a set of guiding questions from the conference organizers that served as launching points for a freewheeling conversation highlighting the speakers' friendship, considerable existing bodies of work, experiences within and outside of academia, and emerging lines of thought. The speakers explored the multiple ways in which academic institutions excluded and harmed students and instructors from historically marginalized groups, with particular attention paid to the experiences of girls and women of color.

Neither an interview nor a debate, this keynote was a rare opportunity to witness two scholar-friends riff off, tease, challenge, and affirm each other. In its comparatively unpredictable nature (especially since the organizers of the conference expected that the keynoters would amend or reject the provided questions as they saw fit), its focus on an exchange between scholars who were also friends, and its rejection of the association of intellectual firepower with the formality usually surrounding keynotes (both participants sat at a table, ignoring the available podium), the conversation constituted a meaningful break with usual protocols, including those related to vocalizations. The keynoters deployed the sound of their voices to disrupt the soundscape of the (feminist) philosophy conference, which continues with exceedingly few exceptions to conform to racialized white sonorous norms.

Eschewing those norms, and refusing to deploy the code-switching so often required of scholars of color, Drs. Dotson and Cooper sonorously voiced their racialized identities through a variety of vocal gestures and traits: interrupting and overlapping, verbal and nonverbal utterances of support or disagreement, regional accents, and individualized, distinct vocalizations (such as Dr. Dotson's signature chuckle that erupts, and then is somehow immediately revoked, a nonverbal utterance that elegantly and efficiently communicates: this would be funny if it weren't so horrific). The constant juxtaposition of informal language with scholarly terms provided a sonorous contrast between the short, monosyllabic staccato of expletives and the sustained legato of academic phrases such as "the multistability of oppression." In an extended riff on the ways in which academic rigor can and in fact must be deployed to arrive at an appropriately nuanced understanding of the history of Black feminist thought, Dr. Cooper began a series of increasingly intense and urgent sentences with "Rigor demands...," using anaphora to invoke both classical forms of rhetoric and recognizably Black forms of oratory (Leeman and Duffy 2012: 5–6). As Drs. Dotson and Cooper expounded on their own relation to the demands and possibilities of Black excellence, their sonorous vocalizations simultaneously instantiated and laid claim to that excellence, marrying the prestige of the keynote address to an unapologetically Black set of vocal sounds and gestures.

By defying the racialized sonorous norms usually accompanying keynote addresses, Drs. Dotson and Cooper created space for members of the audience— especially, but not only, the people of color in the audience—to participate in that defiance. Abandoning the silence usually required of audiences, the gathered group responded frequently to the speakers with a variety of sonorous actions, some vocal (laughing, affirmative humming, groaning) and some not (snapping, clapping). Even the periods of quiet on the part of the audience were in response to the speakers' vocal qualities, and so rather than registering as a kind of generic sonorous deference to established norms, they contributed to a complex and dynamic sonorous texture that both honored and was produced by the particular material, embodied voices and receiving bodies in the room. Central to that texture was the fact that the audience, while still majority white, not only included more women of color than is common at philosophy conferences (including feminist philosophy conferences), but multiple African American female-identified philosophers who either had already or would present papers of their own. The keynote speakers were not just speaking about Black women thinkers; they were clearly speaking to Black women thinkers, and to specific Black women thinkers—academics and teachers who regularly struggle with and against racist practices and norms, including the contemporary sonic color line of the academy. By refusing to engage in the code-switching that the persistently white institutions of higher education so often require of students and faculty of color, Drs. Dotson and Cooper enlisted the vocal and listening practices developed in and supportive of communities of color, thus centering the vocal and aural identities of the women of color present. The white listening ear, actively sidelined, was asked only to do the work necessary to remain in the sonorous interaction, or not, as it wished—most centrally, the speakers rejected the dominant sonorous norms of the academy by refusing to shape their sounded voices in accordance to the (always implicit, always masquerading as neutral) demands of the white listening ear.

The second keynote of FEAST 2019 was provided by Dr. Talia Bettcher, a prominent philosopher with expertise in trans philosophy and philosophy of language. The tensions that had erupted in the field of feminist philosophy in the wake of the Tuvel controversy two years prior continued to fester, although they were perhaps not quite as acutely felt as they had been at FEAST 2017 when the continued existence of the premier journal of feminist philosophy, *Hypatia*, seemed to hang by a thread.[4] Inviting a transwoman philosopher to provide a keynote address clearly established that in the disciplinary controversies that had raged since then, FEAST was positioning itself as a trans-friendly professional organization. Dr. Bettcher's address itself also staked out some crucial commitments regarding vocal politics.

One of the most striking aspects of Dr. Bettcher's address was its almost complete refusal to use any written text. With the exception of reading two quotations verbatim from her iPad, Dr. Bettcher spoke for more than forty minutes without any notes or text (Drs. Dotson and Cooper were similarly untethered, but the fact that Dr. Bettcher's address was an individual presentation rather than a dialogue makes the fact even more notable). Crossing back and forth at the front of the room with a handheld microphone, Bettcher spoke with unusual immediacy about complex theoretical frameworks, working her way through texts both historical and contemporary, allowing the audience to witness the voicing of her ideas, not as recitation of words on a static page, but as sonorously emergent, marked in timbre, intonation, volume, and tempo by the relation of the thoughts to each other, the relative importance or complexity of those thoughts, and the audience's responses to them. And in case there was any confusion about the importance of the audience's ability to follow along with Bettcher's analysis, she periodically paused her talk to ask the audience: are you following me? Are we okay? The query was no mere rhetorical device, nor was it a pro forma gesture of civility, as was evident from the length of the pause, and how it was accompanied by Dr. Bettcher's visual scanning of the audience. Such a genuine invitation to request clarification was a linguistic and vocal recognition that the content of Bettcher's address needed to be marked by what her audience was or was not grasping.

The sonorous qualities of Bettcher's address—its explicitly conversational tone, accompanied by a clear framework and sense of direction—created an intellectual, intervocal environment that was neither purely improvisational (Bettcher clearly had a sense of where she was going, and what she needed to accomplish, and her analysis was obviously undergirded by years of research and careful thought) nor purely linguistically predetermined (as evidenced by the complete lack of written text). Bettcher was engaging in a dynamic intervocality that allowed the gathered audience to receive her ideas as vocalized in the moment for a particular group of receiving, aural bodies. Bettcher let her audience hear her think.

It is important to note that none of the ways in which these addresses was undertaken were necessary or obligatory by virtue of the identities, vocal and otherwise, of the scholars who provided them. It would be yet another instantiation of intervocal injustice if keynoters who identify as members of social groups historically and currently marginalized within academia could be heard only if they eschewed traditional forms of address. And although there were certain sonorous elements to the conversation between Dr. Dotson and Dr. Cooper that registered (accurately or not) as being related to some shared roots in Black sonic culture, to reduce the sonorous meanings of their vocalizations to a presumed belonging in a specific social group would be to underestimate both the differences in their lived experiences as African American women (differences, such as regional location, class, etc., that are likely to show up in their voices) and their own idiosyncratic vocal gestures. With regard to Dr. Bettcher, her privileging of intervocal immediacy and emergence is at best tangentially related to her identity as a transwoman; although, as we have discussed in earlier chapters, voice and the politics of voice are deeply meaningful within trans communities, the vocal cultures at work in them are not as saturated with accrued meanings as those produced, as Jennifer Stoever (2015) has argued, by centuries of the sonic color line and the workings of the white listening ear under white supremacy in the United States.

In describing these two keynote addresses in the way that I have, I recognize that I risk presenting them as paradigms of vocal justice that effectively undermine the exclusionary sonorous norms of philosophical conferences. And indeed, I do hold that these keynotes were important sites of sonorous resistance to vocal injustice, particularly forms of vocal injustice at the intersection of anti-Black racism, sexism, and transphobia. However, even these sites of resistance replicated other forms of vocal injustice without problematizing them. Neither keynote was signed by a professional signed language interpreter; as a relatively small organization with limited funds, FEAST would be unlikely to provide such interpretation as a matter of course, although the organization is currently seeking funding sources that would support this and other accessibility accommodations (personal correspondence with Christine Wieseler, Chair of FEAST's Access Committee, March 20, 2020). While the conference organizers emphasized throughout the conference the need for all speakers to use the microphone, attendees with various degrees of hearing loss still found it difficult to hear the speakers' voices clearly. The sources of this difficulty weren't always obvious; perhaps the amplification was of a murky quality, or the cavernous rooms made it difficult to focus the amplified sound, or the speakers spoke too quickly. Despite these persistent manifestations of vocal injustice, the sonorous aspects of these two keynote addresses were significant and effective interventions in a persistently sonorously oppressive site of philosophical activity.

Conclusion

As sites of philosophical engagement, the classroom and the conference can be understood either as counterarguments to Cavarero's characterization of the persistent devocalization of philosophy or as instantiations of her recommended course of action, that is, as progressive steps toward the revocalization of philosophy. I have suggested that the recentering of voice in philosophical practices has different ramifications for each: for teaching, it would serve to heighten the value of teaching as philosophical practice and challenge the dominance of the lecture as a standard pedagogical approach, while for conferences, it would serve to question dominant sonorous norms to render the conference more inclusive to various participants, particularly those who have been marginalized by structural inequalities such as sexism, racism, classism, ableism, ageism, homophobia, and transphobia. Perhaps most generally, this chapter has sought to serve as an example of the kinds of analyses, questions, and insights that can be generated when sonorous and vocal (in)justice is applied as a conceptual framework. On that point, I am in utter agreement with Cavarero; philosophy has ignored sound and voice for too long, and overcoming that deficit is essential to transforming the discipline into a more inclusive and just site of intellectual inquiry.

Conclusion: Shifting Vocal Soundscapes in the Age of Trump and Covid-19

Our central theoretical frameworks—intervocality, respiratory responsibility, envoicing, vocal generosity—generate new ethical insights into challenges of our time, particularly as they establish the material voice as a site of contemporary social, political, and ecological dynamics as well as a zone of potential. In this final chapter, we examine multiple instantiations of the current sonorous body politic, drawing connections among specific archetypes (the politician, the cowboy), disparate genres (the public political hearing, the stage of musical theatre), and newly politicized, ethically fraught acts (social isolation, masking). We are particularly interested in transformations in vocal politics: how new and emerging vocalizations can produce new political realities and understandings, and how a global pandemic places into acute relief our responsibility for each other's breath and well-being. The overarching argument of this work has been that the soundedness of human vocalization is ethically, socially, and politically meaningful, and that paying close and careful attention to workings of the sound of human vocalizations illuminates important insights about injustice, inequality, and structures of human interaction. The Trump era, and its collision with an unprecedented social, economic, and health crisis, featured rapidly shifting soundscapes that revealed hidden weaknesses in the current political order and new possibilities for resistance and flourishing.

We begin with shifts in the sound of white cishet male authority, identifying new vocal iterations on both political and theatrical stages that, respectively, double down on and mock white male supremacy. We then turn our attention to the politics of breath and voice in the age of Covid-19, exploring the political under- and overtones of mask-wearing and other responses to a pandemic that has rendered shared air a threat to public health.

Gendered Vocal Performances on the Political Stage

Joshua Gunn (2010) notes a contemporary and historical association of uncontrolled speech with femininity and measured, controlled speech with masculinity. Although Gunn does not articulate this dynamic explicitly, it seems clear that the privileging of controlled speech and masculinity goes both ways: that is, controlled speech gains value via its association with masculinity, and masculinity gains value via its association with controlled speech. Noting the damaging effects of Howard Dean's "scream" on his political candidacy, Gunn demonstrates that engaging with uncontrolled speech can make a politician seem untrustworthy, and insufficiently self-controlled; more specifically, the body from which such speech emanates is not sufficiently managed and contained by the mind, and thus is dangerously associated with the feminine (Gunn 2010: 12). Barack Obama's perceived eloquence rested on his careful management of emotions, a mandate both raced and gendered (22). By contrast, unsurprisingly, Hillary Clinton's vocalizations were consistently subjected to the "terrible catch-22" (25) that plagues virtually all female-identified public figures: if one performs femininity well, one does not register as a strong leader, but if one does not perform femininity well, one is disliked. "What I want to suggest is that performances of femininity are principally vocal and related, not to arguments, but to *tone*; not to appearance, but to *speech*; not to good reasons, but to *sound*. This implies that the ideology of sexism is much more insidious, much more deeply ingrained than many might suppose: we don't simply *think* in discriminatory ways, *we hear in sex*" (25, emphasis in the original).

There is much in Gunn's analysis that rings true. Yet recent political events have undermined the notion that privileged white masculinity always or even consistently finds its voice in self-controlled tones, emotional restraint, and something recognizable as eloquence. To the contrary: white male supremacy has found its voice in the scream, the furious bellow, the sneer and the delightful deployment of mocking tones. The vocal performances of the public figures involved in two controversies that instigated public hearings before Congress and received widespread public attention—the 2018 confirmation process of Supreme Court nominee Brett Kavanaugh, and the 2019 House impeachment inquiry—trouble the neat association between controlled, reasoned masculine voices and social and political power.

The confirmation hearings of Brett Kavanaugh were dominated by the emergence of accusations that he had sexually assaulted a young woman while he was in high school, some thirty years prior to his nomination. Dr. Christine Blasey Ford testified to the Senate Judiciary Committee (then chaired by Republican Chuck Grassley), describing in painstaking detail her experience of being assaulted by Kavanaugh. Kavanaugh then also appeared before the committee, and defended himself against the accusations. The differences in the vocal performances of Ford and Kavanaugh were so striking, and so unmistakable, that they received significant attention in the mainstream media (Poniewozik 2018). Ford spoke in a calm, direct voice that only occasionally and slightly shook with nervousness and trepidation. Her voice had a consistent gentleness to it, as well as a resolute eagerness to please, and her expertise as a neuroscientist undergirded her patient explanations of how memories of trauma are stored. As many public commentators noticed, Ford was in many ways the ideal victim: white, educated, reasonable, not hysterical.

Kavanaugh, by contrast, used his opening statement to launch a furious, emotionally charged, partisan attack on the proceedings, as well as a defiant defense of his character. Alternating between rage and self-pity, he yelled, cried, and spat out his words in tones dripping with disdain. Photos captured his face screwed up in rage, an astonishing image for a candidate for the nation's highest court, whose justices are supposed to be paragons of impartiality and rationality. Kavanaugh consistently adopted a puerile tone of surly opposition; when Senator Amy Klobuchar asked whether he had ever experienced a blackout, he (not once but twice) threw the question back at her: "Have you?" He subsequently apologized for the question, but it, and the tone with which it was hurled, was typical of his testimony. Ford, on the other hand, could afford no such outbursts. Maintaining any hope of credibility and legibility required her to stay constant and centered, working through her own feelings in the most dutiful of ways; if she clamped down on her breathing and became stoic, any hope of empathy would be lost, but if she erupted in leaky emotionality, the charge of hysteria would surely follow. Kavanaugh could fling his hot-headed anger in every direction, but Ford's trauma was hers and hers alone to manage.

Interestingly, the vocal performances of Ford and Kavanaugh were widely analyzed in the mainstream media and consistently described in ways similar to our description above. Unable to paint Ford as overemotional and thus entirely or intentionally unreliable, Republicans were forced to come up with an alternative interpretation of her testimony that left her motives and honesty (if not the credibility of her memory) largely unchallenged. Similarly, the explosive emotionality of Kavanaugh's testimony was noted, and some pundits providing live coverage of the hearings wondered aloud whether he had doomed his own nomination (Siddiqui 2018). Such concerns were quickly shown to be unfounded, and Brett Kavanaugh was confirmed as a Supreme Court Justice on October 6, 2018.

At first glance, it would seem as though Ford followed a certain gendered script in terms of her vocal performance, while Kavanaugh departed from one. Ford was deploying a voice that, while still recognizably female-identified, was striving to avoid the vocal gestures and traits that are used to invalidate testimony from women. The vocal mandates that she enacted so artfully (be clear, but not confrontational; direct, but not oppositional; descriptive, but not emotional) is itself a gender script, a demand that female-identified persons modulate their tones and registers in relation to an entrenched set of listening practices designed to receive their speech (particularly speech about experiences of sexual assault) with a hermeneutics of suspicion. Ford, like Anita Hill before her, shaped her vocalizations in response to a complex, interlocking set of systemic injustices, in order to wrest from a hostile environment some scraps of the credibility it was so eager to deny her.

Kavanaugh, on the other hand, seems to abandon the very vocal traits Gunn describes. Where are the measured tones, the soothing, calm forthrightness that reflects order and temperance? How can brittle emotionality teetering on the edge of hysteria (and sometimes seeming to take the plunge) serve the purposes of male supremacy? How can adopting the vocal characteristics of a hyperprivileged teenager—the defiance, the proud proclaiming of his love of beer, the how-dare-they overtones of entitlement—serve as evidence for his suitability for a position revered for its somberness? Something seems amiss.

The public hearings included in the House of Representatives impeachment inquiry in November 2019 raised similar questions. Although these hearings were also sharply adversarial, with the Democratic House leadership leading the investigation into allegations that the Trump administration withheld Congressionally approved foreign aid for Ukraine for the purposes of domestic political gain, the witnesses did not align neatly along pro- and anti-Trump lines. Even witnesses called by Republican members of the committee revealed damning evidence against the administration (Durkee 2019), as did Republican questioning of witnesses called by Democratic members of the committee (Stahl 2019). Those witnesses called by the committee who plausibly could have defended the administration's actions (such as secretary of state Mike Pompeo, or White House chief of staff Mick Mulvaney) refused to testify.

Yet the gendered politics of voice emerged in this context as well, and again, were widely remarked upon by mainstream media. In particular, the vocal performances of Marie Yovanovitch and Fiona Hill were heralded as the new "voices of female authority" (Hesse 2019), as both diplomats enacted vocal gestures that aligned well with the standards for vocal male authority. They utilized the lower registers common to women of their age, and spoke directly, with little to no emotion and the confidence borne of decades-long careers. Unlike Ford, their vocal traits and gestures did not seem designed to navigate the minefield of sexist assumptions about female-identified voices, their credibility and authority. Screw the minefield, they seemed to say; I know what I'm talking about, and you can take it or leave it.

There was no dearth of normative masculine vocal performances in these hearings. Providing damning evidence against the administration, Bill Taylor and Lt. Col. Alexander Vindman utilized the direct, emotionally uninflected vocalizations that Gunn associates with masculine authority; Taylor's testimony in particular was compared favorably to Walter Cronkite (McLaughlin 2019), thus associating him with a paradigm of vocal masculine trustworthiness. However, the testimony of Gordon Sondland, the ambassador to the European Union (and major donor to the Trump campaign) who was given a leading role in interactions with Ukraine, and who testified to the clear existence of a quid pro quo in relation to the congressionally approved funds in question, veered from the vocal norms that Taylor and Vindman enacted. Appearing as the jovial, easygoing dilettante, Sondland's humorous asides and casual cheer lent his vocal performance an almost playful nonchalance. Although such a vocal performance is recognizably masculine (we know immediately that we are in the presence of the hail fellow well met), it is nevertheless at odds with the serious, stately tones of normative masculine, political authority.

And so, as we survey these two sites of public testimony, we see a wide scope of gendered vocal performances: Ford as a navigator of dangerous vocal waters, attempting to speak her feminine identity and derive as much credibility as possible from a testimonially unjust situation; Kavanaugh as the defiantly aggrieved, victimized male raging against the forces that would deny him his due; Taylor and Vindman as the self-possessed statesmen, using the comforting low tones of masculine authority; Sondland as the friendly, easygoing guy with whom you'd like to have a beer; and Yovanovitch and Hill, rejecting the demands of the deferential, accommodating feminine voice, adopting distinctly masculine vocal norms.

Moreover, gender is not the only identity factor at work here: no fewer than three of the witnesses (Vindman, Yovanovitch, and Hill) identified explicitly and proudly as immigrants, and their immigrant status was widely reported and commented upon (Gessen 2019). Yet it matters that the immigrant status of the witnesses was communicated primarily through the content of their speech, and that by and large, it was not visually or, for two out of the three, aurally perceivable. Only Hill's voice is inflected with a recognizable (working-class) British accent—one that is generally subject to neither anti-immigrant nor socioeconomic bias in the United States, which is at least in part why she chose to start her career here (Morrison 2019). All three present as racialized white, and thus distinguished from the immigrants vilified and targeted by the policies of the Trump administration. Thus, although the immigrant witnesses in these hearings attempted to counter the anti-immigrant sentiment predominant in the Trump administration, by presenting their immigrant status as an indicator of their reliability and commitment to US political values, their ability to do so rested significantly on the fact that they neither looked nor sounded like the types of immigrants regularly described as dangerous, polluting, and parasitic.

In some ways, the vocal performances of the female-identified persons in these two sites are easier to analyze in relation to vocal injustice than those of their male-identified counterparts. Ford, Yovanovitch, and Hill are all responding to vocal stereotypes and unjust listening practices in their attempts to secure social and political credibility. Although all three used the measured tones normatively associated with masculine trustworthiness, Ford's vocal performance was widely viewed as more deferential and accommodating, perhaps because she was seeking to establish a new kind of credibility (as a survivor of sexual violence), whereas Yovanovitch and Hill were simply displaying their well-established credibility as seasoned, experienced diplomats. The sheer act of aspiration on the part of a female-identified public figure, understood as a potentially transgressive request for masculine-coded social goods (Manne 2018) frames vocalizations in particular ways.

The vocal performances of Kavanaugh and Sondland are more puzzling. That the performances succeeded is beyond question; Kavanaugh emerged not only unscathed but victorious, and Sondland's reputation as a successful businessman was untarnished. Yet both departed from dominant vocal masculine norms within the political context, Kavanaugh most dramatically. Why didn't the masculine authority usually shored up by a familiar and recognizably masculine voice erode in the face of Kavanaugh's lack of temperateness and Sondland's informality?

The persistence of Kavanaugh's distinctly masculine authority reveals a fundamental misunderstanding within the standard story of gendered vocal dynamics. As we have argued elsewhere in this work, intervocality establishes that practices of receiving sound co-construct, together with the sonorous elements produced by the emanating body, vocal events, and their political meanings. Such an approach undermines the assumption that if female-identified persons vocalized in ways associated with masculine-identified persons, they would earn the same social privileges that those male-identified voices do (just speak low and confidently, ladies, and that raise is yours!). Kavanaugh's vocal performance indicates that the white male supremacy that shapes vocal politics can be pushed even further. Given that white male supremacy is grounded in the (only rarely spoken or admitted) notion that male-identified beings are simply superior by virtue of their sheer existence, there is something untoward about the possibility that a contingent trait of masculinity, one subject to change or even loss, is the source of prestige and worth. Extreme forms of male supremacy are thus under pressure to discard the trappings of authority, in order to communicate more clearly the stable, ontological grounding of their superiority.

When Kavanaugh discards the masculine vocal norms of reasonableness, emotional control, and even lower pitch, he does not undermine his masculine claim to that which he deserves. Instead, he strengthens it, in multiple ways. First, the very fact that such a paradigm of reasonableness has lost his temper is read as a signal that something has gone terribly awry in the social order; given the greater social credence given to male anger, his lack of emotional control registers as compelling evidence that he has, in fact, been grievously wronged (see Chapter 4). Second, his flouting of political and institutional norms—for example, hurling partisan invective in a supposedly nonpartisan procedure addressing his suitability for a position that requires one to be resolutely nonpartisan—aligns with a distinctly masculine independence, a refusal to subordinate oneself to the seemingly petty demands of institutions. This is a distinctly Trumpian form of masculinity, and it is no accident that many commentators wondered if Kavanaugh's fairly uncharacteristic performance was enacted at the behest of the president himself. What Kavanaugh's successful vocal performance reveals with astonishing clarity is that claims of male entitlement can, and perhaps even must, demonstrate their independence from gendered vocal mandates.

The success of Sondland's vocal performance is both similar to and distinct from Kavanaugh's. Importantly, and unlike Kavanaugh, Sondland is not aspiring to a specific position to which he clearly thought he was entitled; nor was he at risk of losing his economic status, and as someone with no apparent political aspirations, he had little to gain by ingratiating himself with either Trump or the voters. At most, he seemed to be hoping to limit his vulnerability to prosecution, particularly regarding possible charges of lying to Congress. Just like Kavanaugh, however, Sondland's affect, of which his vocal performance was a crucial element, flouted expectations and social norms. His warm, joking tones indicated an unwillingness to be molded by the intimidating institutional setting. Even as his testimony was roundly described as explosive and damning, his bodily posture and vocalizations insisted on his ability and right to be his own casual, friendly self, seemingly impervious to the weighty procedure in which he had become entangled.

Kavanaugh's and Sondland's vocal performances can be interpreted as a shedding of the masculine vocal mandate to sound like the ideal, trusted voice in favor of an insistence on their own particularity in the face of institutional pressures and demands. Moreover, their particularity, institutional norms and standards be damned, lays claim to their distinctly masculine prestige and social value. Their very departure from, even rejection of, the vocal traits associated with traditional forms of masculine power render them the most masculine men of all.

Envoicing on the Dramatic Stage: A Sonically Woke *Oklahoma!*

The vocal politics of the political sphere, as meaningful as they are, are likely unmarked by intention and purpose. The theatre, however, offers the possibility of engaging actively with the politics of vocal sound to unsettle even the most canonical of works and to challenge audiences to confront whom they've become in relationship to those works. Broadway's 2019 genre-busting revival (Fish and Kluger 2019) of Golden Age musical *Oklahoma!* (Hammerstein 1943) challenged a host of American myths, and did so in part through upending conventions in the vocal art form.

The historical archetypal American voice associated with self-contained social and political persuasiveness, charisma, and charm is preserved and memorialized in the masculine hero of the genre, a sonorously rich baritone leading man who, in this case, represents the voice of a young, unapologetically optimistic, and confident nation certain of its inalienable rights to both land and freedom. Alfred Drake, John Raitt, and Gordon MacRae's performances of the cowboy Curly in the 40s–50s are case studies in a deep, sustained, resonant, controlled, open-throated sound reflective of hegemonic certainty and nationalistic pride. Their nearly operatic vocal performances take up a large swath of acoustic space, simultaneously filling and being contained by the land around them: their voices seem to say not only that they "belong to the land" but that the land belongs to them. Their vocal surety, balanced and full "chiaroscuro" tone, and seamless vibrato assure the listener of the stability of both body and land. More matter than air, these are the voices that "ground" us in earth.

The controlled voice of traditional male authority lives here in opposition to the feminizing elements of air/breath (Allen 2020) and nature/the wild—a civilizing, stabilizing force against the wildness of the American frontier. As a settler at the moment just before Indian Territory becomes reconstituted as a state, Curly's voice and body are closely aligned with a racialized and masculine "myth of stable land" that lies at the heart of geopolitics, wherein national identity is literally "rooted in the earth" (Nieuwenhuis 2016: 310 and 313, Allen 2020). When Curly is arrested for his role in an accidental death, his implicit integrity exempts him from accountability, and his superior ideals (individual responsibility, self-control, independent spirit) place him, necessarily, above the law. Curly is above the law because he is A Good Guy, and We are Great because We are America.

In their astute reimagining of *Oklahoma!* (Fish and Kluger 2019), in which no text from the original is changed, director Daniel Fish and musical director Daniel Kluger echo Sondland's and Kavanaugh's vocal performances in the political arena by pivoting away from archetypal norms of masculine authority, but this time in a critical mode. They, instead, elicit vocalizations that expose but do not redeem the usually hidden and denied particularity on which such authority is founded. By embracing the campfire/cowboy musical idioms and vocal twang originally conceived in Lynn Riggs's source material *Green Grow the Lilacs* (1930), Fish and Kluger recast the singing cowboy as emerging from a specific social and political location, rejecting the Cowboy as an icon of both American paternalism and masculine rugged individualism. Unlike the particularity through which Sondland and Kavanaugh lay claim to the right to be unbeholden to social and political norms, Curly's unmasking reveals him as an untrustworthy scamp turned tease, bully, tormentor, and then cold-blooded murderer. During his kangaroo-court style acquittal, his defenders inform the local judge that "we ain't gonna let you send the boy to jail on his wedding night, we just ain't" (Hammerstein 1943); Lindsey Graham deployed similar vocal gestures when he breathlessly stated during Kavanaugh's confirmation hearings that "if you really wanted to know the truth, you shur as hell wouldna dun watcha dun to this guy" (CNN 2018). Curly has become the personification of American Exceptionalism, unimpeachable by nature, and American Individualism, held in esteem for simply being unapologetically himself, but the ideals are now heard as dangerous and morally depraved constructs.

Like Sondland, there is a new casualness to Curly's voice, a forced ease, a celebration of prestige that comes by almost throwing status away and flouting norms of vocal behavior. No longer an open-throated operatic baritone, actor Damon Duanno of the revival is a twangy, playful high tenor, slight in body, virtuosic in range, even self-indulgent, somewhat mockingly adventurous in his vocalisms. The myth of the (generic) frontiersman at one with the wide open spaces of new land, all deep inner capacity, full of hope and open to the future, is now shattered; this Curly is not in harmony at all, really, as he flexes his (extremely tenuous) white masculine prestige wherever he can. This Curly is thin-skinned, cocky but not confident, on no side but his own, quick on the draw and fully dangerous. The fact that he still possesses considerable charm— his songs rope us in with their unabashed display of vocal skill—is tempting and troubling in equal measure, particularly for members of his new audience who may longingly identify with his maverick spirit.

Fish and Kluger reveal the holes in the myth of the self-contained, self-assured national identity: there is a psychic toll to be paid for this stolen land, a land now rendered unsafe and unstable. The American refusal to recognize its own mythology as such is implicated in a costly insistence that the nation's geographical borders, as well as the bodies of its people, could or should be impermeable, an insistence that denies vulnerability, porousness, availability, and access to air itself in profound ways. We hear Duanno's new cowboy in our (right-wing) political leaders: style and little substance, delusional about their self-made nature, quick to inflict violence on an unassimilable (or invisible, unheard) other, brittle and prone to self-pity as they paradoxically insist on the superiority of their kind (shouldn't such natural superiority be self-evident, and not quite so in need of proclamations?).

Respiratory Responsibility in the time of Covid-19

The role of the image of the body of land that is the indivisible United States, and the archetype of the sturdy, surefooted, free American individual in the context of the pandemic crisis cannot be overstated. The "borders" of the United States are constructed along the lines of a long-standing and paradoxical myth: they are at once impenetrable (before she became Trump's press secretary, Kayleigh McEnany claimed that "we will not see diseases like the coronavirus come here" [Smith and Holden 2020]) and deeply vulnerable to influxes of undesired migration/asylum-seekers/immigration. Framing such influxes as "invasions" further justifies increasingly militarized responses to border-crossings, and, conveniently, denies the dependence of the US economy on those very border-crossers. Such border anxiety is at the heart of the national identity, which takes the nation to be both highly vulnerable to social and economic contamination and yet invulnerable to changes in the global climate, geopolitics, and the spread of infectious diseases. Translating this anxious identity into "America First" policies has, unsurprisingly, targeted immigrant populations, placing enormous physical and psychological pressures on their communities prior to the emergence of the pandemic, and disproportionately intensifying the threats that the pandemic poses to their survival.

The resistance to and denial of the material aspects of vulnerability are at issue here. Where "America" begins/ends (as an idea or a geographical and historical entity) is no longer clearly defined. A deadly virus moved through those "feminine" elements of air and water—through air sacs in lungs, water vapor between bodies, through air and sea travel—into our "masculine" land borders and solid selves, permeating the borders of individual bodies and infecting millions of people. Through breath, our vulnerability had never been experienced more acutely, as exhortations to maintain social distance in an attempt to flatten the curve of infection thrust us into a new understanding of shared air and intervocality (or, in rejecting those exhortations, a refusal to take up respiratory responsibilities). A new politics of breath emerged around questions of mask-wearing, shared space, "breathing life" into the economy (whilst the death toll was rising) by opening the country in the midst of a pandemic which not at all ironically attacked the respiratory systems of the most vulnerable of citizens. On an embodied level, too, there was a performance of breath and voice by Trump and others in the right-wing establishment that translated the myth of the self-contained, fully autonomous, decidedly masculine individual into a politics of breath.

Refusing to wear a mask in the time of Covid-19—as many GOP leaders did, including those who were confined in close quarters with hundreds of their colleagues while the Capitol was under siege—perpetuated the myth of immunity to contagion at the core of American Exceptionalism. Such refusal is a choice born of privilege, of course, particularly the privilege of not being a "frontline" worker (a phrase that, of course, implies a wartime scenario wherein casualties are both expected and necessary) for whom the lack of a mask intensifies the significant risk of infection. Conspicuously rejecting the mask while urging the public to do the opposite frames such protective measures as contrary to masculine power, authority, and strength. To admit one's codependency on anything (even air itself) is a surrender for leaders who overidentify with self-sufficient masculine American independence, and so mask-wearing itself becomes gendered: it feminizes as it seeks to protect others, admits vulnerability, and marks nondominant bodies, made more vulnerable by unjust social and economic structures, as weak and inferior. It also becomes racialized, as fiercely protecting one's right not to wear a mask becomes closely associated with a white identity that defines itself as impervious to claims of responsibility to others and disease, with both being viscerally rejected as the sorts of bodily burdens that whiteness promises to preclude.

Air, breath, and voice are central to understanding the injustices of the Covid-19 pandemic specifically, as a refraction of long-standing systemic injustices in the United States. Fatal contraction of the virus is more likely in communities with the worst air pollution (Wu et al. 2020), which are also often immigrant and lower socioeconomic communities composed of ethnic minorities. The people in these communities are more likely to have underlying health conditions such as heart disease, diabetes, or chronic lung disease, rendering contraction of the virus even more threatening (Gerretsen 2020). That their jobs were designated as essential only intensified the economic coercion: the pay did not significantly increase, and since their jobs were still available, they were not free to seek unemployment benefits. The virus itself attacks the lungs, making voicing increasingly difficult throughout the sometimes long progression of the disease. Early reports on the effects of Covid-19 in "Long Haul" patients (Davis et al. 2020) indicate that 90 percent experienced ongoing breathing problems, 50 percent had disturbances in their speech and language, and 25–30 percent struggled with changes in their voices. For those hospitalized with severe symptoms, planning for advanced care (end-of-life) directives becomes urgent, as they may well not be able to speak for themselves (if breath is difficult, speaking is impossible), and nobody privy to their end-of-life intentions will be present to speak for them. In the final of moments of life with coronavirus, voice, with the body, is rendered inert.

Toward a More Vocally Just World—A Portal

A political war is underway between the notion of the self as contained and autonomous, neither infecting nor infectable, and the self as fully relational, interconnected, and thus vulnerable. Intervocality, which acknowledges vulnerability, susceptibility, and the politics of shared air, water, and matter, has become a site charged with the possibility of bodily harm and holding the promise of life-affirming, embodied connection with others. The polarity is a stark one: deep longings for the felt experience of embodied vibrations of sound have emerged out of physical (if not social) isolation and distance, just as evidence continues to surface indicating that in-person human sound remains, in the absence of effective treatments, a dangerous prospect. The materiality of sound has never been more clear: its air, water vapor, vibrations, and even pathogens render it now, in the most tangible of ways, the intimate, ineffable, stuff of shared bodies.

Voices singing out from balconies in unison in Italy, public sing-alongs in the South End of Boston, opera singers performing in New Orleans, Broadway and Blues singers belting from windows of apartment buildings in New York and Madrid, musicians of all kinds filling the airwaves with sound that permeates social distance borders: in the early days and weeks of the pandemic, the aural realm emerged as a significant source of healing, joy, community, and pleasure. Virtual duets, ensembles, and choir performances abounded, unshackled from spatial and temporal restrictions. Yet such productions of co-voicing are—by virtue of streaming technology that makes perfect timing impossible—not *events* at all, but video content that has been edited to seem synchronous. The reassembling of the original cast of *Hamilton* to perform together "in real time" on John Krasinski's *Some Good News* appealed to the viewer craving reconnection to community, but that same viewer would be deeply disappointed to learn that such unison performance could not have taken place in real time, and is a mere simulacrum of synchronicity.

Despite the communication challenges that the pandemic has wrought, a world of technologically enabled vocal interactions has simultaneously opened up, making commonplace video chats, classes, religious services, workshops, and conversations both personal and professional across time zones. New forms of vocal interactions, of course, present new challenges. Casual, socially distant in-person conversations require more vocal energy to counter the muffling effects of a mask, and a higher physical engagement to understand and be understood without familiar facial cues. Zoom, the platform most used in the United States for online learning and conferencing, has been designed to resist unison of sound, insisting as it does that only one speaker can (or should) attempt to speak at a time (thus replicating distinctly white conversational norms). Gone are the voices that meet each other in agreement, nonverbal affirmations, audible breath, or simultaneous laughing: it is nearly impossible to speak "with" another person. The technology only "understands" conversations as consisting of discrete, individuated turn-taking (often with inevitable "lag" causing real bodies and screens alike to "freeze" in wait) but not speaking-with another, nor as a group: it is only solo, not really a duet, not at all a chorus. The dramatic power of voices together, in real time, is suspended.

The dangers of close bodily encounters of vocal sound have led to the banning of singing in churches in Germany and the indefinite cancelation of choir rehearsals across the globe, partly in response to the "choir outbreak" of Covid-19 in Washington state (Read 2020). There is evidence that "singing, to a greater degree than talking, aerosolizes respiratory droplets extraordinarily well. Deep-breathing while singing facilitated those respiratory droplets getting deep into the lungs" (Bromage 2020). The multisensory nature of receiving sound has become a politically charged minefield, and formal political structures, at least in the United States, hardly seem up to the task of guiding their citizens through it. The lifting or maintenance of restrictions designed to preserve health are highly variable, rarely reliant on clear benchmarks and reliable data, and wholly tied to the politics of the country, state, and county carrying them out. Which people and which societal elements matter to those politics is becoming terrifyingly obvious.

Thinking into this Great Pause as a portal for change, there is the opportunity to "break with the past and imagine [the] world anew" (Roy 2020). The significant reduction in air pollution caused by the global pandemic, at least in the short term, could perhaps allow a collective, global intake of precious breath to inspire and animate new, more equitable ways of being in a more breathable world. What will be released through collective exhale? Arundhati Roy describes the threshold of change in this moment as

> a gateway between one world and the next. We can choose to walk through it, dragging the carcasses of our prejudice and hatred, our avarice, our data banks and dead ideas, our dead rivers and smoky skies behind us. Or we can walk through lightly, with little luggage, ready to imagine another world. (2020)

To walk differently requires us to breathe differently, to listen and hear differently, to generate and receive vocalizations differently, to redeploy those zones of interaction and co-constitution toward better, more just ends—ends that recognize the deep intersectionality of systemic inequalities such as racism, economic injustice, the environmental extractionism of colonialism, misogyny, and cisnormativity. Sounding bodies are ethical and political bodies, immersed in but not reducible to intricate networks of power and identity, capable of generating new ways of sonorous being-with that reveal the contingency of unjust systems and make new worlds possible.

Notes

Introduction

1 The feminist literature on embodiment and related bodily phenomena is extensive. For an excellent overview, see Lennon (2014); for some important and representative examples, see Bordo (1993), Braidotti (1994), Butler ([1993] 2011), Collins (2008), Garland Thompson (1997), Gatens (1996), Grosz (1994), Rich (1979), Weiss (1999), and Wendell (1996).

1 Voice

1 Eastern philosophies and practices of the body, such as those in Japan, Korea, China, and India, place emphasis on the visceral and organ-based understanding of the bodily processes, grounding concepts such as breath and energy (*ki*, *chi*, or *prana*: which from a Western point of view might be considered abstractions) as physically experienced within (and beyond) the body. Therefore, the insight that breath is material is neither culturally novel nor unprecedented; our point here is that even within the mind-body dualism of dominant Western understandings of physiology, the event of breath and voice is determinedly physical and therefore, material, although often not recognized as such. For more see Tara McAllister-Viel's multicultural account of the phenomena of breath (2009).

2 In the field of phenomenology, intentionality refers not to a person's motivation or purpose, but to a sense of directionality; consciousness, for example, is revealed as intentional once we recognize that consciousness is always consciousness *of something*.

2 Vocal Injustice

1 See "Women in Media in the US—Statistics and Facts" (https://www.statista.com/topics/3220/women-in-media/) for extensive statistical information about the

underrepresentation of women in US media. The same website includes statistical information on LGBTQ characters represented in broadcast networks (https://www.statista.com/statistics/789894/lgbtq-character-inclusion-broadcast-network/), streaming providers (https://www.statista.com/statistics/789908/lgbtq-character-inclusion-streaming-content-providers/), and cable networks (https://www.statista.com/statistics/699407/lgbtq-characters-cable-sexual-orientation/). For statistics on the lack of racial and ethnic diversity in Hollywood and television, see Hunt et al. (2014).

2 Linklater relies on a common misinterpretation of Descartes's famous point here. The importance of the *cogito* for Descartes is not ontological, but epistemological; he is not establishing that the thinking self is the central or primary self, but rather that the act of thinking provides evidence for the existence of the self. That is, the fact that I think allows me to *know* that I exist (whatever kind of entity or being I may be) (Newman 2019).

3 At first glance, it may seem that Cavarero's critique of the devocalization of philosophy is at odds with Derrida's critique of phonocentrism, discussed briefly in the introduction of this work. In fact, the objects of the two thinkers' critiques are distinct. Cavarero is aiming her critique at dominant practices of philosophy, that is, the vehicles by which philosophical knowledge and insight were shared and valued. Derrida, by contrast, is aiming his critique at the content of philosophies of language and of self, theories which either argued for or implied that vocalized language represented an unmediated fullness of presence and identity, untainted by the absences, gaps, and hermeneutic requirements that writing represents. Even Cavarero's close association between voice and identity does not, in our view, constitute an example of Derrida's phonocentrism, because her theory does not require that the voice accurately or completely express an individual's self. Her interest is in the uniqueness of the individual voice, not in its expressive nature.

4 Our criticism of Cavarero here is distinct from Emily Wilbourne's concern (2010: 5) that Cavarero's privileging of the voice allows it to stand in for the individual body and perhaps serve to express in an authentic way the interior truth of the embodied individual. We share Wilbourne's wariness of conceptualizing the voice as a mediating phenomenon that allows an unvarnished, interior essence to be presented, untainted and untouched by the sonorous medium, to an exterior world. But we agree with Ryan Dohoney (2011) that Cavarero, at least, does not make that specific mistake. As mentioned in the previous endnote, for Cavarero, the voice is unique in its facticity, not in its expressive function.

3 The Ethics of Envoicing

1 Jerzy Grotowski describes his method of actor education as a "via negativa—not a collection of skills but an eradication of blocks" ([1968] 2002: 17), in which the approach is an undoing of resistance in order to release unedited, non-habitual bodily impulses: "the body vanishes, burns, and the spectator sees only a series of visible impulses" (16).

2 The video of this piece is no longer available online; a snippet of it can be seen at http://genderfork.com/2009/voice-lessons-learned/.

4 The Gendered Voice

1 The terms "uptalk" (upward inflection pattern) and "vocal fry" (also known as "creaky voice") feverishly entered the mainstream lexicon beginning roughly around 2013, initiating the "war on female voices" (Marcotte 2015) during which author Naomi Wolf notably wrote an article exhorting young women to reclaim their power by rejecting these so-called "destructive" speech patterns (Wolf 2015); in the same year National Public Radio's *This American Life* featured a remarkable segment responding to the vitriolic letters from listeners criticizing the speaking voices of their young female-identifying presenters (Glass 2015). Significant debate has taken place on the subject, including criticism that points to the sexism and oppression inherent in policing women's voices (Gross 2015, Riley 2015), articulations of the patriarchal double-bind presented to powerful female voices (Thompson 2018), and countersuggestions that credit young female voices for being innovative, trendsetting, and full of linguistic ingenuity (Quenqua 2012, Arana 2013).

2 In their extensive examination of the gendering of language, Eckert and McConnell-Ginet offer a useful recontextualization of the phenomenon of "uptalk." They suggest that in lieu of the familiar notion that it is a merely a sign of insecurity or feigned weakness in feminine speech, that "the story is much more complex ... [uptalk, as well as tag questions] can also be used to open up the conversational floor to other participants, to provide a space for others' contributions, and also to show aggression. And its gendering may have at least as much to do with how others interpret them as with differences in who produces them" (2013: 144).

5 Envoicing in Sex, Maternity, and Childbirth

1 According to Pierce's study, 86 percent of participants who were taught how to tone in pregnancy used it in labor; 61 percent found it helpful in alleviating pain; and 50 percent said it helped them stay focused and energized (1998: 43).

2 We acknowledge, of course, that childbirth is not an everyday, quotidian activity for anyone. Nor do we intend to dismiss the exceptional intensity of the experience for most. The point is, on a social-global-political level, it is the norm: giving birth *happens* every minute of every day, to the tune of approximately 4.3 childbirths per second worldwide (Central Intelligence Agency 2020).

3 In preparation for a well-documented Hollywood birth, six-foot high birthing boards containing the words "Be silent and make all movements slow and understandable" served to safeguard the home (WebMD 2006).

6 Ethical Spotlight: Envoicing in Voice Pedagogy

1 Berry, Linklater, and Rodenburg's scholarship is not limited to their printed work, as they have disseminated ideas in many formats: video/DVD, talks, masterclasses, interviews, and in creative research through the live, more ephemeral practice of voice coaching, teaching, and teacher training. When referencing these master trainers, I imply the totality of their legacy and ongoing scholarship, including—but not limited to—the following published texts: Berry (1973, [1987] 1992, 2001, 2008), Linklater ([1976] 2006, 1992), and Rodenburg ([1992] 2015, [1993] 2018, [1997] 2000, 2002).

2 Tara McAllister-Viel (2019) uses the term "natural/free" to represent a branch of training emerging from the shared Anglo-American voice pedagogies (43) of Berry, Rodenburg, and Linklater, who, though they do not represent a unified approach to voice, do share similar artistic and intellectual influences, close interactions, lineage, and common values. See Chapter 2 of this book for a more detailed description of Linklater's pedagogy.

3 Nirmal Puwar uses the term, originally conceived by Charles Mills (1999), to describe the "white, male, upper/middle class body" that is "so naturalised ... that it acts to deny any conception of this subject as classed, gendered and—particularly— raced" (2004: 5–6).

4 Rodenburg teacher certification also comes with a >$20k pricetag.

5 Christine Adaire notes, "Frequently, the voice coach is regarded with suspicion or fear. I've sometimes heard coaches referred to as the 'Voice and Speech Police'" (Adaire et al. 2018: 347).

6 Yoga Nidra is an integrative restoration, relaxation, and mindfulness practice centered around the somatic awareness of body and breath. It is important to acknowledge the complexities of oppression within the Western context of yoga practice, and it is offered here respectfully as both an ancient tantric practice popularized in the modern era by Swami Satyananda Saraswati (1976), but also a research-proven method to counter stress-related illness and chronic pain. For the full scope of research, visit https://pubmed.ncbi.nlm.nih.gov/?term=yoga%20nidra.

7 See Adaire et al. (2018) for more about the vocal needs of gender diverse actors.

8 Phonetician Sameer ud Dowla Khan asserts that vocal fry is used "extensively in languages like Danish, Vietnamese, Burmese, Hmong, and many indigenous languages of Mexico and Central America (such as Zapotec, Mazatec, and Yukatek Maya) … and as you might imagine, speakers of those languages do not suffer from medical problems in the throat any more than speakers of other languages" (2015: para 5).

7 Ethical Spotlight: Envoicing in/and Philosophy

1 Fourteen percent of American Philosophical Association members reporting on their employment status identified as adjunct, part-time, or visiting professors, with another 25 percent falling outside of any clear category. These numbers likely undercount the proportion of precariously employed philosophy instructors, who are less likely to be able to afford the dues of a professional organization. See https://www.apaonline.org/page/demographics.

2 Obviously, not all philosophy classes rely primarily on lectures. Seminars, for example, are explicitly designed to encourage students' vocal participation. In many large universities, however, discipline-specific seminars only become available as students advance through their majors (as if to emphasize that they must earn their right to speak by mastering introductory material). Given that philosophy majors are more likely than university students as a whole to identify as white (by a fairly small margin; see Schwitzgebel 2017a), male (by a significant margin; see Schwitzgebel 2017b), and economically privileged (Pinsker 2015), such seminars are less accessible to students who identify with historically marginalized groups. Elite, well-funded universities, regardless of size, have developed first year seminars, often interdisciplinary and not infrequently taught by philosophers. But such programs are less likely at non-elite, underfunded universities, whose student bodies tend to have higher numbers of students from lower socioeconomic backgrounds. In other words: whether a student gets to participate vocally, in a substantial and meaningful way, in a class that engages with philosophical ideas and texts is significantly influenced by the student's social and economic standing.

3 The American Philosophy Association (APA) regularly publishes demographic information on its membership; although not every philosopher working in the United States is a member of the APA, it is by far the largest professional organization connected to the discipline. Its data in 2018 indicated that approximately 74 percent of its members were male (a proportion confirmed by the data available at http://women-in-philosophy.org/) and 76 percent were white. Fewer than 6 percent of APA members identified themselves to the organization as LGBTQIA, and fewer than 5 percent did so as disabled. See https://www.apaonline.org/page/demographics. A study conducted by the APA Committee on the Status of Black Philosophers and the Society of Young Black Philosophers revealed that there were only 156 Black philosophers (defined as either having earned or in the process of earning a PhD) in the United States; approximately 20 percent of that number are graduate students, and almost 10 percent are unaffiliated, leaving approximately 109 philosophy instructors of color in the entire country (Botts et al. 2014).

4 The controversy stemmed from *Hypatia*'s publication of a controversial article by Rebecca Tuvel that compared transgenderism (the term used by the author, contrary to practices within trans studies) to transracialism, and the subsequent apology for (but not retraction of) the article by the journal's associate editors (including coauthor Cahill), who noted the article's failure to engage sufficiently with the scholarly work of trans philosophers (see Zamudio-Suaréz 2017).

References

AAPAC (2020), "The Visibility Report: Racial Representation on NYC Stages," *American Theatre Wing*, September 30. Available online: http://www.aapacnyc.org/ (accessed January 20, 2021).

Abbany, Zulfikar (2019), "Sexy Siri, You Made a Fool of Everyone," *DW News*, November 2. Available online: https://p.dw.com/p/3D7Ur (accessed June 11, 2020).

Adaire, Christine, Delia Kropp, Sandy Hirsch, and Rebecca Root (2018), "Meeting the Needs of Gender Diverse Actors: Personal, Clinical, and Artistic Perspectives," in Richard Kenneth Adler, Sandy Hirsch, and Jack Pickering (eds.), *Voice and Communication Therapy for the Transgender/Gender Diverse Client: A Comprehensive Clinical Guide*, 3rd ed., 337–57, San Diego, CA: Plural.

Adams, Sarah LaChance (2014), "Maternity as Dehiscence in the Flesh in the Philosophy of Maurice Merleau-Ponty," in *Mad Mothers, Bad Mothers, and What a 'Good' Mother Would Do: The Ethics of Ambivalence*, 109–55, New York: Columbia University Press.

Adams, Sarah LaChance, and Paul Burcher (2014), "Communal Pushing: Childbirth and Intersubjectivity," in Kristin Ziler and Lisa Folkmarson Käll (eds.), *Feminist Phenomenology and Medicine*, 69–80, Albany, NY: SUNY Press.

Alcoff, Linda Martín (2006), *Visible Identities: Race, Gender, and the Self*, New York: Oxford University Press.

Allen, Irma Kinga (2020), "Thinking with a Feminist Political Ecology of Air-and-Breathing-Bodies," in Rebecca Oxley and Andrew Russell (eds.), *Body & Society: Special Issue: Interdisciplinary Perspectives on Breath, Body and World*, 26 (2): 79–105.

ALRA (2020), "MFA Linklater: Teaching Practice Promotional Video (2:15)," Academy of Live and Recorded Arts. Available online: https://alra.co.uk/courses/mfa-linklater-teaching-practice-voice-and-theatre-arts (accessed March 18, 2020).

Al-Saji, Alia (2014), "A Phenomenology of Hesitation: Interrupting Racializing Habits of Seeing," in Emily S. Lee (ed.), *Living Alterities: Phenomenology, Embodiment, and Race*, 133–72, Albany, NY: SUNY Press.

Anastasia, Andrew (2014), "Voice," *Transgender Studies Quarterly*, 1 (1–2): 262–3.

Anderson, Hanah, and Matt Daniels (2016), "Film Dialogue from 2,000 Screenplays, Broken Down by Gender and Age," *The Pudding*, April. Available online: https://pudding.cool/2017/03/film-dialogue/index.html (accessed March 18, 2020).

Annenberg Inclusion Initiative (2020), "Inequality in 1,300 Popular Films: Examining Portrayals of Gender, Race/Ethnicity, LGBTQ & Disability from 2007 to 2019,"

USC Annenberg and the Annenberg Foundation, September 2020. Available online: http://assets.uscannenberg.org/docs/aii-inequality_1300_popular_films_09-08-2020.pdf (accessed January 20, 2021).

Appelbaum, David (1990), *Voice*, Albany, NY: SUNY Press.

Arana, Gabriel (2013), "Creaky Voice: Yet Another Example of Young Women's Linguistic Ingenuity," *Atlantic*, January 10. Available online: https://www.theatlantic.com/sexes/archive/2013/01/creaky-voice-yet-another-example-of-young-womens-linguistic-ingenuity/267046/ (accessed March 18, 2020).

Austin, J. L. (1962), *How to Do Things with Words*, 2nd ed., ed. J. O. Urmson and M. Sbisá, Cambridge, MA: Harvard University Press.

Aziato, Lydia, Angela Kwartemaa, and Kitimdow Lazarus (2017), "Labour Pain Experiences and Perceptions: A Qualitative Study among Post-partum Women in Ghana," *BMC Pregnancy Childbirth*, February 22, 17: 73. Available online: https://bmcpregnancychildbirth.biomedcentral.com/articles/10.1186/s12884-017-1248-1 (accessed March 19, 2020).

Bacharach, Sondra (2018), "Finding Your Voice in the Streets: Street Art and Epistemic Injustice," *Monist*, 101 (1): 31–43.

Baker, Sarah (2018), "The Sounds of Silence during Labor," BirthWorks, International. Available online: https://birthworks.org/the-sounds-of-silence-during-labor/ (accessed March 18, 2020).

Balcerski, Thomas (2020), "#LadyGraham Went Viral—and Not Just Because of Lindsey Graham's Politics," *Washington Post*, June 10. Available online: https://www.washingtonpost.com/outlook/2020/06/10/ladygraham-went-viral-not-just-because-lindsey-grahams-politics/ (accessed June 13, 2020).

Banai, Pavela I. (2017), "Voice in Different Phases of Menstrual Cycle among Naturally Cycling Women and Users of Hormonal Contraceptives," *PLoS One*, 12 (8): e0183462. Available online: https://journals.plos.org/plosone/article?id=10.1371/journal.pone.0183462 (accessed June 10, 2020).

Barrett, Lisa Feldman, and Eliza Bliss-Moreau (2009), "She's Emotional. He's Having a Bad Day: Attributional Explanations for Emotion Stereotypes," *Emotion*, 9 (5): 649–58.

Barthes, Roland (1977), "The Grain of the Voice," in *Image Music Text*, trans. Stephen Heath, 179–89, London: Fontana Press.

Bauman, H-Dirksen L. (2008), "Listening to Phonocentrism with Deaf Eyes: Derrida's Mute Philosophy of (Sign) Language," *Essays in Philosophy*, 9 (1), Article 2. Available online: https://commons.pacificu.edu/eip/vol9/iss1/2/ (accessed March 19, 2020).

Bauman, H-Dirksen L., and Joseph J. Murray (2014), "Deaf Gain: An Introduction," in H-Dirksen L. Bauman and Joseph J. Murray (eds.), *Deaf Gain: Raising the Stakes for Human Diversity*, xv–xlii, Minneapolis: University of Minnesota Press.

Beachum, Lateshia (2020), "Publisher Apologizes for 'Auditory Blackface': A Minstrel-Like Performance of a Black Woman's Essay," *Washington Post*, November 28.

Available online: https://www.washingtonpost.com/arts-entertainment/2020/11/28/fireside-black-essay/ (accessed December 22, 2020).

Beard, Mary (2017), *Women & Power: A Manifesto*, New York: W.W. Norton.

Bernhard, Nina H. (2011), "One Ship in the Night," *Mosaic: A Journal for the Interdisciplinary Study of Literature*, 44 (1): 177–80.

Berry, Cicely (1973), *Voice and the Actor*, New York: Wiley Publishing.

Berry, Cicely ([1987] 1992), *The Actor and the Text*, New York: Applause.

Berry, Cicely (2001), *Text in Action*, London: Virgin.

Berry, Cicely (2008), *From Word to Play*, London: Oberon Books.

Berry, Cicely, Kristin Linklater, and Patsy Rodenburg (1997), "Shakespeare, Feminism and Voice: Responses to Sarah Werner," *New Theatre Quarterly*, 13 (49): 48–52.

Berry, Richard (2006), "Will the iPod Kill the Radio Star?," *Convergence*, 12 (2): 143–62.

Blair, Rhonda (1993), "Not … But/Not-Not-Me: Musings on Cross-Gender Performance," in Ellen Donkin and Susan Clement (eds.), *Upstaging Big Daddy: Directing Theater as If Gender and Race Matter*, 291–307, Ann Arbor: University of Michigan Press.

Bonenfant, Yvon (2010), "Queer Listening to Queer Vocal Timbres," *Performance Research*, 15 (3): 74–80.

Bonnie, Richard J., Emily P. Backes, Margarita Alegria, Angela Diaz, and Claire D. Brindis (2019), "Fulfilling the Promise of Adolescence: Realizing Opportunity for All Youth," *Journal of Adolescent Health*, 65: 440–2.

Bordo, Susan (1993), *Unbearable Weight: Feminism, Western Culture and the Body*, Berkeley, CA: University of California Press.

Boston, Jane (1997), "Voice: The Practitioners, Their Practices, and Their Critics: Reassessing the Controversy in Its Historical Context," *New Theatre Quarterly*, 13 (51): 248–54.

Boston, Jane (2018), *Voice*, London: Macmillan.

Bottomley, Andrew J. (2015), "Podcasting, *Welcome to Night Vale*, and the Revival of Radio Drama," *Journal of Radio & Audio Media*, 22 (2): 179–89.

Botts, Tina Fernandes, Liam Kofi Bright, Myisha Cherry, Guntur Mallarangeng, and Quayshawn Spencer (2014), "What Is the State of Blacks in Philosophy?," *Critical Philosophy of Race*, 2 (2): 224–42.

Bourdieu, Pierre (1977), *Outline of a Theory of Practice*, Cambridge: Cambridge University Press.

Bourdieu, Pierre (1984), *Distinction: A Social Critique of the Judgement of Taste*, trans. Richard Nice, Cambridge, MA: Harvard University Press.

Bourdieu, Pierre (1993), *The Field of Cultural Production: Essays on Art and Literature*, Randal Johnson (ed.), New York: Columbia University Press.

Braidotti, Rosi (1994), *Nomadic Subjects: Embodiment and Sexual Difference in Contemporary Feminist Theory*, New York: Columbia University Press.

Braithwaite, Patia (2019), "Biological Weathering and Its Deadly Effect on Black Mothers," *Self*, September 19. Available online: https://www.self.com/story/weathering-and-its-deadly-effect-on-black-mothers (accessed March 18, 2020).

Brescoll, Victoria L., and Eric Luis Uhlmann (2008), "Can an Angry Woman Get Ahead? Status Conferral, Gender, and Expression of Emotion in the Workplace," *Psychological Science*, 19 (3): 268–75.

Brewer, Gayle, and Colin A. Hendrie (2011), "Evidence to Suggest That Copulatory Vocalizations in Women Are Not a Reflexive Consequence of Orgasm," *Archives of Sexual Behavior*, 40 (3): 559–64.

Bromage, Erin (2020), "The Risks—Know Them—Avoid Them," Erinbromage.com, May 20. Available online at https://www.erinbromage.com/post/the-risks-know-them-avoid-them (accessed June 16, 2020).

Brook, Peter (1968), *The Empty Space*, New York: Scribner.

Brown, Stan (2000), "The Cultural Voice," *Voice and Speech Review*, 1 (1): 17–18.

Bultynck, Charlotte, Charlotte Pas, Justine Defreyne, Marjan Cosyns, Martin den Heijer, and Guy T'Sjoen (2017), "Self-Perception of Voice in Transgender Persons during Cross-Sex Hormone Therapy," *Laryngoscope*, 127 (12): 2796–804.

Burke, Teresa Blankmeyer (2017), "Choosing Accommodations: Signed Language Interpreting and the Absence of Choice," *Kennedy Institute of Ethics Journal*, 27 (2): 267–99.

Burke, Teresa Blankmeyer, and Brenda Nicodemus (2013), "Coming Out of the Hard of Hearing Closet: Reflections on a Shared Journey in Academia," *Disability Studies Quarterly*, 33 (2). Available online: https://dsq-sds.org/article/view/3706 (accessed March 19, 2020).

Butler, Judith (1990), *Gender Trouble: Feminism and the Subversion of Identity*, London: Routledge.

Butler, Judith ([1993] 2011), *Bodies That Matter: On the Discursive Limits of Sex*, New York: Routledge.

Cahill, Ann J. (2001), *Rethinking Rape*, Ithaca, NY: Cornell University Press.

Cahill, Ann J. (2010), *Overcoming Objectification: Toward a Carnal Ethics*, New York: Routledge.

Cahill, Ann J., and Christine Hamel (2019), "Toward Intervocality: Linklater, the Body, and Contemporary Feminist Theory," *Voice and Speech Review*, 13 (2): 130–51.

Carson, Anne (1995), "The Gender of Sound," in *Glass, Irony, and God*, 119–42, New York: New Directions.

Cartei, Valentina, Alan Garnham, Jane Oakhill, Robin Banerjee, Lucy Roberts, and David Reby (2019), "Children Can Control the Expression of Masculinity and Femininity through the Voice," *Royal Society Open Science*, 6 (7): 190656. Available online: https://www.ncbi.nlm.nih.gov/pubmed/31417760 (accessed May 18, 2020).

Cartei, Valentina, and David Reby (2013), "Effect of Formant Frequency Spacing on Perceived Gender in Pre-pubertal Children's Voices," *PloS One*, 8 (12): e81022.

Available online: https://www.ncbi.nlm.nih.gov/pmc/articles/PMC3849092/ (accessed May 18, 2020).

Cavarero, Adriana (2005), *For More Than One Voice: Toward a Philosophy of Vocal Expression*, trans. Paul A. Kottman, Stanford, CA: Stanford University Press.

Central Intelligence Agency (2020), *The World Factbook 2020*, Washington, DC. Available at https://www.cia.gov/library/publications/resources/the-world-factbook/index.html (accessed April 15, 2020).

Cheng, William (2016), *Just Vibrations: The Purpose of Sounding Good*, Ann Arbor: University of Michigan Press.

Cixous, Hélène, Deborah Jenson, Susan Rubin Suleiman, and Sarah Cornell (1991), *"Coming to Writing" and Other Essays*, Cambridge, MA: Harvard University Press.

Cler, Gabriel J., Victoria S. McKenna, Kimberly L. Dahl, and Cara E. Stepp (2020), "Longitudinal Case Study of Transgender Voice Changes under Testosterone Hormone Therapy," *Journal of Voice*, 34 (5): 748–62.

Cleveland Clinic (2020), "Voice Changes: What Can They Tell You as You Age?" December 31. Available online: https://health.clevelandclinic.org/voice-changes-what-can-they-tell-you-as-you-age/ (accessed January 21, 2021).

CNN (2018), "Lindsey Graham Erupts: Kavanaugh Hearing an Unethical Sham," *YouTube*, September 27. Available online: https://www.youtube.com/watch?v=RTBxPPx62s4 (accessed June 16, 2020).

Colaianni, Louis (2011), "Bearing the Standard: Issues of Speech in Education," *Voice and Speech Review*, 7 (1): 199–208.

Collins, Patricia Hill (2004), *Black Sexual Politics: African Americans, Gender, and the New Racism*, New York: Routledge.

Collins, Patricia Hill (2008), *Black Feminist Thought: Knowledge, Consciousness, and the Politics of Empowerment*, New York: Routledge.

Cook, Rena (2012), "American Speech: Honoring the Authentic Voices of Your Students," *Teaching Theatre*, 23 (2): 24–7.

Coronel, Joy Lanceta, Jacqueline Springfield, and Joshua Feliciano-Sanchez Moser (2020), "Strategies for Guiding Actors' Accent and Linguistic Needs in the Twenty-First Century," *Voice and Speech Review*, 14 (2): 196–212.

Cosyns, Marjan, John Van Borsel, Katrien Wierckx, David Dedecker, Fleur Van de Peer, Tine Daelman, Sofie Laenen, and Guy T'Sjoen (2013), "Voice in Female-to-Male Transsexual Persons after Long-term Androgen Therapy," *Laryngology*, 124 (6): 1409–14.

Cottom, Tressie McMillan (2019), *Thick: And Other Essays*, New York and London: New Press.

Cox, Gordon (2020), "Listen: How to Make Anti-Racist Theatre," *Variety*, June 9. Available online: https://variety.com/2020/legit/news/listen-how-to-make-anti-racist-theater-1234629085/ (accessed January 20, 2021).

Crawley, Ashon T. (2017), *Blackpentecostal Breath: The Aesthetics of Possibility*, New York: Fordham University Press.

Crowell, Rachel (2020), "The Latest: TikTok Math Questions: Rachel Crowell's Take," *American Mathematical Society blog*, September 23. Available online: http://www.ams.org/news?news_id=6391.

Dahl, Kimberly L., and Leslie A. Mahler (2020), "Acoustic Features of Transfeminine Voices and Perceptions of Voice Femininity," *Journal of Voice*, 34 (6): 961.e19–26.

Damasio, Antonio (1995), *Descartes' Error: Emotion, Reason and the Human Brain*, New York: Harper Perennial.

Damasio, Antonio (1999), *The Feeling of What Happens: Body and Emotion in the Making of Consciousness*, New York: Harcourt Brace.

Davies, Shelagh, Viktória G. Papp, and Christella Antoni (2015), "Voice and Communication Change for Gender Nonconforming Individuals: Giving Voice to the Person Inside," *International Journal of Transgenderism*, 16 (3): 117–59.

Davis, Hannah E., Gina S. Assaf, Lisa McCorkell, Hannah Wei, Ryan J. Low, Yochai Re'em, Signe Redfield, Jared P. Austin, and Athena Akrami (2020), "Characterizing Long COVID in an International Cohort: 7 Months of Symptoms and Their Impact," *medRxiv*, December 27. Available online: https://doi.org/10.1101/2020.12.24.20248802 (accessed January 21, 2021).

DeCasper, Anthony J. and William P. Fifer (1980), "Of Human Bonding: Newborns Prefer Their Mothers' Voices," *Science*, 208 (4448): 1174–6.

Derrida, Jacques (1976), *Of Grammatology*, trans. Gayatri Chakravorty Spivak, Baltimore, MD: Johns Hopkins University Press.

Diamond, Susan L. (1996), *Hard Labor*, New York: Forge.

Diprose, Rosalyn (2002), *Corporeal Generosity: On Giving with Nietzsche, Merleau-Ponty, and Levinas*, Albany, NY: SUNY Press.

Dohoney, Ryan (2011), "An Antidote to Metaphysics: Adriana Cavarero's Vocal Philosophy," *Women & Music*, 15: 70–85.

Dohoney, Ryan (2015), "Echo's Echo: Subjectivity in Vibrational Ontology," *Women & Music*, 19: 142–50.

Dolan, Jill (1993), "Geographies of Learning: Theatre Studies, Performance, and the 'Performative,'" *Theatre Journal*, 45 (4): 417–41.

Dolan, Jill (2001), *Geographies of Learning: Theory and Practice, Activism and Performance*, Middletown, CT: Wesleyan University Press.

Dolar, Mladen (2006), *A Voice and Nothing More*, Cambridge, MA: MIT Press.

Dotson, Kristie (2012), "How Is This Paper Philosophy?," *Comparative Philosophy*, 3 (1): 3–29.

Dunn, Leslie C., and Nancy A. Jones (1994a), "Introduction," in Leslie C. Dunn and Nancy A. Jones (eds.), *Embodied Voices: Representing Female Vocality in Western Culture*, 1–13, Cambridge: Cambridge University Press.

Dunn, Leslie C., and Nancy A. Jones, eds. (1994b), *Embodied Voices: Representing Female Vocality in Western Culture*, Cambridge: Cambridge University Press.

Duranti, Alessandro, Elinor Ochs, and Bambi B. Schieffelin, eds. (2011), *The Handbook of Language Socialization*, West Sussex, UK: John Wiley & Sons.

Durkee, Alison (2019), "'Unacceptable': Volker Revises Testimony As GOP's Hand-Picked Impeachment Witnesses Fail to Deliver," *Vanity Fair*, November 20. Available online: https://www.vanityfair.com/news/2019/11/kurt-volker-tim-morrison-impeachment-testimony (accessed June 16, 2020).

Dwyer, Jim (2017), "Remembering a City Where the Smog Could Kill," *New York Times*, February 28. Available online: https://www.nytimes.com/2017/02/28/nyregion/new-york-city-smog.html (accessed March 18, 2020).

Eckert, Penelope, and Sally McConnell-Ginet (2013), *Language and Gender*, 2nd ed., New York: Cambridge University Press.

Edmundson, Anne, ed. (2006), "Silent Birth Now a Noisy Controversy," *WebMD*. Available online: https://www.webmd.com/baby/features/silent-birth-now-noisy-controversy#3 (accessed March 18, 2020).

Ehrick, Christine (2015), "Vocal Gender and the Gendered Soundscape: At the Intersection of Gender Studies and Sound Studies," *Sounding Out!*, February 2. Available online: https://soundstudiesblog.com/2015/02/02/vocal-gender-and-the-gendered-soundscape-at-the-intersection-of-gender-studies-and-sound-studies/ (accessed March 18, 2020).

Eidsheim, Nina Sun (2015), *Sensing Sound: Singing & Listening as Vibrational Practice*, Durham and London: Duke University Press.

Eidsheim, Nina Sun (2019), *The Race of Sound: Listening, Timbre & Vocality in African American Music*, Durham and London: Duke University Press.

Eko, Hannah (2018), "As a Black Woman, I'm Tired of Having to Prove My Womanhood," *BuzzFeed*, February 27. Available online: https://www.buzzfeednews.com/article/hannaheko/aint-i-a-woman (accessed May 19, 2020).

Epstein, Rebecca, Jamilia Blake, and Thalia González (2017), *Girlhood Interrupted: The Erasure of Black Girls' Childhood*, Washington, DC: Georgetown Law on Poverty and Inequality. Available online: https://www.law.georgetown.edu/poverty-inequality-center/wp-content/uploads/sites/14/2017/08/girlhood-interrupted.pdf (accessed January 14, 2021).

Evans, Fred (2009), *The Multivoiced Body: Society and Communication in the Age of Diversity*, New York: Columbia University Press.

Fasoli, Fabio, and Peter Hegarty (2020), "A Leader Doesn't Sound Lesbian!: The Impact of Sexual Orientation Vocal Cues on Heterosexual Persons' First Impression and Hiring Decision," *Psychology of Women Quarterly*, 44 (2): 234–55.

Firestone, Shulamith ([1970] 2003), *The Dialectic of Sex: The Case for Feminist Revolution*, New York: Farrar, Straus and Giroux.

Fischer, Julia, Stuart Semple, Gisela Fickenscher, Rebecca Jürgens, Eberhard Kruse, Michael Heistermann, and Ofer Amir (2011), "Do Women's Voices Provide Cues of the Likelihood of Ovulation? The Importance of Sampling Regime," *PloS One*, 6 (9): e24490. Available online: https://www.ncbi.nlm.nih.gov/pmc/articles/PMC3177841/ (accessed June 10, 2020).

Fish, Daniel (Director), and Daniel Kluger (Music Supervisor) (2019), *Oklahoma!* (2019 Broadway Cast Recording), Oscar Hammerstein (Book/Lyrics), and Richard Rodgers (Music), Decca Broadway release, UMG Recordings, Inc.

Fisher, Linda (2010), "Feminist Phenomenological Voices," *Continental Philosophy Review*, 43 (1): 83–95.

Flynn, Jill, Kathryn Heath, and Mary Davis Holt (2014), "Women, Find Your Voice," *Harvard Business Review*, June. Available online at: https://hbr.org/2014/06/women-find-your-voice (accessed April 19, 2020).

Forno, Erick, and Juan C. Celedón (2009), "Asthma and Ethnic Minorities: Socioeconomic Status and Beyond," *Current Opinion in Allergy and Clinical Immunology*, 9 (2): 154–60.

Foucault, Michel (1977), *Discipline and Punish: The Birth of the Prison*, trans. Alan Sheridan, London: Allen Lane.

Frijda, Nico, K. Richard Ridderinkhof, and Erik Rietveld (2014), "Impulsive Action: Emotional Impulses and Their Control," *Frontiers in Psychology* 5. Available online: https://www.frontiersin.org/articles/10.3389/fpsyg.2014.00518/full (accessed March 19, 2020).

Garland-Thompson, Rosemarie (1997), *Extraordinary Bodies: Figuring Physical Disability in American Culture and Literature*, New York: Columbia University Press.

Gatens, Moira (1996), *Imaginary Bodies: Ethics, Power and Corporeality*, London and New York: Routledge.

Gelb, Michael J. (1996), *Body Learning: An Introduction to the Alexander Technique*, 2nd ed., New York: Henry Holt.

Gerretsen, Isabelle (2020), "How Air Pollution Exacerbates Covid-19," BBC, April 17. Available online: https://www.bbc.com/future/article/20200427-how-air-pollution-exacerbates-covid-19 (accessed June 16, 2020).

Gessen, Masha (2019), "The Immigrant Witnesses of the Impeachment Hearings," *New Yorker*, November 24. Available online: https://www.newyorker.com/news/our-columnists/the-immigrant-witnesses-of-the-impeachment-hearings (accessed June 16, 2020).

Gill, Mary (1994), "Accent and Stereotypes: Their Effect on Perceptions of Teachers and Lecture Comprehension," *Journal of Applied Communication Research*, 22 (4): 348–61.

Gilligan, Carol (1982), *In a Different Voice: Psychological Theory and Women's Development*, Cambridge, MA: Harvard University Press.

Gingras, J. L., E. A. Mitchell, and K. E. Grattan (2005), "Fetal Homologue of Infant Crying," *Archives of Disease in Childhood: Fetal and Neonatal Edition*, 90 (5): F415–18.

Ginther, Amy Mihyang (2015), "Dysconscious Racism in Mainstream British Voice Pedagogy and Its Potential Effects on Students from Pluralistic Backgrounds in UK Drama Conservatoires," *Voice and Speech Review*, 9 (1): 41–60.

Glaser, Eliane (2015), "The Cult of Natural Childbirth Has Gone too Far," *Guardian*, March 5. Available online: https://www.theguardian.com/commentisfree/2015/mar/05/natural-childbirth-report-midwife-musketeers-morcambe-bay (accessed March 18, 2020).

Glass, Ira (2015), "If You Don't Have Anything Nice to Say, SAY IT IN ALL CAPS: Freedom Fries," January 23, *This American Life*, produced by National Public Radio and WBEZ Chicago, podcast, MP3 audio, 8:30. Available online: https://www.thisamericanlife.org/545/if-you-dont-have-anything-nice-to-say-say-it-in-all-caps/act-two (accessed June 3, 2020).

Gorodeisky, Kerein (2016), "19th Century Romantic Aesthetics," in Edward N. Zalta (ed.), *The Stanford Encyclopedia of Philosophy*. Available online: https://plato.stanford.edu/archives/fall2016/entries/aesthetics-19th-romantic/ (accessed March 18, 2020).

Górska, Magdalena (2016), "Breathing Matters: Feminist Intersectional Politics of Vulnerability," Dissertation, Linköping University, Linköping.

Górska, Magdalena (2018), "Feminist Politics of Breathing," in Lenart Škof and Petri Berndtson (eds.), *Atmospheres of Breathing*, 247–62, Albany, NY: SUNY Press.

Graddol, David, and Joan Swann (1989), *Gender Voices*, Oxford: Blackwell.

Gross, Terry (2015), "From Upspeak to Vocal Fry: Are We Policing Young Women's Voices?," July 23, *Fresh Air*, produced by National Public Radio, podcast, MP3 Audio, 36:38. Available online: https://www.npr.org/2015/07/23/425608745/from-upspeak-to-vocal-fry-are-we-policing-young-womens-voices (accessed March 18, 2020).

Grosz, Elizabeth (1994), *Volatile Bodies: Towards a Corporeal Feminism*, London: Routledge.

Grotowski, Jerzy ([1968] 2002), *Towards a Poor Theatre*, New York: Routledge.

Gunn, Joshua (2010), "On Speech and Public Release," *Rhetoric and Public Affairs*, 13 (2): 1–41.

Hambrick, Greg (2007), "Is Lindsey Graham Gay?," *Charleston City Paper*, September 12. Available online: https://www.charlestoncitypaper.com/charleston/is-lindsey-graham-gay/Content?oid=1111370 (accessed June 13, 2020).

Hammerstein, Oscar (1943), *Oklahoma!*, New York: Random House.

Hamraie, Aimi (2016), "Universal Design and the Problem of 'Post-Disability' Ideology," *Design and Culture*, 8 (3): 285–309.

Hancock, Adrienne B. (2017), "An ICF Perspective on Voice-Related Quality of Life of American Transgender Women," *Journal of Voice*, 31 (1): 115.e1–8.

Hancock, Adrienne, and Lauren Helenius (2012), "Adolescent Male-to-Female Transgender Voice and Communication Therapy," *Journal of Communication Disorders* 45 (5): 313–24.

Hancock, Adrienne B., Julianne Krissiner, and Kelly Owen (2011), "Voice Perceptions and Quality of Life of Transgender People," *Journal of Voice*, 25 (5): 553–8.

Hancock, Adrienne B., and Benjamin A. Rubin (2015), "Influence of Communication Partner's Gender on Language," *Journal of Language and Social Psychology*, 34 (1): 46–64.

Hanly, Peter (2009), "Hegel's Voice: Vibration and Violence," *Research in Phenomenology*, 39: 359–73.

Harbin, Ami (2014), *Disorientation and Moral Life*, New York: Oxford University Press.

Harris, Hunter (2018), "How *Sorry to Bother You* Found (and Used) Its White Voice," *Vulture*, July 18. Available online: https://www.vulture.com/2018/07/boots-riley-sorry-to-bother-you-found-and-used-its-white-voice.html (accessed March 18, 2020).

Hartman, Saidiya (2019), *Wayward Lives, Beautiful Experiments: Intimate Histories of Riotous Black Girls, Troublesome Women, and Queer Radicals*, New York: W.W. Norton.

Havis, Devonya (2009), "Blackness beyond Witness: Black Vernacular Phenomena and Auditory Identity," *Philosophy and Social Criticism*, 35 (7): 747–59.

Hayes, Bill (2020), Tweet, August 27. Available online: https://twitter.com/billdotmu/status/1298982019687313408?s=21&fbclid=IwAR0qtBAFMpTAS8BWZCrmw5qIE2XkjKV3CT8rX4x4wjCMcAo_yluN9maRFic (accessed December 22, 2020).

Haynes, Phyllis (2010), Interview with Kristin Linklater on Studio 1 Network. Video. Available online at: https://www.youtube.com/watch?v=L4X5gVENkn4 (accessed April 19, 2020).

Hearns, Liz Jackson, and Brian Kremer (2018), *The Singing Teacher's Guide to Trans Voices*, San Diego: Plural Publishing.

Helou, Leah B., and Sandy Hirsch (2018), "Considerations for Discharge and Maintenance," in Richard Kenneth Adler, Sandy Hirsch, and Jack Pickering (eds.), *Voice and Communication Therapy for the Transgender/Gender Diverse Client: A Comprehensive Clinical Guide*, 3rd ed., 359–74, San Diego, CA: Plural.

Hendrickson, Jonathan (2020), "What Joe Biden Can't Bring Himself to Say," *Atlantic*, January/February. Available online: https://www.theatlantic.com/magazine/archive/2020/01/joe-biden-stutter-profile/602401/.

Henry, John Patrick, I. Javier Ameijeiras, Alexander Libby, Bella Sotomayor, Florian Bouju, and Serene Lim (2019), "Broadway by the Numbers 2019," *ProductionPro*. Available online: https://production.pro/broadway-by-the-numbers (accessed January 20, 2021).

Hesse, Monica (2019), "What Does Female Authority Sound Like? Marie Yovanovitch and Fiona Hill Just Showed Us," *Washington Post*, November 22. Available online: https://www.washingtonpost.com/lifestyle/style/what-does-female-authority-sound-like-marie-yovanovitch-and-fiona-hill-just-showed-us/2019/11/22/b5041d06-0cbc-11ea-8397-a955cd542d00_story.html (accessed June 16, 2020).

Heyes, Cressida (2007), *Self-Transformations: Foucault, Ethics, and Normalized Bodies*, New York: Oxford University Press.

Hill, Evan, Ainara Tiefenthäler, Christiaan Triebert, Drew Jordan, Haley Willis, and Robin Stein (2020), "8 Minutes and 46 Seconds: How George Floyd Was Killed in Police Custody," *New York Times*, May 31. Available online: https://www.nytimes. com/2020/05/31/us/george-floyd-investigation.html (accessed June 3, 2020).

Hoffman, Kelly M., Sophie Trawalter, Jordan R. Axt, and M. Norman Oliver (2018), "Racial Bias in Pain Assessment and Treatment Recommendations, and False Beliefs about Biological Differences between Blacks and Whites," *Proceedings of the National Academy of Sciences of the United States of America*, 113 (16): 4296–301.

Holdsworth, Elizabeth, and Allison A. Appleton (2020), "Adverse Childhood Experiences and Reproductive Strategies in a Contemporary U.S. Population," *American Journal of Physical Anthropology*, 171 (1): 37–49.

Hubbard, L. Ron ([1950] 2007), *Dianetics: The Modern Science of Mental Health*, Los Angeles: Bridge Publications.

Hughes, Susan M., Franco Dispenza, and Gordon G. Gallup Jr. (2004), "Ratings of Voice Attractiveness Predict Sexual Behavior and Body Configuration," *Evolution and Human Behavior*, 25 (5): 295–304.

Hunt, Darnel M., Ana-Christina Ramón, and Zachary Price (2014), *2014 Hollywood Diversity Report: Making Sense of the Disconnect*, Los Angeles: Ralph J. Bunche Center for African-American Studies at UCLA. Available online: https:// socialsciences.ucla.edu/wp-content/uploads/2017/09/2014-Hollywood-Diversity-Report-2-12-14.pdf (accessed December 30, 2020).

Ihde, Don (2007), *Listening and Voice: Phenomenologies of Sound*, 2nd ed., Albany, NY: SUNY Press.

Irigaray, Luce (1999), *The Forgetting of Air in Martin Heidegger*, trans. Mary Beth Mader, Austin: University of Texas Press.

Irigaray, Luce (2004), "Before and Beyond Any Word," in Luce Irigaray (ed.), *Key Writings*, 134–41, London and New York: Continuum.

Irwig, Michael S. (2017), "Testosterone Therapy for Transgender Men," *Lancet Diabetes and Endocrinology*, 5 (4): 301–11.

Ivry, Tsipy (2010), *Embodying Culture: Pregnancy in Japan and Israel*, New Brunswick, NJ: Rutgers University Press.

Izdebski, Krzysztof (2008), "Erotic and Orgasmic Vocalization: Myth, Reality, or Both?," in *Emotions in the Human Voice*, Vol. 1: Foundations, 1–30, San Francisco, CA: Plural.

Jacobi, Tonya, and Dylan Schweers (2017), "Female Supreme Court Justices Are Interrupted More by Male Justices and Advocates," *Harvard Business Review*, April 17. Available online: https://hbr.org/2017/04/female-supreme-court-justices-are-interrupted-more-by-male-justices-and-advocates (accessed March 18, 2020).

James, Robin (2010), *The Conjectural Body: Gender, Race, and the Philosophy of Music*, Lanham, MD: Lexington Books.

James, Robin (2015), "Gendered Voices and Social Harmony," *Sounding Out!*, March 9. Available online: https://soundstudiesblog.com/category/gendered-voices-forum/ (accessed March 18, 2020).

James, Robin (2019), *The Sonic Episteme: Acoustic Resonance, Neoliberalism, and Biopolitics*, Durham and London: Duke University Press.

Jordan, Julia (2018), "The Count 2.0," *Dramatists Guild of America*, October 8. Available online: https://www.dramatistsguild.com/advocacy/the-count (accessed January 20, 2021).

Kahn, Sameer ud Dowla (2015), "Open Letter to Terry Gross," July 8. Available online: https://www.reed.edu/linguistics/khan/Khan-LetterToTerryGross.pdf (accessed January 21, 2021).

Karpf, Anne (2017), "Speaking Sex to Power? The Female Voice as a Dangerous Instrument," *Ears Wide Open: Il Paesaggio Sonoro Negli Studi di Cinema e Media*, 14: 27–36. Available online: http://repository.londonmet.ac.uk/1276/ (accessed June 10, 2020).

Keich, Holly (2016), "The Power of Sound in Labor," *Om Baby Center*, February 28. Available online: https://ombabycenter.wordpress.com/2016/02/28/the-power-of-sound-in-labor/ (accessed March 18, 2020).

Kelly, Victoria, Stellan Hertegård, Jenny Eriksson, Ulrika Nygren, and Maria Södersten (2019), "Effects of Gender-Confirming Pitch-Raising Surgery in Transgender Women a Long-Term Follow-Up Study of Acoustic and Patient-Reported Data," *Journal of Voice*, 33 (5): 781–91.

Kim, Christine Sun (2015), "The Enchanting Music of Sign Language." [Video File], August. Available online: https://www.ted.com/talks/christine_sun_kim_the_enchanting_music_of_sign_language (accessed December 20, 2020).

Kim, Ruthanne Crapo, Ann J. Cahill, and Melissa Jacquart (2020), "Bearing the Brunt of Structural Inequality: Ontological Labor in the Academy," *Feminist Philosophy Quarterly*, 6 (1): Article 3.

Kishi, Rieko, Beverly J. McElmurry, Susan Vonderheid, Susan Altfeld, Barbara McFarlin, and Junko Tashiro (2010), "Japanese Women's Experiences From Pregnancy Through Early Postpartum Period," *Health Care for Women International*, 32 (1): 57–71.

Kisilevsky, B. S., S. M. Hains, C. A. Brown, C. T. Lee, B. Cowperthwaite, S. S. Stutzman, M. L. Swansburg, K. Lee, X. Xie, H. H. Ye, K. Zhang, and Z. Wang (2009), "Fetal Sensitivity to Properties of Maternal Speech and Language," *Infant Behavior and Development*, 32 (1): 59–71.

Kleinberger, Rébecca (2018), "Why You Don't Like The Sound of Your Own Voice" [Video File], May 24. Available online: https://www.ted.com/talks/rebecca_kleinberger_why_you_don_t_like_the_sound_of_your_own_voice (accessed March 18, 2020).

Knight, Dudley (1997), "Standard Speech: The Ongoing Debate," in Marian Hampton and Barbara Acker (eds.), *The Vocal Vision*, 155–83, New York: Applause.

Krell, Salomé M.(2011), "Of Rabbit Holes and Aquamarines (Cabbages and Kings)," *Mosaic: A Journal for the Interdisciplinary Study of Literature*, 44 (1): 89–99.

Kristeva, Julia (1982), *Powers of Horror: An Essay on Abjection*, New York: Columbia University Press.

Kristeva, Julia (1984), *Revolution in Poetic Language*, trans. Margaret Waller, New York: Columbia University Press.

Kuhl, Patricia K. (2004), "Early Language Acquisition: Cracking the Speech Code," *Nature Reviews Neuroscience*, 5 (11): 831–43.

Kyratzis, Amy, and Jenny Cook-Gumperz (2008), "Language Socialization and Gendered Practices in Childhood," in Patricia A. Duff and Nancy H. Hornberger (eds.), *Encyclopedia of Language and Education, Vol. 8: Language Socialization*, 145–57, New York: Springer.

Lauzen, Martha M. (2020), "It's a Man's (Celluloid) World: Portrayals of Female Characters in the Top Grossing Films of 2019," Center for the Study of Women in Television and Film. Available online: https://womenintvfilm.sdsu.edu/wp-content/uploads/2020/01/2019_Its_a_Mans_Celluloid_World_Report_REV.pdf (accessed December 21, 2020).

Leavitt, Amy (2020), "Vocal Traditions: Rodenburg Voice and Speech," *Voice and Speech Review*, 14 (1): 96–107.

Leeman, Richard W., and Bernard K. Duffy, eds. (2012), *The Will of the People: A Critical Anthology of Great African American Speeches*, Carbondale, IL: Southern Illinois University Press.

Lennon, Kathleen (2014), "Feminist Perspectives on the Body," in Edward N. Zalta (ed.), *The Stanford Encyclopedia of Philosophy*. Available online: https://plato.stanford.edu/archives/fall2014/entries/feminist-body/ (accessed March 18, 2020).

Levin, Roy J. (2006), "Vocalised Sounds and Human Sex," *Sexual and Relationship Therapy*, 21 (1): 99–107.

Levitt, Rachel (2013), "Silence Speaks Volumes: Counter-Hegemonic Silences, Deafness, and Alliance Work," in Sheena Malhotra and Aimee Carrillo Rowe (eds.), *Silence, Feminism, Power: Reflections at the Edges of Sound*, 67–81, New York: Palgrave Macmillan.

Liberman, Mark (2007), "The Perils of Mixing Romance with Language Learning," *Language Log*, November 7. Available online: http://itre.cis.upenn.edu/~myl/languagelog/archives/005093.html (accessed March 18, 2020).

Lieberman, Philip (1967), *Intonation, Perception, and Language*, Cambridge, MA: MIT Press.

Linklater, Kristin (1976), *Freeing the Natural Voice*, 1st ed., New York: Drama Book Specialists.

Linklater, Kristin (1992), *Freeing Shakespeare's Voice: The Actor's Guide to Talking the Text*, New York: Theatre Communications Group.

Linklater, Kristin (2006), *Freeing the Natural Voice: Imagery and Art in the Practice of Voice and Language*, Revised and Expanded 2nd ed., London: Nick Hern Books.

Linklater, Kristin (2009a), "The Alchemy of Breathing," in Jane Boston and Rena Cook (eds.), *Breath in Action: The Art of Breath in Vocal and Holistic Practice*, 101–7, London: Jessica Kingsley.

Linklater, Kristin (2009b), "The European League Institute of the Arts." Available online: https://www.linklatervoice.com/resources/articles-essays/40-the-european-league-of-institutes-of-the-arts (accessed March 18, 2020).

Linklater, Kristin (2010), "The Importance of Daydreaming," *American Theatre*, 27 (1): 43–4, 124–6.

Linklater, Kristin (2018), "Vocal Traditions: Linklater Voice Method," *Voice and Speech Review*, 12 (2): 1–10.

Lipsky, Jon (undated), *Beyond Acting One: A Personalized Approach to Text*. Unpublished Manuscript.

Loeffler, Summer (2014), "Deaf Music: Embodying Language and Rhythm," in H-Dirksen L. Bauman, and Joseph J. Murray (eds.), *Deaf Gain: Raising the Stakes for Human Diversity*, 436–56, Minneapolis: University of Minnesota Press.

Lofgren, Mike (2020), "The GOP Has Become a Death Cult," *Common Dreams*, April 17. Available online: https://www.commondreams.org/views/2020/04/17/gop-has-become-death-cult (accessed June 16, 2020).

Loveday, Leo (1981), "Pitch, Politeness, and Sexual Role: An Exploratory Investigation," *Language and Speech*, 24: 71–88.

Lugones, María (1987), "Playfulness, 'World'-Travelling, and Loving Perception," *Hypatia*, 2 (2): 3–19.

Lugones, María (2003), *Pilgrimages/Peregrinajes: Theorizing Coalition against Multiple Oppressions*, New York: Routledge.

Macharia, Sarah (2015), "Who Makes the News?" *Global Media Monitoring Project 2015*, London and Toronto: World Association for Christian Communication. Available online: http://cdn.agilitycms.com/who-makes-the-news/Imported/reports_2015/global/gmmp_global_report_en.pdf (accessed March 18, 2020).

MacKendrick, Karmen (2016), *The Matter of Voice: Sensual Soundings*, New York: Fordham University Press.

Majewski, W., H. Hollien, and J. Zalewski (1972), "Speaking Fundamental Frequency of Polish Adult Males," *Phonetica*, 25 (2): 19–25.

Mampe, Birgit, Angela D. Friederici, Anne Christophe, and Kathleen Wermke (2009), "Newborns' Cry Melody Is Shaped by Their Native Language," *Current Biology*, December 15, 19: 1994–7.

Manne, Kate (2018), *Down Girl: The Logic of Misogyny*, New York: Oxford University Press.

Marcotte, Amanda (2015), "The War on Female Voices Is Just Another Way of Telling Women to Shut Up," *Daily Dot*, July 24. Available online: https://www.dailydot.com/unclick/vocal-fry-99-percent-invisible-womens-voices/ (accessed June 8, 2020).

Marwick, Arthur (2011), *The Sixties: Cultural Transformation in Britain, France, Italy and the United States, c. 1958–c. 1974*, London: Bloomsbury Reader. Ebook available at: https://books.google.com/books?id=etYOaWh1t4cC.

McAllister-Viel, Tara (2009), "(Re)considering the Role of Breath in Training Actors' Voices: Insights from Dahnjeon Breathing and the Phenomena of Breath," *Theatre Topics*, 19 (2): 165–80.

McAllister-Viel, Tara (2019), *Training Actors' Voices: Towards an Intercultural/Interdisciplinary Approach*, New York: Routledge.

McCance, Dawne, ed. (2011), Kristin Linklater/The Santorini Voice Symposium, special issue of *Mosaic: A Journal for the Interdisciplinary Study of Literature*, 44 (1).

McCarty, T. L., Mary Eunice Romero, and Ofelia Zepeda (2006), "Reclaiming the Gift: Indigenous Youth Counter-Narratives on Native Language Loss and Revitalization," *American Indian Quarterly*, 30 (1&2): 28–48.

McCloskey, Deirdre N. (1999), *Crossing: A Memoir*, Chicago: University of Chicago Press.

McLaughlin, Kelly (2019), "People Are Comparing Ambassador Bill Taylor's Voice to Walter Cronkite's as He Testifies in the Trump Impeachment Hearing," *Business Insider*, November 13. Available online: https://www.businessinsider.com/bill-taylor-voice-walter-cronkite-trump-impeachment-hearing-2019-11 (accessed June 16, 2020).

McNeill, Emma J. M., Janet A. Wilson, Susan Clark, and Jayne Deakin (2008), "Perception of Voice in the Transgender Client," *Journal of Voice*, 22 (6): 727–33.

Meier, Paul (2008), *Accents and Dialects for Stage and Screen*, Lawrence, KS: Paul Meier Dialect Services.

Menakem, Resmaa (2017), *My Grandmother's Hands: Racialized Trauma and the Pathway to Mending Our Hearts and Bodies*, Las Vegas: Central Recovery Press, Ebook available at: https://books.google.com/books?id=OaG4DgAAQBAJ

Metcalf, Stephen (2017), "How John Wayne Became a Hollow Masculine Icon," *Atlantic*, December. Available online: https://www.theatlantic.com/magazine/archive/2017/12/john-wayne-john-ford/544113 (accessed March 18, 2020).

Miller-Frank, Felicia (1995), *The Mechanical Song: Women, Voice, and the Artificial in Nineteenth-Century French Narrative*, Stanford, CA: Stanford University Press.

Mills, Charles (1999), *The Racial Contract*, Ithaca, NY: Cornell University Press.

Monks, James, and Robert M. Schmidt (2011), "The Impact of Class Size on Outcomes in Higher Education," *B.E. Journal of Economic Analysis & Policy*, 11 (1): Article 62.

Moraga, Cherríe (1983), "Preface," in Cherríe Moraga and Gloria Anzaldúa (eds.), *This Bridge Called My Back: Writings by Radical Women of Color*, 2nd ed., New York: Kitchen Table.

Morisseau, Dominique (2017), "Rules of Engagement," program for *Pipeline* at Lincoln Center Theater, June 15–August 27, single-page insert.

Morris, Jeremy Wade, and Eleanor Patterson (2015), "Podcasting and Its Apps: Software, Sound, and the Interfaces of Digital Audio," *Journal of Radio & Audio Media*, 22 (2): 220–30.

Morris, Richard (1997), "Speaking Fundamental Frequency Characteristics of 8- through 10-year-old White- and African-American Boys," *Journal of Communication Disorders*, 30 (2): 101–16.

Morrison, Nick (2019), "Fiona Hill's Master Class Is a Lingering Badge of Shame for Oxford University," *Forbes*, November 27. Available online: https://www.forbes.com/sites/nickmorrison/2019/11/27/fiona-hills-masterclass-is-a-lingering-badge-of-shame-for-oxford-university/?sh=c06a3553037a (accessed January 21, 2021).

Myers, Marc (2018), "Barry White's Music of Love," *Wall Street Journal*, October 11. Available online: https://www.wsj.com/articles/barry-whites-music-of-love-1539265974 (accessed March 18, 2020).

NCVS (National Center for Voice & Speech) (undated), "Voice Changes Throughout Life," NCVS.org. University of Utah. Available online: http://www.ncvs.org/ncvs/tutorials/voiceprod/tutorial/changes.html (accessed May 18, 2020).

Newman, Lex (2019), "Descartes' Epistemology," in Edward N. Zalta (ed.), *The Stanford Encyclopedia of Philosophy*. Available online: https://plato.stanford.edu/archives/spr2019/entries/descartes-epistemology/ (accessed April 24, 2020).

Newman, Michael, and Angela Wu (2011), "Do You Sound Asian When You Speak English? Racial Identification and Voice in Chinese and Korean Americans' English," *American Speech*, 86 (2): 152–78.

Nieuwenhuis, Marijn (2016), "The Emergence of Materialism in Geography: Belonging and Being, Space and Place, Sea and Land," *Social Science Information*, 55 (3): 300–20.

Nygren, Ulrika, Agneta Nordenskjöld, Stefan Arver, and Maria Södersten (2016), "Effects on Voice Fundamental Frequency and Satisfaction with Voice in Trans Men during Testosterone Treatment—A Longitudinal Study," *Journal of Voice*, 30 (6): 766. e23–766.e34.

Nyre, Lars (2015), "Urban Headphone Listening and the Situational Fit of Music, Radio and Podcasting," *Journal of Radio and Audio Media*, 22 (2): 279–98.

Oates, Jennifer, and Georgia Dacakis (2015), "Transgender Voice and Communication: Research Evidence Underpinning Voice Intervention for Male-to-Female Transsexual Women," *Perspectives on Voice and Voice Disorders*, 25 (2): 48–58.

O'Brien, Jane (2013), "How Foetuses Learn Language," *BBC News Magazine*, May 9. Available online: https://www.bbc.com/news/world-us-canada-22457797 (accessed March 18, 2020).

O'Donnell, Kieran J., Nadja Reissland, and Vivette Glover (2017), "New Insights into Prenatal Stress: Immediate- and Long-Term Effects on the Fetus and Their Timing," in Giuseppe Buonocore and Carlo Valerio Bellieni (eds.), *Neonatal Pain: Suffering,*

Pain, and Risk of Brain Damage in the Fetus and Newborn, 75–88, Cham, Switzerland: Springer.

Oppel, Richard A., and Kim Barker (2021), "New Transcripts Detail Last Moments for George Floyd," *New York Times*, April 1. Available online: https://www.nytimes.com/2020/07/08/us/george-floyd-body-camera-transcripts.html (accessed May 14, 2021).

Oram, Daron (2019), "De-Colonizing Listening: Toward an Equitable Approach to Speech Training for the Actor," *Voice and Speech Review*, 13 (3): 279–97.

Oram, Daron (2020a), "Decentering Listening: Toward an Anti-Discriminatory Approach to Accent and Dialect Training for the Actor," *Voice and Speech Review*. Available online: https://doi.org/10.1080/23268263.2020.1842455 (accessed January 3, 2021).

Oram, Daron (2020b), "The Heuristic Pedagogue: Navigating Myths and Truths in Pursuit of an Equitable Approach to Voice Training," *Theatre, Dance and Performance Training*, 11 (3): 300–9.

Ortega, Mariana (2016), *In-Between: Latina Feminist Phenomenology, Multiplicity, and the Self*, Albany, NY: SUNY Press.

Osborne, Michelle (2018), "How American Society Habitually Silences Women of Color Part 1," *YWCA*, July 25. Available online: https://www.ywcaworks.org/blogs/ywca/wed-07252018-1200/how-american-society-habitually-silences-women-color-part-i (accessed June 11, 2020).

Owen, Kelly, and Adrienne B. Hancock (2010), "The Role of Self- and Listener Perceptions of Femininity in Voice Therapy," *International Journal of Transgenderism*, 12 (4): 272–84.

Painter-Morland, Mollie (2011), "Voice as 'Relational Space': Agency beyond Narcissism or the Loss of Self," *Mosaic: A Journal for the Interdisciplinary Study of Literature*, 44 (1): 141–61.

Passie, Torsten, Uwe Hartmann, Udo Schneider, and Hinderk M. Emrich (2003), "On the Function of Groaning and Hyperventilation during Sexual Intercourse: Intensification of Sexual Experience by Altering Brain Metabolism through Hypocapnia," *Medical Hypotheses*, 60 (5): 660–3.

Pemberton, Cecilia, Paul Mccormack, and Alison Russell (1998), "Have Women's Voices Lowered Across Time? A Cross Sectional Study of Australian Women's Voices," *Journal of Voice*, 12 (2): 208–13.

Pierce, Beverly (1998), "The Practice of Toning in Pregnancy and Labor: Participant Experiences," *Complementary Therapies in Nursing and Midwifery*, April, 4 (2): 41–6.

Pierce, Beverly (2001), "Toning in Pregnancy and Labor," *Journal of Prenatal & Perinatal Psychology & Health*, 15 (3). Available online: https://www.questia.com/read/1P3-1373167401/toning-in-pregnancy-and-labor (accessed April 10, 2020).

Pinsker, Joe (2015), "Rich Kids Study English," *Atlantic*, July 6. Available online: https://www.theatlantic.com/business/archive/2015/07/college-major-rich-families-liberal-arts/397439/ (accessed March 18, 2020).

Plett, Casey (2011), "Column 19: Voices," *McSweeney's*, September 23. Available online: https://www.mcsweeneys.net/articles/column-19-voices?fbclid=IwAR2puM Hpn8AyZT1UFStFbMtbk167FvgxF3xwwwAizHMChf8UckLW8l-A28I (accessed March 18, 2020).

Poniewozik, James (2018), "A High-Stakes Hearing Raises Two Voices, One Quiet, One Loud," *New York Times*, September 27. Available online: https://www.nytimes. com/2018/09/27/arts/television/brett-kavanaugh-hearing-television.html (accessed June 16, 2020).

Power, Terri (2016), *Shakespeare and Gender in Practice*, London: Red Globe Press.

Pridgett, Tamara (2020), "What Is Black Girls Breathing?," *Popsugar*, May 20. Available online: https://www.popsugar.com/fitness/what-is-black-girls-breathing-47460703 (accessed June 3, 2020).

Puts, David Andrew (2005), "Mating Context and Menstrual Phase Affect Women's Preferences for Male Voice Pitch," *Evolution and Human Behavior*, 26 (5): 388–97.

Puwar, Nirmal (2004), *Space Invaders: Race, Gender and Bodies Out of Place*, Oxford: Berg.

Quenqua, Douglas (2012), "They're, Like, Way Ahead of the Linguistic Currrrve," *New York Times*, February 27. Available online: https://www.nytimes. com/2012/02/28/science/young-women-often-trendsetters-in-vocal-patterns. html?searchResultPosition=1 (accessed March 18, 2020).

Rao, Delip (2018), "When Men and Women Talk to Siri." Available online: http:// deliprao.com/archives/276 (accessed March 19, 2020).

Read, Richard (2020), "A Choir Decided to Go Ahead with Rehearsal. Now Dozens of Members have COVID-19 and Two Are Dead," *LA Times*, March 29. Available online: https://www.latimes.com/world-nation/story/2020-03-29/coronavirus-choir-outbreak (accessed May 17, 2020).

Reagan, Patricia B., Pamela J. Salsberry, Muriel Z. Fang, William P. Gardner, and Kathleen Pajer (2012), "African-American/White Differences in the Age of Menarche: Accounting for the Difference," *Social Science & Medicine*, 75 (7): 1263–70.

Reby, David, Florence Levréro, Erik Gustafsson, and Nicolas Mathevon (2016), "Sex Stereotypes Influence Adults' Perception of Babies' Cries," *BMC Psychology*, 4, Article 19.

Rée, Jonathan (1999), *I See a Voice: Deafness, Language and the Senses—A Philosophical History*, New York: Metropolitan Books.

Regmi, Krishna (2012), "A Review of Teaching Methods–Lecturing and Facilitation in Higher Education (HE): A Summary of the Published Evidence," *Journal of Effective Teaching*, 12 (3): 61–76.

Rich, Adrienne (1979), *Of Women Born: Motherhood as Experience and Institution*, London: Virago.

Richardson, Elsa (2016), "The History of Our Emotions," *Ladybeard: The Mind Issue*, 23, December. Available online: https://www.refinery29.com/en-gb/elsa-richardson-on-the-history-of-our-emotions (accessed March 18, 2020).

Riggs, Lynn (1930), *Green Grow the Lilacs*, New York: Samuel French.

Riley, Erin (2015), "Naomi Wolf Misses the Point about 'Vocal Fry'. It's Just an Excuse Not to Listen to Women," *Guardian*, July 27. Available online: https://www.theguardian.com/commentisfree/2015/jul/28/naomi-wolf-misses-the-point-about-vocal-fry-its-just-an-excuse-not-to-listen-to-women (accessed March 18, 2020).

Ro, Tony, Timothy M. Ellmore, and Michael S. Beauchamp (2013), "A Neural Link between Feeling and Hearing," *Cerebral Cortex*, 23 (7): 1724–30.

Rodenburg, Patsy [1992] (2015), *The Right to Speak*, New York: Methuen.

Rodenburg, Patsy [1993] (2018), *The Need for Words*, London: Methuen.

Rodenburg, Patsy [1997] (2020), *The Actor Speaks*, London: Methuen.

Rodenburg, Patsy (2002), *Speaking Shakespeare*, London: Palgrave Macmillan.

Roudiez, Leon S. (1984), "Introduction," in Julia Kristeva, *Revolution in Poetic Language*, trans. Margaret Waller, 1–10, New York: Columbia University Press.

Rousuck, J. Wynn. (1996), "Bringing New Voices to Theater: The Company of Women works on Scripting a New Play at the Same Time as It Stages an All-Female 'King Lear' and Conducts Workshops for Women and Girls," *Baltimore Sun*, August 11. Available online: https://www.baltimoresun.com/news/bs-xpm-1996-08-11-1996224120-story.html (accessed March 19, 2020).

Roy, Arundhati Roy (2020), "The Pandemic Is a Portal," *Financial Times*, April 3. Available online: https://www.ft.com/content/10d8f5e8-74eb-11ea-95fe-fcd274e920ca (accessed May 17, 2020).

Rubin, Jeffrey Z. Frank J. Provenzano, and Zella Luria (1974), "The Eye of the Beholder: Parents' Views on the Sex of Newborns," *American Journal of Orthopsychiatry*, 44 (4): 512–19.

Salerno, Jessica M., and Liana C. Peter-Hagene (2015), "One Angry Woman: Anger Expression Increases Influence for Men, but Decreases Influence for Women, during Group Deliberation," *Law and Human Behavior*, 39 (6): 581–92.

Sataloff, Robert T. (2017), *Professional Voice: The Science and Art of Clinical Care*, 4th ed., San Diego: Plural.

Scheper, Jeanne (2016), " 'Voices within the Voice': Aural Passing and Libby Holman's Deracinated/Reracinated Sound," in *Moving Performances: Divas, Iconicity, and Remembering the Modern Stage*, 93–126, New Brunswick, NJ and London: Rutgers University Press.

Schlichter, Annette (2014), "Un/Voicing the Self: Vocal Pedagogy and the Discourse-Practices of Subjectivation," *Postmodern Culture*, 24 (3). Available online: https://muse.jhu.edu/article/589571 (accessed March 18, 2020).

Schwitzgebel, Eric (2017a), "The Racial Diversity of Philosophy Majors," *Daily Nous*, December 21. Available online: http://dailynous.com/2017/12/21/racial-diversity-philosophy-majors-guest-post-eric-schwitzgebel/ (accessed March 18, 2020).

Schwitzgebel, Eric (2017b), "What Proportion of Philosophy Majors Are Women?" *Daily Nous*, December 9. Available online: http://dailynous.com/2017/12/09/women-majoring-philosophy-schwitzgebel/ (accessed March 18, 2020).

Scientology Parent (undated), "Silent Birth Questions and Answers." Available online: http://www.scientologyparent.com/silent-birth/silent-birth-questions-answers/ (accessed March 18, 2020).

Searle, John (1969), *Speech Acts: An Essay in the Philosophy of Language*, Cambridge: Cambridge University Press.

Siddiqui, Sabrina (2018), "Kavanaugh's Angry Testimony Raises Doubts over Future Impartiality," *Guardian*, October 3. Available online: https://www.theguardian.com/us-news/2018/oct/02/kavanaugh-impartial-justice-testimony (accessed June 16, 2020).

Siisiäinen, Lauri (2012), "Confession, Voice and the Sensualization of Power: The Significance of Michel Foucault's 1962 Encounter with Jean-Jacques Rousseau," *Foucault Studies*, 14: 138–53.

Silva, Liana M. (2015), "As Loud as I Want to Be: Gender, Loudness, and Respectability Politics," *Sounding Out!*, February 9. Available online: https://soundstudiesblog.com/2015/02/09/as-loud-as-i-want-to-be-gender-loudness-and-respectability-politics/ (accessed March 18, 2020).

Skitolsky, Lissa (2020), *Hip-Hop as Philosophical Text and Testimony: Can I Get a Witness?*, Lanham, MD: Lexington Books.

Smith, David, and Emily Holden (2020), "'We Won't See Coronavirus Here' … and Other Gems from Trump's New Press Secretary," *Guardian*, April 8. Available online: https://www.theguardian.com/us-news/2020/apr/08/kayleigh-mcenany-donald-trump-press-secretary-quotes (accessed June 3, 2020).

Smith, Paige (2020), "In 2020, Self-Care Is Becoming a More Radical Act," *HuffPost*, December 8. Available online: https://www.huffpost.com/entry/2020-self-care-radical-act_l_5f89b98ec5b69daf5e12b779?dps (accessed January 21, 2021).

Snow, Kimberley (1994), *Keys to the Open Gate: A Woman's Spirituality Sourcebook*, Berkeley, CA: Conari Press.

Sorry to Bother You (2018), [Film] Dir. Boots Riley, USA: Annapurna Pictures.

Stahl, Jeremy (2019), "Fiona Hill Took the Intelligence Committee to School," *Slate*, November 21. Available online: https://slate.com/news-and-politics/2019/11/fiona-hill-trump-impeachment-testimony.html (accessed June 16, 2020).

St. Pierre, Joshua (2012), "The Construction of the Disabled Speaker: Locating Stuttering in Disability Studies," *Canadian Journal of Disability Studies*, 1 (3): 1–21.

St. Pierre, Joshua (2015), "Cripping Communication: Speech, Disability, and Exclusion in Liberal Humanist and Posthumanist Discourse," *Communication Theory*, 25 (3): 330–48.

STAND League (undated), "What Is Silent Birth?" Available online: https://www.standleague.org/facts-vs-fiction/faqs/what-is-silent-birth.html (accessed March 18, 2020).

Sterne, Jonathan (2003), *The Audible Past: Cultural Origins of Sound Reproduction*, Durham, NC: Duke University Press.

Stoever, Jennifer Lynn (2015), *The Sonic Color Line: Race and the Cultural Politics of Listening*, New York: New York University Press.

Subtirelu, Nicholas Close (2015), "'She Does Have an Accent but…': Race and Language Ideology in Students' Evaluations of Mathematics Instructors on RateMyProfessors. com," *Language in Society*, 44 (1): 35–62.

Tannen, Deborah (2007), *You Just Don't Understand: Women and Men in Conversation*, New York: William Morrow.

Terreri, Cara (2015), "Making Noise in Labor and Birth," Lamaze International, September 21. Available online: https://www.lamaze.org/Giving-Birth-with-Confidence/GBWC-Post/making-noise-in-labor-and-birth (accessed March 18, 2020).

Thompson, Rachel (2018), "Stop Telling Women How They Should Talk," *Mashable*, August 22. Available online: https://mashable.com/article/vocal-fry-upspeak-women/#eueOX_6pCSqo (accessed June 8, 2020).

Thoutenhoofd, Ernst Daniël (2000), "Philosophy's Real-World Consequences for Deaf People: Thoughts on Iconicity, Sign Language and Being Deaf," *Human Studies*, 23: 261–79.

Timmons, Jessica (2018), "When Can a Fetus Hear," *Healthline: Parenthood*, January 4. Available online: https://www.healthline.com/health/pregnancy/when-can-a-fetus-hear (accessed March 18, 2020).

Tomasky, Michael (2020), "Trump's Culture Warriors Are a Literal Death Cult Now," *Daily Beast*, April 17. Available online: https://www.thedailybeast.com/trumps-coronavirus-culture-warriors-are-a-literal-death-cult (accessed June 16, 2020).

Tran, Dien, Evren Odcikin, and Rebecca Novick (2019), "The Changing of the Guard: Who's In, Who's Out: The Numbers," *American Theatre*. Available online at https://www.americantheatre.org/2019/04/09/whos-in-whos-out-the-numbers/ (accessed April 19, 2020).

Tremain, Shelley (2013), "Introducing Feminist Philosophy of Disability," *Disability Studies Quarterly*, 33 (4). Available online: https://dsq-sds.org/article/view/3877 (accessed March 19, 2020).

Tremblay, Jean-Thomas (2019), "Feminist Breathing," *differences*, 30 (3): 92–117.

Tygielski, Shelly (2019), "Transforming Self-Care into a Passionate Movement," Mindful.org, March 6. Available online: https://www.mindful.org/transforming-self-care-into-a-passionate-movement/ (accessed June 14, 2020).

Vallee, Mickey (2016), "Hearing Voice: A Theoretical Framework for Truth Commission Testimony," *Law and Critique*, 27: 45–61.

Vihman, Marilyn (1996), *Phonological Development: The Origins of Language in the Child*, Oxford: Blackwell.

Villarosa, Linda (2018), "Why American's Black Mothers and Babies Are in a Life-or-Death Crisis," *New York Times Magazine*, April 11. Available online: https://www.nytimes.com/2018/04/11/magazine/black-mothers-babies-death-maternal-mortality.html (accessed March 18, 2020).

Vogel, Lauren (2019), "Fat Shaming Is Making People Sicker and Heavier," *CMAJ: Canadian Medical Association Journal*, 191 (23): E649. Available online: https://www.ncbi.nlm.nih.gov/pmc/articles/PMC6565398/ (accessed June 13, 2020).

Vrtička, Pascal (2017), "The Social Neuroscience of Attachment," in Agustín Ibáñez, Lucas Sedeño, and Adolfo M. García (eds.), *Neuroscience and Social Science: The Missing Link*, 95–119, Cham, Switzerland: Springer.

Wald, Christina (2007), *Hysteria, Trauma and Melancholia: Performative Maladies in Contemporary Anglophone Drama*, New York: Palgrave Macmillan.

Watson, Kathryn (2017), "How Babies Breathe in the Womb," *Healthline: Parenthood*, March 13. Available online: https://www.healthline.com/health/pregnancy/how-babies-breathe-in-the-womb (accessed March 18, 2020).

Watt, Seth O., Konstantin O. Tskhay, and Nicholas O. Rule (2018), "Masculine Voices Predict Well-Being in Female-to-Male Transgender Individuals," *Archives of Sexual Behavior*, 47 (4): 963–72.

Webb, Alexandra R., Howard T. Heller, Carol B. Benson, and Amir Lahav (2015), "Mother's Voice and Heartbeat Sounds Elicit Auditory Plasticity in the Human Brain before Full Gestation," *Proceedings of the National Academy of Sciences*, 112 (10): 3152–7.

WebMD (2006), "Silent Birth Now a Noisy Controversy," April 13. Available online: https://www.webmd.com/baby/features/silent-birth-now-noisy-controversy (accessed April 15, 2020).

Weiss, Gail (1999), *Body Images: Embodiment as Intercorporeality*, New York and London: Routledge.

Weiss, Gail, Ann V. Murphy, and Gayle Salamon, eds. (2019), *50 Concepts for a Critical Phenomenology*, Evanston, IL: Northwestern University Press.

Wendell, Susan (1996), *The Rejected Body: Feminist Philosophical Reflections on the Disabled Body*, London: Routledge.

Werner, Sarah (1996), "Performing Shakespeare: Voice Training and the Feminist Actor," *New Theatre Quarterly*, 12 (47): 249–58.

Weston, Anthony (2018), *Teaching as the Art of Staging*, Sterling, VA: Stylus.

White, Tracie (2018), "Epidurals Increase in Popularity, Stanford Study Finds," *SCOPE*, June 26. Available online: https://scopeblog.stanford.edu/2018/06/26/epidurals-increase-in-popularity-stanford-study-finds/ (accessed March 18, 2020).

Wilbourne, Emily (2010), "Lo Schiavetto (1612): Travestied Sound, Ethnic Performance, and the Eloquence of the Body," *Journal of the American Musicological Society*, 63 (1): 1–44.

Williams, Camille (2016), "Are Women's Birth Sounds Silenced in the Hospital?" *Huffpost*, April 13. Available online: https://www.huffpost.com/entry/are-womens-birth-sounds-s_b_9678662 (accessed April 10, 2020).

Wilson, Sean, Helen Meskhidze, Peter Felten, Stephen Bloch-Schulman, Julie Phillips, Claire Lockard, and Susannah McGowan (2020), "From Novelty to Norm: Moving Beyond Exclusion and the Double Justification Problem in Student-Faculty

Partnerships," in Lucy Mercer-Mapstone and Sophia Abbot (eds.), *The Power of Partnership: Students, Staff, and Faculty Revolutionizing Higher Education*, 43–60, Elon, NC: Elon University Center for Engaged Learning.

Wolf, Naomi (2015), "Young Women, Give up the Vocal Fry and Reclaim Your Strong Female Voice," *Guardian*, July 24. Available online: https://www.theguardian.com/commentisfree/2015/jul/24/vocal-fry-strong-female-voice (accessed June 8, 2020).

Wu, Xiao, Rachel C. Nethery, Benjamin M. Sabath, Danielle Braun, and Francesca Dominici (2020), "Exposure to Air Pollution and COVID-19 Mortality in the United States," *medRxiv* 2020.04.05.20054502. Available online: https://doi.org/10.1101/2020.04.05.20054502 (accessed May 17, 2020).

Wysocki, Jaroslaw, Ewa Kielska, Piortr Orszulak, and Jerzy Reymond (2008), "Measurements of Pre- and Postpubertal Human Larynx: A Cadaver Study," *Surgical and Radiologic Anatomy*, 30: 191–9.

Yancy, George (2012), *Look, a White! Philosophical Essays on Whiteness*, Philadelphia: Temple University Press.

Yancy, George (2015), "Tarrying Together," *Educational Philosophy and Theory*, 47 (1): 26–35.

Yancy, George (2018), *Backlash: What Happens When We Talk Honestly about Racism in America*, Lanham, MD: Rowman and Littlefield.

Young, Iris Marion (2005), *On Female Body Experience: "Throwing Like a Girl" and Other Essays*, New York: Oxford University Press.

Young, Vershawn Ashanti (2009), "'Nah, We Straight': An Argument Against Code-Switching," *JAC*, 29 (1/2): 49–76.

Young, Vershawn Ashanti, and Y'Shanda Young-Rivera (2013), "It Ain't What It Is: Code Switching and White American Celebrationists," *JAC*, 33 (1/2): 396–401.

Yousman, Bill, Henry Giroux, Janice Welsch, and Mark Traverso (Director) (2006), "Giroux: Culture, Politics & Pedagogy" [Video File], Media Education Foundation. Available online: https://bu.kanopy.com/video/giroux-culture-politics-pedagogy (accessed April 18, 2020).

Yuasa, Ikuko P. (2008), *Culture and Gender of Voice Pitch: A Sociophonetic Comparison of the Japanese and Americans*, London: Equinox.

Yuasa, Ikuko P. (2010), "Creaky Voice: A New Feminine Voice Quality for Young Urban-Oriented Upwardly Mobile American Women," *American Speech*, 85 (3): 315–37. Available online: https://read.dukeupress.edu/american-speech/article-abstract/85/3/315/5885/Creaky-Voice-A-New-Feminine-Voice-Quality-for (accessed June 8, 2020).

Zamudio-Suaréz, Fernanda (2017), "Months After 'Transracialism' Flap, Controversy Still Rages at Feminist Philosophy Journal," *Chronicle of Higher Education*, July 21. Available online: https://www.chronicle.com/article/Months-After/240722 (accessed March 18, 2020).

Zheng, Robin (2018), "Precarity Is a Feminist Issue: Gender and Contingent Labor in the Academy," *Hypatia*, 33 (2): 235–55.

Zimman, Lal (2018), "Transgender Voices: Insight on Identity, Embodiment, and the Gender of Voice," *Language and Linguistics Compass*, 12 (8): e12284. Available online: https://onlinelibrary.wiley.com/doi/epdf/10.1111/lnc3.12284 (accessed March 19, 2020).

Zimmerman, Edith (2019), "Is My Voice Attractive?," *New York Magazine*, January 17. Available online: https://www.thecut.com/2019/01/is-my-voice-attractive.html (accessed June 11, 2020).

Zuckerman, Esther (2018), "Director Boots Riley Breaks Down the Craziest Part of 'Sorry To Bother You'", *Thrillist*, July 5. Available online: https://www.thrillist.com/entertainment/nation/sorry-to-bother-you-ending-explained-boots-riley-interview (accessed March 18, 2020).

Index